# Teaching Writing as Journey, Not Destination

## Essays Exploring What "Teaching Writing" Means

# Teaching Writing as Journey, Not Destination

## Essays Exploring What "Teaching Writing" Means

by

**P.L. Thomas**
*Furman University, Greenville SC*

**INFORMATION AGE PUBLISHING, INC.**
Charlotte, NC • www.infoagepub.com

**Library of Congress Cataloging-in-Publication Data**

CIP record for this book is available from the Library of Congress
http://www.loc.gov

ISBNs:  978-1-64113-512-2 (Paperback)

978-1-64113-513-9 (Hardcover)

978-1-64113-514-6 (ebook)

Printed in the United States of America

# CONTENTS

# SECTION III: BEING A WRITER

# SECTION IV: CHOICE

# SECTION V: CITATION AND RESEARCH PAPERS

# SECTION VI: CREATIVE WRITING

# SECTION VII: DIAGRAMMING SENTENCES

# SECTION VIII: DIRECT INSTRUCTION

# SECTION IX: DISCIPLINARY WRITING

## SECTION XV: LABRANT, LOU

## SECTION XVI: LITERACY AND THE LITERARY TECHNIQUE HUNT

## SECTION XVII: PLAGIARISM

## SECTION XVIII: POETRY

## SECTION XIX: PUBLIC INTELLECTUAL (WRITING FOR THE PUBLIC)

## SECTION XX: PUBLISHING

## SECTION XXI: READING LIKE A WRITER

## SECTION XXII: RUBRICS

## SECTION XXIII: TEACHING ENGLISH

## SECTION XXIV: WRITING PROCESS

# PREFACE

## Creating Space for Writers to Happen

### Kristen Marakoff

I began my education career in fall 2016, teaching English at a rural high school about five minutes down the street from the selective liberal arts college where I received my undergraduate degree. The college has a reputation in the community for being "where the smart people go." I cannot pretend that, by virtue of attending this well-respected college, I hit the ground running as a teacher; I suffered through my first-year learning curve just like everyone else. However, as semesters have passed and I have revised my practice again and again, time has been my best teacher, and the writing crafted in my class has grown stronger. That doesn't mean that I am done growing as a professional; I know that I will continue to interrogate and revise my teaching choices. Regardless, when I look at the writers in my class today, I see their successes, and I'm satisfied. In fact, I'm happy enough with my practice that I have presented on it at teaching conferences on the state and national level. When I do so I often talk to the audience afterwards, and it never fails that someone mentions the college I attended. "Well, you went to Furman, didn't you? No wonder you can teach."

There are a couple of logical fallacies embedded into this assumption, and I would like to unpack them here. First of all, as anyone who has

*Teaching Writing as Journey, Not Destination:*
*Essays Exploring What "Teaching Writing" Means*, pp. xi–xxvi
Copyright © 2019 by Information Age Publishing

attended any higher-education institution of any caliber can attest, there are people who got in because they are brilliant and will do a genuine service to the area of study in their institution, and there are people who got in because they can pay full tuition. Attending a selective university doesn't make you smart, or even mean that you were smart before you got there; it often just means you were lucky or wealthy enough to get in. A person's pedigree is not indicative of their intelligence, and to assume so is only to reinforce an educational caste system which simultaneously rewards already privileged young people for their parents' wealth and bars the vast majority of poor young people from experiences of privilege. I was a smart high school student, and I worked hard at the college I attended, and I can also say unhesitatingly that if my parents had been unable to afford tuition costs of nearly 20,000 dollars a year *after* an over 50% discount in scholarships, I could not have attended the institution I did, through no fault of my own, and without any difference in my intelligence.

But let's assume, for the sake of argument, that my attending a private university meant that I was inherently more intelligent than my public college peers. When people say that my intelligence and natural inclination towards writing is the spur for my students' writing success, they are assuming that smart people are inherently good teachers, and that people who write for a living are inherently good at teaching writing. In short, that being able to teach something is an intrinsic truth of being able to *do* something. It then follows that time spent teaching people to teach is unnecessary and even wasteful, because people who are good at something will, without any augmentation to their skill, be equipped to teach to others what they can naturally do.

## Set Up for Failure: Barriers to Effective Writing Instruction

Let me share with you a capstone moment in my writing instruction at my college, filled with professors who are incredibly intelligent, and who participate actively in their fields through research and written publications of their findings. I was in a history class. The professor had asked us to write a paper on the trading relationships China held during the Tang Dynasty. The professor was a writer. He was working on at least two books; one was based on his extensive knowledge of Ancient and Imperial China and the other was a translation of a Chinese text to English, which he was working on with his wife. The professor was not yet tenured, but his eventual status as associate professor was all but assured, not only because of his impressive CV but also because his three-piece suits (worn every class day) and hourly smoke breaks in the courtyard had already made him a fixture of the campus. He was a dynamic person, and he was a smart and capable writer.

The class had turned in their Tang Dynasty papers, and the professor had just handed them back, graded. To be completely fair, at least half of the class had not done any of the reading, and so knew nothing about the Tang Dynasty. However the other half of us, the ones who had done the reading and worked hard on the essays, were completely dumbfounded by our poor grades. As we sat in our black plastic desks, looking down at the "C's" and "D's" written jerkily in red sharpie, the professor tried to explain:

> Some of you wrote sentences like, *"the book says..."* But, books don't *say* things, right? I mean, some of your sentences just don't make sense. So, you know, before you submit your next papers, read back over them and make sure you're, you know, saying what you mean, and that you're making sense.

This was the extent of the help we were given before we were tasked with writing new papers, this time our term paper. This was tantamount to receiving no help at all, as I'm relatively certain that everyone in the class had written sentences that, to their knowledge at least, made perfect sense. In fact, I can safely say that I have never encountered any student who has written something completely illogical on purpose. We are always *trying* to communicate through our writing, we just don't always do it well. The job of the writing teacher is to help the student succeed in their communicative goals and not just to tell them when they have failed. My professor wasn't capable of doing that. Even though he himself was a good writer, and his intelligence (if it can be judged by an ability to list every Chinese dynasty and their emperors in chronological order and with flawless pronunciation) was not in question, he had never learned how to teach other people to be as brilliant as he was. He could put together beautiful PowerPoint presentations, (he even matched the background shades to accent colors in the portraits of Chinese emperors included on each slide), but that was the limit of his teaching finesse. He was a smart and capable scholar, and I'm sure he could learn and be successful in any endeavor he chose, but no one had taught him to teach, and that meant he couldn't do it very well, most especially when it came to writing.

I don't want you to think that all of my college professors taught composition this way. But most of them did. Even though I was going to a school that was applauded for its teaching and for producing successful graduates, the writing instruction I received was mostly ineffective and frustrating. I don't mean this as a criticism, although I know it sounds like one. Teaching writing is hard. Not only do you need a technical and nuanced understanding of writing for a myriad of different purposes and then effectively communicate these nuances to students, but you also have to resign yourself to the fact that most of your students will fail to apply the vast majority of what you teach to their own writing, at least right away. Teaching writing is mostly an exercise in patience and trust: giving students an opportunity to write themselves through a lot of bad pieces with the expectation that one day they will get better, and that even if they don't, the learning that they did was worth the process. Your goal, then, is to create a space for writers to become writers, instead of a space where students produce functional student papers that reinforce poor writing habits. All of this is a huge amount to ask from a person whose degree is probably based on the content of their subject area (literature, biology, history) and at the most included a couple of freshman composition courses.

To make matters worse, professors and teachers have often never had good writing instruction themselves, and so have no past model to fall back on. It's unfair to hold educators accountable for teaching the skill of writing within their discipline when they have likely never been taught, and have only learned what they do know through natural aptitude. Here, college professors are often more equipped than high school teachers because one of their professional obligations is to write and publish with some frequency, and so they are at least revisiting their own writing practice regularly. There are many high school teachers, however, who haven't written anything since their own college years, not through any fault of their own but because the demands of teaching make it all but impossible. Most of these high school teachers are incredibly self-conscious about their own writing ability because they have been distanced from it for years, and yet we expect them to teach students a process that they do not practice and often do not fully understand themselves. With all of these significant and obvious barriers to good writing instruction, it's difficult to blame instructors when writing instruction is poor. It wasn't the fault of any of my professors or former teachers that writing was mystified for me as a student; I'm sure they were equally mystified by the process as well, and were doing the best they could with the tools they'd been given.

## Writing With Reading and Revision: Creating Space for Genre Awareness

I still became a much better writer throughout my college years in spite of the majority of my professors' poor practices, and this was primarily because I had a few professors who knew how to teach writing. One of them (my favorite of them) wrote this book. All of them emphasized the creation of an environment where students organically discovered their own writing process over direct instruction. Writing is a journey not in creating a specific paper or essay (that's the work of a student proving themselves to a professor), but a journey in discovering your own capacity to write through the crafting of many pieces over time, without a heavy emphasis on the success of any one of those pieces (that's the work of a person who sees themselves as a writer). The best writing professors I had acknowledged this journey, and celebrated failure and success in equal measure, recognizing that both were necessary for the writer's growth.

This isn't as radical as it sounds. Just as different people memorize information differently, so will different students have a different process that works for them in terms of crafting writing (which will shift over time and across genres) and they must have the space to discover that process on their own. A good writing teacher can guide and reassure students without imposing their own process onto the students. In my experience, that has meant actually reinserting parts of the writing process that students don't normally consider "writing," through encouraging students to consider truths about most writers' processes that are often vocalized and then forgotten: namely, the importance of reading in conjunction with writing, and the necessity of revising.

When I consider the importance of reading texts as mentor texts (texts that the writer analyzes to build an awareness of writing within the genre of the studied text, and with a similar purpose) I realize that working as a scholar even at the collegiate level necessitates this type of reading, which is perhaps one of the reasons why I experienced such gains as a writer in college. Even without explicit instruction, college benefits writers because they are forced to do two things in conjunction with one another: read and write. More specifically, we are asked to read and write *within genres* at the same time. In high school English classes, too often we ask students to write the dreaded literary analysis essay, but never ask students to actually read a professional example of literary analysis. It's no wonder, then, that the papers we get back are poor specimens of literary analysis. Students don't know what they're being asked to do. College-level reading, however, authentically provides mentor texts (in the form of critical essays and research papers written by scholars) for students to work from; students are constantly reading and responding to texts of the same genre as those that they are writing, which allows them to organically discover what it means to write from the vantage point of a scholar in that particular field.

I have also found too often that when we ignore mentor texts in high school, writing is reduced to a monolithic skill. In reality, writers require different skills for different types of writing, as well as for different fields and different purposes. Writing a text message to a friend is different to writing a blog post, just as writing about your latest research findings in epigenetics (the biology field) is different from writing a poststructuralist analysis of the latest short story (the English field). And yet, too often, writing is seen as the purview of the English teacher only, and so high school students are only ever exposed to the discipline-specific writing traits of English scholars (despite the fact that few of them will ever enter this narrow field). Collegiate writing experiences, which are inherently differentiated by field, authentically circumlocute the problem of monolithic writing that we do a poor job of even acknowledging in high school classrooms, because students are always writing within disciplines and across all disciplines.

In an attempt to manage the impossible task of teaching students to write in all possible fields for all possible purposes, English teachers often compound the problems implicit in teaching a "one size fits all" model of writing when we give students prescriptive rules to follow. The intention is good. We see that students don't have the first clue about how to write an academic essay, and we also see that we already have the huge burden of teaching the mandated materials or skills that are determined by the department, state, or Common Core, and so we have less than no time to spend on discipline-specific writing. So rather than give students authentic examples of texts in the genre they are writing and allow them to organically discover what it means to write a critical essay in the English discipline, we condense what should be a year-long exploration of genre into a bullet point list of prescriptive rules to follow, such as "never use first-person perspective" or "always include your thesis in the first paragraph." While this is well-intentioned, the results are ultimately detrimental to the student.

Prescriptive writing rules are misleading because they do not acknowledge the very narrow genres in which they are applicable (which is "academic papers written under timed circumstances"). There are very few "rules" in writing, but rather fluid expectations within genres that are broken when they do not serve the communicative purpose of the writer, or when the fashions change (consider, for instance, the postmodern reemergence of first-person perspective in the English discipline). So when we give students prescriptive rules to writing and fail to explain the purpose of these prescriptive rules or their place within very narrow genres, we lead students to thinking that *all* writing follows these rules, when in reality very little real-world writing does. Worse, we encourage them to think like students who are checking off boxes on a rubric to appropriately complete an assignment, instead of encouraging them to think as writers whose goal is to communicate effectively, and to make choices that facilitate that communication.

One of my first successes, then, as a teacher of writing, was to introduce my high school writers to scholarly essays in the English discipline, similar in content and style to the essays they would later be expected to craft. My experience in college English classes, where we would read a text, and then read scholarly essays critiquing the text, and then write to contribute to the critical conversation surrounding the text, was replicated in my high school classroom. The critical essays students turned in were immediately stronger, without any additional instruction on my part. The gains in writing that I didn't make until college my students were making now, just because reading was reintroduced as a central part of writing instruction in the classroom. This is the way it should be. Organic growth in writing from authentic immersion in mentor texts does not have to be, and should no longer be, an exclusively collegiate experience; students can read mentor texts to teach them genre awareness and improve genre-specific writing at any time, and that authentic immersion in texts produces proven gains.[1]

In much the same way that reading mentor texts produces gains in students because it reinserts an essential and authentic part of a writer's process into the classroom expectations, so must other essential parts of writing return to the writing teacher's curriculum. The writing process, like genres of writing, is not monolithic; we shouldn't teach our students *the* writing process, but rather strategies for beginning their writing and then revising it. And when we consider our own experiences with writing, we often find that our own writing processes are far from concrete, and that we constantly adapt our process to meet the needs of our current task. As an example, the process that I undertook to write this preface was radically different from the way that I begin to write a critical analysis of a text for the English discipline, and both of those processes are radically different from the way I begin to write a poem. When I sat down to write this preface, I began by doing a rough outline composed of loose thoughts I knew I wanted to address. But as I wrote, my original thoughts crystalized and I realized I needed to reorganize the entire preface, rewriting significant sections to support what I had only just (3,000 words in) realized was my point. Conversely, when I write an academic essay, I don't begin until I have written an outline so detailed that I essentially only have to insert coordinating conjunctions and punctuation to have a functional essay. And when I write poetry I have no draft or outline at all, but work line by line (normally from a few "root" lines that I think of spontaneously) and follow the direction of my intuition. All of these processes are different, and yet through all of them I have produced meaningful work. We need to give our students the same freedom to discover their own process for each genre, and accept that it will not only be different from their previous writing processes, but also that it will most likely be different from our own.

Once students have *begun* writing, it is immediately appropriate to talk about the process of revision, since it is an aspect of writing that is included in nearly all writing processes. Ironically, it also seems to be the most skipped or glossed over aspect of the monolithic writing process regularly taught in high school and college. When we do address revision in the classroom, too often we teach it as part of a five-step writing process (brainstorm, rough draft, revise, edit, submit) which is a dishonest simplification at best. Many writers (myself included) revise constantly as they work, rereading again and again before they have finished to ensure they are writing themselves into their point, and then over again once their work is completed. The editing phase, then, is simultaneous with the revision process, although the writer will often delete, add, or shift significant portions of the text and render much of their editing work obsolete. Other writers revise only after they have finished their work, or sections of their work, and others will set aside writing for lengths of time after finishing it, rereading only after they have some distance from their project. Still others prefer peer feedback on first drafts before they make any of their own edits, and the list could go on for different revision strategies that writers employ. Then, of course, it goes without saying that as soon as these writers shift genres, all of their processes for revision change as well. Essentially, what teachers should recognize and what students should learn in any writing class is that *how* revision happens is not very important, but *that* revision happens is essential. Almost all good writing goes through multiple, significant revisions, not because that is a rule handed down from the heavens but because writers are invested in the quality of their work, and when they read it they organically want to tweak (or overhaul) it to make it better. Revision isn't a chore; it is a natural impulse that stems from a genuine investment in the communicative value of the writing.

## Reorienting "The Writing Process" Into "The Writing Process(es)"

I hope by this point I have stressed enough the value of allowing students to try on a multiplicity of writing processes, and giving them the space to discover their own. But, just like our students, sometimes it is helpful to have a model of what other people do (either in their writing or in their classrooms) to know that you are on the right track. You will see throughout this book many different practical tips and examples of how to structure a writing-friendly classroom. Just like the different writing processes that different writers employ, none of them is more valuable than the others, only more appropriate in different circumstances. For my circumstances (teaching 20 to 30 juniors and seniors in an English class in a public high school) this is the process I use to foster authentic, genre-specific writing. Use what works for you, discard what doesn't, and feel free to modify as you see fit. It won't hurt my feelings.

All writing assignments begin, in my class, days before students are ever given a new set of expectations, guidelines, or a rubric. Instead, we start with a few class hours dedicated to exploring the new genre that students will eventually be expected to mimic (personal essays, newspaper articles, scholarly works). Students read the texts (as a class, in pairs, individually) and analyze them for (1) the communicative goals of the writers, and (2) the stylistic and/or literary choices the author makes in order to further those communicative goals. This can be more simply put as "what is the writer saying (both literally and figuratively)?" and "how are they saying it?" Additionally, I ask students consider the context of the text. Who is writing? Who are they writing to? When and where were they writing, and what do we know that helps us situate this text historically? All of these questions are considered and interrogated across multiple texts, and as we go, students build a list (both a physical list and an internal set of guidelines) on what this particular genre looks like and how writers tend to construct text within this genre to make meaning.

After students have read multiple mentor texts with an eye to writer's craft (normally over two to three 85-minute class blocks), I then give the students the expectations for the writing assignment. Expectations in my class have three major components: a suggested writing process for that particular assignment, a list of minimum expectations, and the deadlines for each chunked stage. For the suggested writing process, I write down the steps I would go through as a writer myself if I were to write in the genre the students will mimic. However, I stress to my students each time we discuss the assignment that the writing process suggestion on their paper is just that, a suggestion, and that they should modify it as necessary for themselves. The minimum expectations, however, are the aspects of the project that are nonnegotiable for that assignment, and quite possibly for that genre. Most of the time, this list is eerily similar to, and always supplemented by, the list of conventions students have drafted themselves about that genre. For instance, the minimum expectations for a personal essay assignment where I expect students to use the narrative mode would be, "You must have a claim. You must evidence this claim by breaking into the narrative mode at least once. You must attempt to frame your piece so that there is a clear beginning and ending." As we progress throughout the semester, I will also add minimum expectations that the students should have the ability to complete based on prior lessons, such as "the paper must be in standard MLA format. The paper must have all sources properly cited with in-text citations and a Works Cited." It is important, however, to only have two to four minimum expectations per assignment at its onset and to keep those minimum expectations as narrow and achievable as possible. The focus for the students should be on generating good writing, not on checking off boxes on a rubric. The minimum expectations are only what you need the students' first drafts to include, not what they need to be by the time they are finished, so keep this in mind as you draft your own minimum expectations.

The final component of an assignment's expectations are the chunked deadlines for each draft of the project, and it is these deadlines that give each writing unit its framework. Students are expected to show me at least three drafts of each assignment: a preliminary draft, a first submission, and a final submission. I don't use the words "rough" and "final" draft anymore, because I found that students didn't take the rough draft seriously. Instead, they would turn in drafts that were really brainstorming activities, ideas for what the paper would eventually be, or the beginning of incomplete drafts. While that kind of thinking and writing is an important preliminary activity, turning it in as a draft doesn't give me the opportunity to read the actual writing, to give the student effective feedback, or to design relevant mini-lessons for the class. For this reason, students must turn in the completed drafts of their work in order for me to comment.

However, brainstorming, outlining, and drafting out ideas are all activities that I want to encourage in my students because it will help them become better writers, which is why I ask to see students' "preliminary drafts." Preliminary drafts are due two or three days before the first submission is due, and all I am checking for is that the student has put something on paper that demonstrates that they have thought about their writing in advance of the night before the paper is due. Good writing takes time, and it is the teacher's responsibility to create a writing environment that requires students to take extended time to write. In my class, preliminary drafts are not for a grade and are checked only for completion, but failing to turn one in, on time or at all, will result in a final grade cap (for instance, you can't get higher than a B on the final if you turn the preliminary draft in late, no higher than a C if I never see it). As for the actual completion of preliminary drafts, anything the student wants to do to in their own constructed writing process is acceptable (I've had students turn in mind maps, outlines, a few different opening paragraphs, or annotated bibliographies for research papers, among many things). As I said before, I check the preliminary drafts only for completion, but use the time I spend checking preliminary drafts to get a sense of where the student is going, redirect students if necessary, and give informal feedback and suggestions.

The deadline for the first submission, or the first completed draft of the writing, is generally due about a week after students have received the assignment, and two to three days after I've checked the preliminary drafts. That week's class time would have been filled with analyzing a few mentor texts that have similar communicative goals and genres to our own writing (often times I will mix in an excellent student sample here as a mentor text) and then discussing directly how these mentor texts can benefit us in our own writing. The rest of the time is workshop time for the students to write their first submissions, and I am available as a fellow writer to give encouragement or to provide suggestions when the students are stuck. The first submission, when turned in, must meet all of the minimum requirements that were outlined on the assignment expectations, or I will return it back to the author and ask them to review the minimum expectations and resubmit. It is on the first submission, then, that the majority of my feedback occurs. As I look through the student submissions, I will *not* correct any perceived mistakes, but I will write questions to the students, such as "why do you frame your paper this way? How would elaborating on this moment change the essay? What do you want your readers to walk away believing?" I make only enough notes that I will remember what I wanted to talk about with each student, and then any overarching concerns that I want to address to the entire class (anything from constructing narrative with more relevant detail to writing complete sentences) become the topics for my mini-lessons.

The stretch of time between the first submission and the final submission is where the majority of my writing instruction happens. This is because I have found that frontloading crafting technique doesn't work. Although students will say things like "I can't write," or "my writing is bad," they never think that the crafting lesson you are teaching applies to them, unless you can point to concrete moments in their writing where they demonstrate the weakness you are addressing. For that reason, most of my writing mini-lessons happen during the revision stage, which occurs during the two to three weeks after their first submission. During this time, I teach crafting mini-lessons based on the needs of the particular class, return students to even more mentor texts for analysis and discussion of technique and goals, and give students ample workshop time to revise their papers based on what they are learning. Most importantly, I also hold a writing conference with each individual student, early in the revision stage, on their first submission (normally while other students are workshopping or analyzing a mentor text).

Writing conferences are, according to my students, the single most helpful activity we do in class for improving writing. However, they can easily turn discouraging if the time is just used to give students a list of their failings. The word "conferences" implies a communal exchange, with the teacher as a fellow writer and scholar instead of an instructor, and I have found that students make the best revisions to their work when they are included in the discussion of what should be changed. For that reason, I begin every writing conference with the question, "what do you want help revising in your paper?" The students know this question is coming (I tell them before we begin, and after doing it a few times they know the routine) and will enter the conference already knowing what they want to work on and will have questions about how to accomplish it. I also have the list of questions I wrote on the student's paper to facilitate discussion if the student is stuck, and to remind me of the strengths and areas of improvement for that particular paper. As the student and I talk, I will write a revision plan for the student based on our discussion. For instance, if the student and I talk about adding more detail to a narrative, revising the opening paragraphs to include a personal experience, and switching perspective towards the end of the paper back to an authorial address, then I will write this down in a bulleted list on the student's first submission. I will then ask the student, at the end of our discussion, whether or not they feel that they can accomplish the revisions in the plan. If students have questions about craft specific to those revisions, then I can answer them immediately, but more often than not the student feels empowered by the discussion to get to work right away.

The revision plan becomes the student's individual, second set of minimum expectations; when the final is turned in, I will look at the revision plan the student and I crafted together, and make sure that they attempted the revisions we discussed. Students also know that after the writing conference they are free to return new drafts (or partial drafts) to me at any point until the final submission and I will continue to give them feedback. Conversely, when students turn in a final submission, (at the end of the revision stage) I do not give them any feedback other than their grade. If students want to continue working on the piece, they schedule another writing conference with me, we make a new revision plan, and the student rewrites the paper. I then regrade the paper, and the old grade is replaced by the new one. Students can complete this process as many times as they like until they are happy with their work, or until the grading period ends. Although it seems like this process would be a lot of work for the teacher, in reality you will know the student's paper so well by the second or third conference that it takes much less time to check revisions and give suggestions. More importantly, allowing students to revise until *they* are happy with their work teaches students to think as writers and artists, who must decide for themselves when a work is complete. Allowing multiple revisions also ensures our students' grades match their achievement levels and personal agency, and doesn't penalize students for taking a little longer to reach the same goals as their peers.

At the end of the two to three weeks of revision and the day students are set to turn in their final submissions, there is one final activity we do as a class: sharing. Students write differently (and better) when they know they have an authentic audience outside of just their teacher, just as writers write more conscientiously for a publishable article than for an entry in a journal. During the class period where students will share their work, students take their papers and divide into groups of four, which I allow them to select. Then one student, without prefacing or hedging, will read their piece to their group. When they have finished, the students will go around the group and each member will share one aspect of the writing that they enjoyed. Then, another student will share their work, and they will repeat this process until every group member has shared and received feedback from each of their peers. Finally, the group will vote one of the four students to share their paper with the rest of the class, meaning that everyone will read their paper out loud to a small group, but only five or six students will read their paper to the entire class. I find this type of sharing more effective because it allows everyone to share their work in a safe environment, as there are many students who never get the benefits of reading their work to an audience because they are afraid of speaking to the whole class. It also, by giving students encouragement in a small group setting, encourages students to *want* to share with the whole class because they have already heard positive feedback from their peers. This method of sharing also cuts back on the boredom and time suck of every student reading their paper out loud to the class. After all the students who wish to share with the class have done so, I encourage students to write thank-you notes to the students whose work they admired, or whose sharing they appreciated.

It is during this final class period of presenting our work, before we abandon a piece of writing and move on to the next assignment, that I most recognize the value of teaching writing as content. By including sharing as an integral part of the writing process, the class dynamic changes from a room full of disconnected students to a community of peers and fellow writers. Last year in one of my classes, a quiet boy, whose name isn't Chris but who I'll call Chris for this story, and who didn't participate much in class, was voted to share his piece of writing with the whole group. He was nervous, but his peers encouraged him, telling him that his piece "was the best of all of ours," and that they "loved his topic." So despite his reservations, Chris stood in front of the class and read to us an essay about people judging him: because he had a nose ring, because he wore dark clothing, because he was a teenager, because he was quiet and unassuming. He peppered the narrative aspects of the essay with tangential stories about his friends, who were good people even though others immediately judged them to be, based on appearances, as "goth" and "up to no good." He ended his essay with a plea to the class to not judge others before getting to know them, and to give people a chance regardless of their appearance. As Chris read, he stuttered a little, blushed, and caught a few more errors in that final submission from the process of reading aloud. But even with those hang-ups and Chris's fears, the class clapped and snapped enthusiastically when he finished. One outspoken girl at the back of the class shouted over the applause, "Now I *liked* that one!"

We finished the rest of the student readings and then wrote our thank you notes. As students completed them, they walked to their peers' desks and quietly placed the notes on the corner. I noticed that Chris's desk was getting quite a few visitors. By the end of the period, Chris had over a dozen notes from his peers. As I was wrapping class up, telling students to finish their notes and thanking them all for their sharing and their reception of other students' writing, I look over at Chris, reading each letter. He was sobbing. He told me later that he felt like the class listened to him and accepted him, and that he had never felt or even expected to feel that way in a high school setting. That moment, the writing community of trust and security that it fostered, and the risks my students afterwards felt comfortable taking in their writing, never would have been possible if students were not encouraged to share.

## Writing as a Process, Not a Product

I've just shared with you almost everything I know about teaching writing. It's rather depressing to realize that all of my tips and strategies on writing instruction can fit into just a few pages of text, but I know that as I continue to teach that my writing units will become more sophisticated and more effective, and they will look a little different each year. And my students will continue to achieve more and more, but it will not be because the techniques that I use will necessarily be better, but because I will be better as a teacher. In the same way, this text will provide you with tons of strategies for teaching writing, developed over years and years of being a writing teacher. But the actual strategies themselves aren't actually what is important. What's important is that a space is created where students feel that their work is legitimate and considered valuable. Writing conferences, multiple submissions, sharing spaces, and any other strategies you glean from this book are ultimately only different avenues towards the goal of fostering an environment where students don't think of themselves as students, but as writers and truth-tellers. And as long as you are getting to that space, and students feel secure and important, you are doing what you're supposed to be doing, regardless of the strategies you employ and regardless of the final quality of student work.

I would like to share one final story of my experience learning to write as a student. I was a high school junior, taking a survey course of British literature. We were assigned to choose a tale from *The Canterbury Tales* that we hadn't read as a class, read the scholarly critiques of it, and write our own critical analysis. As a future English major and anglophile, I loved writing that paper. The final product was a 14-page essay composed in a single-sitting flurry of perceived brilliance on a neighbor's couch, while the kids I was supposed to be babysitting took advantage of my distraction (bordering on neglect) by hosting lightsaber fights so violent that their dog Molly cowered under a chair. The paper was a comparison of "The Knight's Tale" to "The Wife of Bath's Tale." I found it on an old flash drive a few months ago, and it was really, really terrible. I actually used the word "plethora" in it. But I didn't, until I read it again, remember how terrible it was. What I remembered was that my teacher, Mr. Lentz, treated me like a legitimate writer, and told me that the paper was good, and helped me work to make it stronger. When I got to college I took a class on *The Canterbury Tales* where we read the entire text in Middle English, and then essentially had the same assignment that I had my junior year of high school. When I set out to write this college term paper, I didn't even think about that first paper I wrote in high school. There would have been nothing about it that I could have salvaged. Like I said, it was very terrible. But that doesn't mean that doing that assignment as a high school student was a waste. Far from it. Every paper we ever write is sitting behind us as experience to help us with that next paper or piece of writing, and because I had a positive experience with that first paper, I was more confident when it came time to write the college term paper. I received encouragement, even if I didn't really deserve it. What Mr. Lentz did for me, what I hope I did for Chris, and all that any of us can do as teachers, is make the experience of writing a positive one.

Unfortunately, just because we create safe environments for writers doesn't mean that all of our students are going to become writers. The reality is that many of our students will leave high school (or college, four years later) and never write again. Once again, we must value the process over the product. When we allow students to experience themselves as real writers in an environment that allows them to be writers rather than students, we will inevitably have some (many) who finish our class and decide that they still don't want to write. We must trust that the experience was worthwhile for them, even if they make the choice to not immediately use it. And for a very few students, the writing environment they are exposed to in your class will serve as a catalyst for their writing selves, and students who never thought they would *choose* to write, will. When they do, the practice and experience you've made room for will sit behind them as gentle encouragement. Because ultimately, all you can do is establish an environment where students enjoy writing and can tap into their inherent compulsion to write, if they have it. Your goal, then, as a teacher of writing, is not to be a perfect teacher. It is not to provide more effective feedback than my college professors did. It is not to devise an infallible writing unit, or to bridge the gap between the teacher who writes and the writing teacher. It is not even to have students who are producing good pieces of writing. Our job is to create growing space for writers, writers who used to be students.

# ENDNOTE

1. Purcell-Gates, V., Duke, N. K., & Martineau, J. A. (2007). Learning to read and write genre-specific text: Roles of authentic experience and explicit teaching. *Reading Research Quarterly, 42*(1), 8–45.

# INTRODUCTION

## Teaching Writing as Journey, Not Destination

You'd think after 34 years of teaching writing at both the high school and college levels, I would have a pretty firm handle on everything. *You'd* think that, maybe, but not me.

On the last class session of my first-year writing seminars during fall semester 2017, I asked my students what had worked and not worked over the course of four or so months. They were perceptive in what they shared, and as a result, I began to redesign significantly both the course schedule and the time spent on many of my practices. Their feedback, thankfully, was mostly positive—as one student shared in her final reflection that is colored with a bit of hyperbole:

> I will never use any of the writing techniques that I was taught all four years of high school. My high school teachers failed me as a college writer. I am grateful that I got Dr. Thomas as a teacher considering that he was very willing to help you and was understanding that we are freshman and will make many mistakes. Talking to my friends outside of my class who have writing seminars this semester their professors expected them to know everything that needed to make them a strong college writer.

*Teaching Writing as Journey, Not Destination:*
*Essays Exploring What "Teaching Writing" Means,* pp. xxvii–xxxii
Copyright © 2019 by Information Age Publishing
All rights of reproduction in any form reserved.

Confirming the gap between how students view writing after high school and the expectations of academic writing for undergraduates and scholars, her feedback also speaks to a truism about learning to write (*being* a writer) and learning to teach writing (*being* a teacher of writing): both are journeys, and not destinations.

In this introduction to a volume collecting a wide range of essays on my own journey to be a writer and to teach writing, I want to discuss the patterns expressed by my two seminars, and consider briefly how that will impact my practice in future first-year writing and other writing-intensive courses. Their feedback included the following:

- **Students emphasized the effectiveness of professor/student essay conferencing.** I have at the college level greatly adjusted how I respond to essays compared to my previous career teaching high school English (note that now I have about 24 first-year students over two courses that meet M, W, F, and my high school load was 100–125 students over five classes that met M-F). I have all essays submitted as electronic Word files, and I then offer some track change edits/revisions and include comments. However, I now provide very brief, and never exhaustive, feedback on these drafts, and instead require students to conference (at least once after the first final draft submitted and my feedback returned) so we can discuss the essay and create a revision plan. I have always felt this is more effective so when these two seminars overwhelmingly con-firmed the power of conferences, I am now planning *more class time* dedicated to conferencing since requiring additional out-of-class conferences, they said, would be burdensome (scheduling these now are a bit of a challenge).
- **However, students noted peer-conferencing was less effective as currently implemented.** My standard process has been to have students bring hard copies of their first final essay submission on the due date (the electronic version is due by e-mail attachment before that class session) in order to have peer-conferencing in class. These students felt this process was not effective, and instead, want peer feedback *after* my feedback. I have always struggled with peer conferencing, and this means I have work left to do on this journey.
- **Students recognized the value of writing teachers sharing their own writing as models for student writing.** One of the most conscientious students shared quickly in the class debrief that she appreciated me sharing my writing and talking through what and how I write in order to model for them how to draft their essays. The other students were enthusiastic in agreement, and I feel

this was a strong endorsement of the power of *teaching writing as a writer*. While I am happy with this part of my teaching, I think I can increase the intentionality of this approach—sharing an ongoing draft of a piece in real time during the semester, for example, instead of all final pieces.

- **Students valued writing workshop time in class because they could interact immediately with the professor while drafting.** My course daily schedule and overarching course pattern tend toward the first half of the course being more traditional (class lessons and discussion, especially reading like a writer [see Chapters 23 and 53] with mentor texts), and then the second half including quite a few class sessions devoted to workshop time for students to draft, research, read, conference, etc., during the class hour. Although I have always valued workshop time for students, the expectations, especially at the college level, that class is about professor-oriented and content-based instruction still weigh on my own consideration about appropriate use of class time. These students confirmed the value of workshop time in class, noting especially having me there to help.

- **Students appreciated a composition course remaining primarily focused on learning to write and not on content acquisition and traditional practices such as taking tests.** A problem for the first-year writing seminars at my university, since switching away from more traditional composition courses anchored in the English department, has been professors outside of English teaching writing seminars as introductory disciplinary content courses. When talking with their first-year peers in other first-year writing seminars, my students came to appreciate the writing focus of my courses—mentioning, for example, that other students have been taking tests and involved in other activities (such as very narrowly prompted essays) more common in disciplinary content courses.

- **Students asked for more class sessions dedicated to brainstorming for every essay assigned.** One definite improvement I will incorporate is providing a more structured class session for brainstorming all four essays. This set of students acknowledged they very much benefitted from the one intense brainstorm session for the cited scholarly essay, and added that they felt this process would have been effective for all of the writing assignments.

- **Students appreciated but struggled with choice of types of essays and topics.** I have been a strong proponent and practitioner of allowing students choice in both the kinds of essays they write and their topics. The problem I have encountered teaching college students at an academically selective college is that these students *prefer* prompt-driven writing (that is the dominant experience they have had as students, and many have been successful within that context), and most of their writing have been *absent* any choice. An ongoing goal for my practice remains *how to help students build the writer's toolbox necessary for being capable of the choice they deserve* as scholars and writers.

- **Students admitted that drafting, and required drafts, were helpful for improving the quality of their essays and thinking.** One of the most shocking lessons I have learned with my current university students is their resistance to drafting. But that resistance is grounded not in any sort of laziness or even procrastination (although they bring the procrastination-still-produces-A's habit from high school); it is mostly their fear of turning in work, in their words, "that isn't perfect yet." Because I employ a minimum requirements approach (instead of traditional grades; see **Section XIII. Grading,** Chapters 33, 34, 35) that emphasizes drafting, most of my students do comply with those minimum expectations; however, far fewer students embrace the unlimited opportunity for drafting essays that would certainly improve their grades and improve them as writers. While I have been fairly successful with students drafting as required, I must continue to find strategies for helping them appreciate drafting more fully (I will touch on this below).

- **Students viewed feedback on their drafts positively and appreciated prompt replies and thorough feedback.** The same student I quoted above about me sharing my writing also embraced one of the foundational jokes of all the classes I teach: I tell students if I do not respond immediately to an e-mail (or text) or if they do not have their essays returned in less than one day of submission, I didn't receive the e-mail, text, or essay—or I am dead. There is a scene in the film version of *Mosquito Coast* in which the Harrison Ford character is whipping up the locals in the land he has bought, noting that he wants them to work hard but he will always be working harder. That is a teacher commitment I have always worked by. While I have learned to temper the amount of feedback I offer (but still have some tone problems), I remain prompt in how I respond to students and their work. Students appreciate my standards for my response to their writing by often embodying higher standards for themselves.

Not directly addressed by my students' feedback, I have an additional broad concern that I plan to address as I revise these seminars since I always revise my writing seminars (and all courses I teach) with each new semester. My minimum requirement technique meets some of my instructional goals, but it fails at helping students develop their own sense of the *quality* of their work and their *deserved* grades (which I must assign despite not grading throughout the semester).

I have long rejected rubrics (see **Section XXII. Rubrics,** Chapters 54, 55), but I also do appreciate the need for teachers at all levels to make expectations clear for students—both in how the teacher states explicit expectations and how students identify their own expectations. "Minimum" seems to be less effective for the population of students I teach (the "do all this or fail" is a deficit approach and does not really match the aspiration of high-achieving students who are mostly in courses for the A).

This is quite tentative, but here are some evolving thoughts on how to help students understand the A/B divide in the quality of their essays and their overall course grade:

- **A work:** Participating by choice in multiple drafts and conferences *beyond* the minimum requirements (first full essay submission, conference, revised essay submission); essay form and content that are nuanced, sophisticated, and well developed (typically more narrow, well-defined than broad); a high level demonstrated for selecting and incorporating source material in a wide variety of citation formats; submitting work as assigned and meeting due dates (except for illness, etc.); attending and participating in class-based discussions, lessons, and workshops; completing assigned and choice reading of course texts and mentor texts in ways that contribute to class discussions and original writing.

- **B work:** Submitting drafts and attending conferences as detailed by the minimum requirements (first full essay submission, conference, revised essay submission); essay form and content that are solid and distinct from high school writing (typically more narrow, well-defined than broad); a basic college level demonstrated for selecting and incorporating source material in a wide variety of citation formats; submitting work as assigned and meeting most due dates; attending and participating in class-based discussions, lessons, and workshops; completing assigned and choice reading of texts and mentor texts in ways that contribute to class discussions and original writing.

Just as my students should come to embrace writing as a journey, I discover every time I teach writing that, yes, teaching writing is also a journey and not a destination.

I have much left to do.

•

The chapters that follow are intended as a cohesive body of essays that explore and debate the enduring and current challenges of teaching writing, specifically at the high school and undergraduate college levels, but these essays also are offered as stand-alone readings and resources for practicing teachers, instructors, and professors who are on a shared journey with me as teachers of writing and as writers.

As an educator in my fourth decade of teaching, I have come to embrace critical pedagogy because it is an overarching philosophy of teaching and learning that holds sacred human agency and acknowledges the foundational importance of literacy in that human agency. Running through this volume, then, is a commitment to reading and re-reading the world as well as writing and re-writing the world, concepts emphasized throughout Paulo Freire's canon. Specifically, writing and re-writing the world is about power—resisting the powers that oppress and embracing the powers that liberate.

Hand-in-hand with my commitments to being a critical teacher and writer is an existential awareness that informs the journey metaphor throughout these essays. The journey is, as Albert Camus stresses in "The Myth of Sisyphus,"[1] the *thing itself* that gives us our happiness, without any promise of a destination. As existential philosophers argue, human passion and human suffering are inseparable, and thus, to struggle as Sisyphus does is not torture but the very real condition necessary for being fully human. Many see this view of life as dark, negative, but I offer here the notion that to be a writer and to be a teacher of writing are both fulfilling endeavors *in the acts themselves*, not in some promise of and end, a final state of perfect.

Finally, I offer in this collection my own perpetual counterargument to Kurt Vonnegut's claim writing is unteachable (see Chapter 8)—a touchstone you will encounter often in the coming pages.

## ENDNOTE

1. Camus, A. (1991). *The myth of Sisyphus and other essays* (J. O'Brien, Trans.). New York, NY: Vintage.

# SECTION I

## ACCOUNTABILITY, STANDARDS, AND HIGH-STAKES TESTING OF WRITING

# CHAPTER 1

# ADVENTURES IN NONSENSE

## Teaching Writing in
## the Accountability Era

> No, it's all nonsense, believe me. I had no idea how
> much nonsense it was, but nonsense it all is.
>
> Anna Scott, *Notting Hill*

Everything that is wrong with edujournalism and the teaching of writing in the accountability era can be found in *Education Week/Teacher*: the anemic examination of the five-paragraph essay (or see also when journalists discover a field in the same way Columbus discovered America) and Lucy Calkin's interview about the state of teaching writing (or when edugurus package and promote educommerce).[1] Both of *Education Week/Teacher* pieces frame how the teaching of writing now faces greater demands from the nearly equally maligned and praised Common Core. But neither piece admits that the Common Core is at best on life support or that their claim puts the cart before the horse. You see, the teaching of writing should be driven by the field of composition—the decades of expertise that can be found in the scholarship of writers and teachers of writing as well as foundational and powerful organizations such as the National Writing Project (NWP) and the National Council of Teachers of English (NCTE).

---

*Teaching Writing as Journey, Not Destination:*
*Essays Exploring What "Teaching Writing" Means*, pp. 3–6
Copyright © 2019 by Information Age Publishing

The Common Core is little more than bureaucratic nonsense; these standards serve the needs of educommerce, but do not reflect the field of literacy, do not meet the needs of teachers or students. And thus, these standards, the high-stakes tests inevitably linked to all standards, and the coverage of writing in *EdWeek*, as Anna Scott opined, *it's all nonsense*.

A little history here: Flash back to 2005 when Thomas Newkirk detailed in *English Journal* that the "new" SAT writing section had already resulted in "students [being] coached to invent evidence if they were stuck" (p. 22).[2] In other words, writing was reduced to conforming to the 25-minute, one-draft prompted assessment in *one* high-stakes test. Newkirk confirmed what George Hillocks found about the accountability movement's negative impact on writing:

> [W]hen students have been subjected to this instruction for eight to ten years, they come to see the five paragraph theme and the shoddy thinking that goes with it as the solution to any writing problem. Directors of freshman English at three Illinois state universities have complained about the extent of the problem. The English department at Illinois State University publishes a manual advising their incoming freshmen that while the five para- graph essay may have been appropriate in high school, it is not appropriate in college and should be studiously avoided. It shuts down thinking.
>
> This is a crucial time in American democracy. We are faced with problems that demand critical thinking of all citizens. We need to help students examine specious arguments and know them for what they are. Our tests encourage the opposite. They encourage blurry thinking and obfuscation. As a society, we cannot afford to spend valuable classroom time on vacuous thinking and writing. (p. 70)[3]

So let's consider the state of writing instruction in K–12 public schools— and let's try looking at the overwhelming evidence as detailed by Applebee and Langer.[4] In my review[5] (excerpted below) of this research, I detail both what we know about the state of teaching writing and what the roadblocks are to effective writing pedagogy.

In Chapter Two (Writing Instruction in Schools Today), Applebee and Langer lay the foundation for what becomes the refrain of their analysis of teaching writing in idle and high school:

> Overall, in comparison to the 1979–80 study, students in our study were writing more in all subjects, but that writing tended to be short and often did not provide students with opportunities to use composing as a way to think through the issues, to show the depth or breadth of their knowledge, or to make new connections or raise new issues.... The responses make it clear that relatively little writing was required even in English.... [W]riting on average mattered less than multiple-choice or short-answer questions

in assessing performance in English.... Some teachers and administrators, in fact, were quite explicit about aligning their own testing with the high-stakes exams their students would face. (pp. 15–17)

And those concerned about or in charge of education reform policy should use this study and analysis as a cautionary tale about the unintended and negative consequences of the current 30-year accountability era that has failed No Child Left Behind (NCLB) and its call for scientifically based education policy. Since the central message about the gap between best practice and the day-to-day reality of writing in U.S. middle and high schools is consistent in Applebee and Langer's work, I want to highlight several key points and then conclude with a couple caveats that help inform teachers and policy makers:

- Across disciplines, students are being asked to write briefly and rarely, with most writing falling within narrow templates that are unlike discipline-based or real-world writing.
- Teachers tend to know about and embrace the value of writing to learn content, but rarely implement writing to achieve rich and complex examinations of prior or new learning.
- Student technology savvy is high (notably related to social media), while teacher technology savvy remains low. Technology's role in teaching and learning is detailed as, again, narrowed by high-stakes testing demands and "primarily ... used to reinforce a presentational mode of teaching" (p. 116). These findings call into question advocacy for greater investments in technology absent concern for how it is implemented as well as raising yet another caution about ignoring research showing that technology (especially word processing) has the potential to impact writing positively if implemented well.
- While English language learners (ELLs) tend to be one category of students targeted by education reform and efforts to close achievement gaps, high-stakes testing and accountability stand between those students and the potential effectiveness of extended process writing in writing workshop experiences.
- Like ELL students, students in poverty suffer the same fate of disproportionately experiencing narrow learning experiences that focus on test-prep and not best practice in writing instruction:

    By far the greatest difference between the high poverty and lower poverty schools we studied stemmed from the importance that teachers placed and administrators placed on high-stakes tests that students faced. In the higher poverty schools, fully 83% of teachers across subject areas reported state exams were important in shaping curriculum and instruction, compared with 64% of their colleagues in lower poverty schools. (p. 149)

- One important counter-narrative to the education reform focus on identifying top teachers is that Applebee and Langer note that when teachers have autonomy and implement best practice, high-poverty students outperform comparable high-poverty students in classrooms "with more traditional approaches to curriculum and instruction," driven by test-prep (p. 148).

The problem with teaching writing is not that teachers lack knowledge of good writing pedagogy (although that certainly is a concern), but that accountability and high-stakes testing (read: Common Core and whatever the next wave is) have supplanted teacher autonomy and the expertise in the field of teaching writing. The five-paragraph essay was never good writing pedagogy, and abdicating the field of composition to Common Core—or any set of standards, any high-stakes testing—and the concurrent educommerce proves to be nonsense that feeds the foundational problems with teaching writing.

Period.

## ENDNOTES

1. Sawchuk, S. (2016, June 20). Is the five-paragraph essay history. *Education Week/Teacher*. Retrieved from https://www.edweek.org/tm/articles/2016/06/20/is-the-five-paragraph-essay-history.html ; Lind, D. (2016, July 11). Here's why I'm skeptical of Roland Fryer's new, much-hyped study on police shootings. *Vox*. Retrieved from https://www.vox.com/2016/7/11/12149468/racism-police-shootings-data ; Rebora, A. (2016, June 20). Remodeling the workshop: Lucy Calkins on writing instruction today. *Education Week/Teacher*. Retrieved from https://www.edweek.org/tm/articles/2016/06/20/remodeling-the-workshop-lucy-calkins-on-writing.html
2. Newkirk, T. (2005, November). The new writing assessments: Where are they leading us? *English Journal, 95*(2), 21–22.
3. Hillocks, G., Jr. (2003). Fighting back: Assessing the assessments. *English Journal, 92*(4), 63–70.
4. Applebee, A. N., & Langer, J. A. (2013). *Writing instruction that works: Proven methods for middle and high school classrooms*. New York, NY: Teachers College Press.
5. Thomas, P.L. (2014, January 10). Review: Writing instruction that works: Proven methods for middle and high school classrooms. *Teachers College Record*. Retrieved from http://www.tcrecord.org/Content.asp?ContentId=17375

CHAPTER 2

# WHY YOU CANNOT TRUST COMMON CORE ADVOCACY

I used to show my high school students a passage from Aristotle that was essentially a "kids today" rant, noting he wrote in the 300s B.C. So I generally have little patience with anyone damning contemporary youth as if this generation is somehow quantifiably worse than the ones before. That is so much drivel.

"Why Americans can't write"[1] falls squarely in that sub-genre, but, alas!, that is just a mask for its real purpose: propagandizing for the Common Core. Before we look at the nonsense in this really bad piece of writing that claims students today can't write, we must note that the writer, Natalie Wexler, chairs the board of trustees for the Writing Revolution, self-described as "a national not-for-profit organization dedicated to teaching students from underserved school districts to think clearly and reflect that thinking in their writing."[2] And here is the key bit of information: Who sits on the advisory board? David Coleman, grand architect of the ELA Common Core.

So Wexler claims writing is in dire circumstances based on data from The National Assessment of Educational Progress (NAEP). The problem here is that in my own analysis of the writing section of NAEP,[3] I have shown that the test is so badly constructed that we can draw *no valid claims about writing at all*.

If Wexler were credible on writing quality by American students, she would be aware that we have significant research on how students are being taught writing and what the consequences of those practices are.[4] Wexler would also know that, yes, students are not writing as much as they need to write, and in many ways, students arriving at college do not have the background in writing they should or that they need to write well in college. But the real interesting part of that research is the cause of both our failure to teach writing well and students underperforming as writers in college: the *standards and testing movement* has effectively dismantled the composition movement that began in the 1970s and 1980s, notably because of the National Writing Project.

In short, Applebee and Langer found that *teachers across several disciplines know more than ever about best practices in teaching writing*, but because of high-stakes accountability, students are unlikely to receive that instruction or the practice they need to be competent young writers. Therefore, it is easy and valid to extrapolate that there is no doubt that simply changing the standards will not change the corrosive impact the accountability movement has had on writing. Neither Common Core as standards nor the related high-stakes test will save writing, but they are both poised to continue ruining writing instruction.

We are left only with this: Wexler's piece is yet more heinous Common Core propaganda, cloaked in the weakest of sheep's clothing—a really bad piece of writing claiming students today cannot write.

## ENDNOTES

1. Wexler, N. (2015, September 24). Why Americans can't write. *The Washington Post* retrieved from https://www.washingtonpost.com/opinions/why-americans-cant-write/2015/09/24/6e7f420a-6088-11e5-9757-e49273f05f65_story.html
2. https://www.thewritingrevolution.org/
3. Schmidt, R., & Thomas, P.L. (2009). *21st century literacy: If we are scripted, are we literate?* Heidelberg, Germany: Springer.
4. Applebee & Langer (2013).

# CHAPTER 3

# MISGUIDED READING POLICY CREATES WRONG LESSONS FOR STUDENTS AS WRITERS

Having taught writing to teenagers and young adults at the high school and undergraduate levels for over 30 years now, I have a standard approach to the first few classes: We identify and then unpack and challenge the lessons the students have learned about writing. For these foundational lessons to work, however, I have to gain the trust of my students so that they are open and honest about the real lessons (or more accurately framed as "rules" they have conformed to implementing). One of the best moments in this process is when I very carefully ask them to explain to me how they decide when to use commas.

Usually someone is willing to confess: "I put commas when I pause." And then I ask who else uses that strategy, and essentially every time most, if not all, of the students raise their hands. Next, I help them trace just how this completely flawed rule entered into their toolbox as writers. I note that when they were first learning to read, especially when they were being taught to read aloud, teachers in the first, second, and third grades likely stressed how we pause slightly at commas and a bit more at periods when reading aloud. Students usually nod their heads, recalling those early lessons, and even specific teachers.

The next part is tricky and really important. Throughout elementary, middle, and high school, then, students receive a good deal of direct

*Teaching Writing as Journey, Not Destination:*
*Essays Exploring What "Teaching Writing" Means*, pp. 9–11
Copyright © 2019 by Information Age Publishing

grammar instruction, often framed as rules (although this is a key problem with such instruction), often done in isolation (the ultimate fatal flaw of grammar instruction), and almost universally offered well before students have reached the level of abstract reasoning (brain development) necessary to understand how grammar works as a system.[1]

Throughout most of my teaching career at the high school level, students were issued a traditional grammar text (Warriner's), and in that text, commas had an entire chapter and something like 47 rules. Since most students were uninterested, unmotivated, and incapable of understanding all that dense information on commas, they simply did what most humans would do—fabricate something they could manage from the information they understood. Thus many students flip a *reading aloud guideline* that associates commas with pausing into a horribly inadequate "rule" for punctuating sentences.

As a teacher of writing, then, I am vividly aware of how we have traditionally misled students with both our reading and our writing policies, significantly grounded in prescriptive and mechanistic approaches to language—approaches that teach the wrong lessons and do more harm than good. That awareness leads me to recognize that the Common Core movement, and the next generation of standards in their wake, is likely to increase that problem, not address the need to implement effective and thoughtful reading and writing policy.

For one example is the concern raised in "Common Core calls for kids to read books that 'frustrate' them. Is that a good idea?" by Russ Walsh:[2]

> The Common Core, in its pursuit of "college and career readiness," calls for ramping up the complexity of texts read by children in all grades after second grade. Some reading educators, including University of Illinois Professor Emeritus Tim Shanahan, have argued that this means we should not be focused on having students read in texts at their instructional level, but in texts that are at their frustration level.

This call for students reading at the "frustration level," sadly, is nothing new. Student have typically been required to read texts that don't match either their language development or their background or perceptions of existence—works that are to them needlessly complex and difficult simply to comprehend (much less interpret).

Take for example nearly any student reading Shakespeare or Nathaniel Hawthorne's *The Scarlet Letter*. Setting aside that plays were never intended to be read texts, both of these works are variations of English so far removed from contemporary students that (just as they have done with comma/pausing rules) they decide that all good writing must be impenetrable—arcane words, labyrinthine sentences. As a result, when I stress that good writing must be specific, concrete, coherent, and above all else *clear*, students are baffled.

Common Core, again, appears to me nothing new; "close reading" is New Criticism repackaged.[3] But I do fear that calls for students reading at frustration levels are likely to perpetuate the very worst of traditional reading policies and practices. Reading and writing are the core of all learning, and as such, we should take much greater care that our reading and writing policy is grounded in healthy and effective approaches to literacy. We must also recognize that our reading practices feed our writing practices.

As has been all too common in formal schooling, Common Core and the entire standards movement appear poised to once again drive misguided reading policy that will teach our students the wrong lessons as young writers. And if nothing else, that puts me at a constant frustration level.

## ENDNOTES

1. Warner, AL. (1993, September). If the shoe no longer fits, wear it anyway? *English Journal*, 76-80.
2. Walsh, R. (2014, September 22). Common Core calls for kids to read books that 'frustrate' them. Is that a good idea? [Web log]. The Answer Sheet. *The Washington Post*. Retrieved from https://www.washingtonpost.com/news/answer-sheet/wp/2014/09/22/common-core-calls-for-kids-to-read-books-that-frustrate-them-is-that-a-good-idea/
3. New Criticism, Close Reading, and Failing Critical Literacy Again https://radicalscholarship.wordpress.com/2014/02/02/new-criticism-close-reading-and-failing-critical-literacy-again/

CHAPTER 4

# REFORMED TO DEATH

## Discipline and Control Eclipse Education

An enduring gift of being a student and a teacher is that these experiences often create lifelong and powerful personal and professional relationships. Reminiscing about these experiences, however, is often bittersweet because we are simultaneously reminded of the great promise of education as well as how too often we are completely failing that promise. After writing about my two years as a co-lead instructor for a local writing project summer institute, a former student I discussed called me, and we found ourselves wading deeply into the bittersweet.

She has in the intervening years been a co-facilitator in the same workshop where I taught her now almost two decades ago; she also has worked in many capacities providing teachers professional development and serving as a mentor to preservice teachers completing education programs and certification requirements.

As we talked, the pattern that emerged is extremely disturbing: the most authentic and enriching opportunities for teachers are routinely crowded out by bureaucratic and administrative mandates, often those that are far less valid as instructional practice. In my chapter on de-grading the writing classroom,[1] I outlined how the imposition of accountability ran roughshod over the rise of the National Writing Project (NWP), which embodied both the best of how to teach writing and a gold standard approach to profes-

*Teaching Writing as Journey, Not Destination:*
*Essays Exploring What "Teaching Writing" Means*, pp. 13–16
Copyright © 2019 by Information Age Publishing

13

sional development. What is best for teachers and what is best for students, however, are mostly irrelevant in the ongoing high-stakes accountability approach to education reform, a process in which discipline and control eclipse education.

Local sites of the NWP are crucibles of how the reform movement is a death spiral for authentic and high-quality teaching and learning as well as teacher professionalism. At the core of the NWP model is a charge that teachers must experience and become expert in that which they teach; therefore, to guide students through a writing workshop experience, teachers participate in extended summer writing workshop institutes.

While NWP site-based institutes and other programs thrived against the weight of the accountability era, that appears to be waning under the weight of accountability-based mandates *that are in a constant state of reform*; teachers are routinely required to seek *new* certification while they and their students must adapt to a perpetually different set of standards and high-stakes tests. That bureaucracy is often Orwellian since "best practice" and "evidence-based"—terminology birthed in authentic contexts such as the NWP—have become markers for programs and practices *that are aligned with standards and testing*, not with the research base of the field. The logic is cripplingly circular and disturbingly misleading.

This erosion and erasing of teaching writing well and effectively is paralleled all across the disciplines in K–12 education, in fact—although how writing is particularly ruined in standards- and testing-based programs and practices remains our best marker of accountability as discipline and control, not as education. I want to end here by staying with writing, but shifting to the sacred cow of the reform movement: evidence.

High-stakes testing of writing has been a part of state accountability and national testing (NAEP and, briefly, the SAT) for more than 30 years since A Nation at Risk ushered in (deceptively) the accountability era of K–12 public education in the United States. What do we know about high-stakes testing as well as the accountability paradigm driven by standards and tests?

George Hillocks[2] has documented that high-stakes testing of writing *reduces* instruction to training students to conform to anchor papers, template writing, and prescriptive rubrics. In other words, as I noted above, "best practice" and "evidence-based" became whether or not teaching and learning about writing conformed to the way students were tested—not if students had become in any way authentic or autonomous writers, and thinkers. My own analysis of NAEP tests of writing[3] details that standardized data touted as measuring writing proficiency are strongly skewed by student reading abilities and significant problems with the alignment of the assessment's prompts and scoring guides.

And now, we have yet more proof that education reform is fundamentally flawed, as Jill Barshay reports:

> "[T]he use of the computer may have widened the writing achievement gap," concluded the working paper, "Performance of fourth-grade students in the 2012 NAEP computer-based writing pilot assessment." If so, that has big implications as test makers, with the support of the Department of Education, move forward with their goal of moving almost all students to computerized assessments, which are more efficient and cheaper to grade.[4]

Not only does high-stakes testing of writing fail the research base on how best to teach composition, but also the pursuit of efficiency[5] continues to drive all aspects of teaching and learning, effectively contradicting the central claims of reformers to be pursuing seemingly lofty goals such as closing the achievement gap.

Writing instruction and assessment are prisoners of the cult of proficiency that is K–12 education reform, and are just one example of the larger accountability machine that has chosen discipline and control over education. Reform has become both the means and the ends to keeping students and teachers always "starting again," "never [to be] finished with anything," as Gilles Deleuze[6] observed.

Barshay ends her coverage of the Institute of Education Sciences (IES) study on computer-based writing assessment with a *haunting fear about how evidence drives practice in a high-stakes accountability environment*, a fear I guarantee will inevitably become reality: "My fear is that some educators will respond by drilling poor kids in the QWERTY keyboard, when the time would be better spent reading great works of literature and writing essays and creative stories." As long as reforming and accountability are the masters, we will continue to make the wrong instructional decisions, we will continue to be compelled to make the wrong decisions.

## ENDNOTES

1. Bower, J., & Thomas, P.L. (Eds.). (2016). *De-testing and de-grading schools: Authentic alternatives to accountability and standardization* (Revised ed.). New York, NY: Peter Lang.

2. Hillocks, G., Jr. (2003). Fighting back: Assessing the assessments. *English Journal, 92*(4), 63–70; Hillocks, G., Jr. (2002). *The testing trap: How state writing assessments control learning*. New York, NY: Teachers College Press.

3. Schmidt, R., & Thomas, P.L. (2009). *21st century literacy: If we are scripted, are we literate?* Heidelberg, Germany: Springer.

4. Barshay, J. (2016, January 11). Using computers widens the achievement gap in writing a federal study finds. *The Hechinger Report*. Retrieved from http://hechingerreport.org/online-writing-tests-widen-achievement-gap/

5. Ball, A., Christensen, L., Fleischer, C., Haswell, R., Ketter, J., Yageldski, R., & Yancey, K. (2005, April 16). The impact of the SAT and ACT timed writing tests. Urbana, IL: National Council of Teachers of English; NCTE Position Statement on Machine Scoring. (2013, April 20). *The National Council of Teachers of English*. Retrieved from http://www2.ncte.org/statement/machine_scoring/

6. Deleuze, G. (1992). Postscripts on the societies of control. *October, 59*, 3–7.

# SECTION II

## BEING A WRITING TEACHER

# CHAPTER 5

# A COMMUNITY OF WRITING TEACHERS

The purposeful teaching of writing that led to and then sprang from the formation of the National Writing Project (NWP) and its affiliated sites has always emphasized the importance of a community of writers. And while the summer institutes offered through NWP sites—where I was saved as a writing teacher and then fortunate to be a co-lead instructor for two summers years later—create over several weeks for teachers writing workshop experiences that include forming communities of writing teachers, I fear that in the high-stakes environment of most K–12 public schools and then in the departmentalized environments of higher education the existence of those communities of writing teachers are rare, if not entirely absent.

I entered full-time teaching in the fall of 1984 as a beginning teacher and want-to-be writer. On that first day, I saw my job as a public school English teacher primarily focusing on the teaching of writing. While my students over the next 18 years would be quick to admit I had high expectations, possibly too high, for them—demanding a great deal of writing as well as significant growth as writers and thinkers—I also had high expectations for me as a writing teacher. Every day, I feared I was doing that work less effectively than I could, and I was constantly evolving, growing, changing—notably after attending the Spartanburg Writing Project (SWP) summer institute.

*Teaching Writing as Journey, Not Destination:*
*Essays Exploring What "Teaching Writing" Means*, pp. 19–21
Copyright © 2019 by Information Age Publishing

Several years after I entered higher education as a teacher educator, my university moved to a first-year seminar format, opening the door for professors from any discipline to teach first-year writing—but the university failed to consider that the teaching of writing is a complex skill set, not something just anyone can do because they has an advanced degree.

Just shy of a decade into the first-year seminar commitment, then, the university has made curricular changes (including requiring one additional upper-level writing course), and was a part of the first Faculty Writing Fellows (FWF) program that includes professors from English, education, psychology, biology, computer science, philosophy, sociology, history, and so forth. This year-long faculty seminar has allowed us to spend our time thinking deeply about the challenges of teaching writing at the university level.

The faculty members in these seminars have a wide range of experiences and backgrounds in teaching writing, and that diversity has significantly opened my eyes wider to the challenges of teaching writing. Since I am working my way into the fourth decade as a teacher of writing, I have a much different perspective than early-career professors in disciplines such as psychology or computer science. When I discuss my strategies for reading like a writer where I highlight the rhetorical and aesthetic aspects of writing, professors from philosophy or biology, for example, say "I can't do that" or "I don't do that."

From these exchanges, then, we begin to discuss how professors can and do address first-year writing differently—but that those differences are not a problem because no writing teacher can accomplish everything in one writing course. To paraphrase Thoreau, a writing teacher is not charged with doing everything, but something. As John Warner has explained, "I do my best to help students succeed for the future writing occasions they'll confront in college and beyond, but the truth is, I cannot properly prepare them for what's coming."[1]

And thus, we have begun to stress among our faculty that any one writing course is not an inoculation that will cure writing ills. In fact, we are working hard to dissuade professors of deficit views about students, grammar, writing, and such. Just as any writer is always a writer-in-progress, all teachers of writing are writing-teachers-in-progress.

As a writer and writing teacher, I am still learning, and here are some of the lessons I have begun to see during our FWF experience:

1.  Regardless of background or level of experience, everyone teaching writing needs purposeful preparation for writing instruction.
2.  To teach writing, we must all be willing to investigate our attitudes about language as well as our own experiences as both student writers and writers in our disciplines.

3. We should form a community of writers for our students, but our schools must provide for all teachers of writing that same ongoing *community of writing teachers*.
4. Writing is a complex skill that can and should be taught at all levels of formal education with the full recognition that no one can ever be *finished* learning to write.
5. Teaching writing is a discipline itself, a field rich in evidence but mostly defined by the perpetual problems of how to foster writers in hundreds of different writing situations. Each writing student is a new and unique challenge, not a flawed or incomplete student to be "fixed."
6. The pursuits of writing and teaching writing are greatly enhanced by equal parts passion and humility.

Finally, what has been most rewarding about the FWF experience and our community of writing teachers is that I am chomping at the bit for my *next* fall first-year writing courses where once again, I will be doing some things differently, and I trust, better.

## ENDNOTE

1. Warner, J. (2015, December 15). I cannot prepare students to write their (history, philosophy, sociology, poly sci., etc.) papers [Web log]. Just Visiting. *Inside Higher Ed.* Retrieved from https://www.insidehighered.com/blogs/just-visiting/i-cannot-prepare-students-write-their-history-philosophy-sociology-poly-sci-etc

# CHAPTER 6

# FOSTERING THE TRANSITION FROM STUDENT TO WRITER

Just past midterm in my first-year writing seminar one fall, I asked my two sections of students to brainstorm about what behaviors that worked for them in high school have failed to work for them in the first semester of college—focusing specifically on their roles as academic writers. Part of this exercise has been supported by my adopting Keith Hjortshoj's *The Transition to College Writing* as well as my instructional commitment to providing my students overt opportunities to set aside their student behaviors and adopt writer (scholar) behaviors.

The responses were illuminating about both how often high school fails students and that many of my students have in fact begun to understand the important transition from high school to college. Several students confronted the need to start their essays much earlier, spending more time on drafting their work (and adding not to write the night before the work is due), but one student offered an excellent recognition about the need for writers to have a primary audience and then to shape their purpose with that audience in mind; he framed that response against the superficial ways in which he had been allowed to consider audience as a reader in high school.

Just a few days after this exercise with my first-year students, as a co-leader of a year-long faculty seminar on teaching writing, my colleagues had an equally enlightening discussion about our experiences with learning

*Teaching Writing as Journey, Not Destination:*
*Essays Exploring What "Teaching Writing" Means,* pp. 23–25

to write throughout our formal education, reaching from K–12 through graduate school. Some key patterns included that many of us had our writing graded, but received little feedback designed to prompt revision, and that many of us had some of the best direct writing instruction during our graduate school experiences, notably while writing a thesis/dissertation. Ultimately, we identified that many professors were attempting to teach courses (first-year composition) that we never took ourselves and teach pedagogy that we had never experienced as students.

And then came a really key discussion: We acknowledged that our own writing—and especially our own engagement in writing—was at its best when we had authentic audiences and were working with topics of our choice. Of course, we then moved to confronting that these are the qualities our own students need (even deserve) to become the sort of young writers and scholars that we envision.

These discussions pushed me, after over 30 years teaching writing, to think about a recent conference I had with a first-year student whose work/writing and classroom behavior remain trapped in high school. He is not engaged in class, and when we conferenced about his second essay—I was compelled to note in my comments on the paper that few professors would accept the essay since the formatting was shoddy and the work did not meet the basic requirements of the assignment—I first asked if he had read the sample essays I provided for the assignment. He immediately said that he had not, and seemed completely unconcerned that he hadn't.

I have no desire to ascribe blame, but this student (and most of my students about whom I have concern for their success) is almost completely disengaged from the course except to comply and move on. In other words, the quality of his writing and behavior in class are not necessarily representations of his ability but are reflections of the absence of what we discussed in our faculty seminar. He doesn't see anything authentic about his audience or purposes as a writer in this class.

Here I must stress the warning I often share with teachers-to-be and current teachers in my graduate courses: We must not require 100% success in order to embrace a practice. Now, that said, here are the strategies I have developed over those 30-plus years that are designed to foster the transition from *student* to *writer/scholar*:

- Balance giving students choice with providing them the sort of structure that builds toward the larger writing goals of the course. My first-year writing seminar is a semester-long course that requires students to submit four original essays of about 1,250–1,500 words each. For several years, the essays were all open-ended assignments with students deciding the type and content of each essay. That was a failed approach. Now, I move the student from a personal narrative, then to an online essay that uses hyperlinks for citation and incorporates images and/or videos, then to a disciplinary-based traditionally cited (APA, MLA, etc.) essay, and then to a final essay that we determine the type based on the student's needs once we have the first essays to consider.

- Focus investigations of texts in class on reading like a writer (see Chapters 23, 54) so that we always acknowledge the primary audience of the text and how the writer shapes the purpose of the writing to that primary audience. Students are provided many authentic models for the types of writing they are writing. Our class sessions examining both text and then the essay assignments are anchored in real-world essays (including published academic essays) that we mine for how writers write.

- Provide feedback on essays and in individual conferences that support revision strategies that are actionable and manageable. Increasingly, I have reduced marking and comments on essay drafts, and then dedicated individual conferences to asking students about their essays while working toward making sure the student has a clear revision plan once the conference is completed. It is during these conferences that I can confront whether or not the student is authentically engaged in an essay—and seek ways to make sure the student has a genuine reason to write and revise further.

Again, nothing in teaching will be 100% successful, but I believe we are doing our students a great disservice if we simply give into fatalism and continue to allow writing to be assignments that students dutifully complete in order to receive course credit. My commitment as a teacher of writing is to foster a transition from student to writer that serves my students well as young people on a journey to their own autonomy—and even happiness.

That means I am on a journey as well as a teacher of writing.

# CHAPTER 7

# WHO CAN, WHO SHOULD TEACH WRITING?

My transition from public high school English teacher to university professor overlapped with my university debating and then voting to change its
core curriculum and academic calendar. I sat in many contentious faculty
meetings mostly listening as faculty held forth about the pros and cons of
both the established core/calendar and the proposed core/calendar. One
thing that I witnessed was that faculty are quite protective of their own
disciplines—but are apt to step carelessly on disciplines outside their area
of expertise.

For example, the faculty were considering dropping the traditional first-
year composition approach that is taught exclusively by English faculty for
a first-year seminar approach that allowed and required faculty across all
disciplines to teach the writing-intensive seminars for first-year students.
As someone who taught high school English for almost 20 years—most
of that time spent learning the complex craft of teaching writing through
trial-and-error and dedicating much of my own energy to learning how to
teach writing by studying the research against my own practices—I heard
faculty repeatedly trample the field of composition, in terms of speaking
as if the field doesn't exist as well as stating directly and indirectly that
"anyone can teach writing because we all are scholars."

Let's jump ahead about 10 years. The faculty did adopt a new core and
calendar, including the first-year seminar structure. After a decade, we

*Teaching Writing as Journey, Not Destination:*
*Essays Exploring What "Teaching Writing" Means,* pp. 27–30
Copyright © 2019 by Information Age Publishing

reconsidered the first-year seminar model, and much of the motivation for that reflection is that who can and who should teach writing have become significant problems—ones not anticipated well or addressed adequately. A few academic years ago, due to my interest in the first-year seminars and teaching writing, I was named Faculty Director, First Year Seminars in order to help provide the sort of faculty support that had been lacking. Also, we have a First Year Oversight Committee, but that oversight has focused primarily on approving new courses and monitoring funding for seminars—although the committee has managed faculty workshops over the summer to address course development and teaching writing.

As a transition, we have implemented year-long Faculty Writing Fellows seminars, including 12 faculty and three seminar facilitators to begin building a purposeful approach to supporting faculty who teach writing across the curriculum. Just as I remain in search of how to teach writing well to students of all ages (there is no finish line), I also can attest that teaching faculty at any level how to teach writing is a perpetual and nearly overwhelming struggle.

First, then, I want to highlight a couple foundational issues and questions that must be addressed when any school is considering who can and who should teach writing:

- Initially, acknowledge that composition is a disciplinary field[1] that is not the same as English as a discipline. In fact, many K–12 teachers and college professors with credentials/degrees in English are primarily skilled in literary analysis, not teaching writing. As well, even when we acknowledge composition as a field, we should also recognize that it is typically a marginalized field. That marginalization includes assigning new/beginning teachers to teach composition and so-called "remedial" writing as a sort of gauntlet they must endure to earn *better* course assignments. In higher education, adjuncts and *teaching* assistants are disproportionately charged with the teaching of writing also.

- The larger questions of who can and who should teach writing are much more complex than many schools admit. All educators at every educational level have attained a degree of literacy that equips them for the ability (can) to teach writing, but flipping that *can* to *should* is where schools often make a fundamental mistake. Faculty charged with teaching writing purposefully but without a formal background in composition must *want* to teach writing and then must receive sustained and organized instruction and support in how to teach writing.

If schools committed to writing across the curriculum, expanding writing-intensive courses, or embracing "anyone can teach writing" manage the two hurdles above, however, several additional problems are sure to exist:

- Faculty without composition backgrounds tend to view "teaching writing" as correcting grammar, mechanics, and usage "errors." This dynamic requires establishing common language among faulty teaching writing (for example, do not say "writing" to mean "grammar") and then couching that common terminology in a robust examination of linguistics that confronts the tension between prescriptive grammarians and descriptive grammarians. That tension typically can be predicted in that the general public and educators without composition backgrounds skew toward prescriptive grammar (rules-based) while composition best practices tend to be driven by a descriptive grounding in linguistics (conventions-based).

- Without addressing that tension above, then, I am convinced the process to expand who can and should teach writing is doomed to failure. How to accomplish that, however, is another matter entirely. That tension is likely to manifest itself in a trap: Faculty without composition backgrounds will often note that they feel unprepared to teach "writing" (which is code for correcting grammar, mechanics, and usage), but when they are introduced to best practice in teaching writing and descriptive linguistics, they balk. The result is: "Teach me how to teach writing, but I don't want to hear about how to teach writing; I want to correct my students' horrible grammar."

- That trap means the first step to learning how to teach writing is giving faculty the opportunity to investigate their own attitudes toward language, and then to invite them to set aside, as Connie Weaver calls it, the "error hunt."[2] Teaching writing begins with having a rich and healthy attitude about language, and then coming to understand that teaching writing is not simply teaching grammar and that the question is not *if* we address grammar, mechanics, and usage, but *how*, *when*, and *why* (and that the *why* is to foster students as writers, not grammarians).

- Even those of us with formal backgrounds in teaching writing face a significant hurdle shared with many educators without that formal background: It is very difficult to teach writing in the context of best practices (for example, writing workshop) if the teacher has not been a participant in best practices such as a writing workshop. One of the most powerful elements of the National Writing Project's professional development model has been summer workshops that provide just that experience. Faculty designated for teaching writing must be provided some extended opportunities to examine themselves as writers, participating in writing workshop and the practices they will bring to their own students.

- All of the problems above should also be within a *formal mission and concurrent goals for writing* shared within the school/college and among faculty. Both faculty and students are likely to be more successful if everyone has core goals to maintain a manageable focus for teaching writing. However, that mission and those goals must acknowledge that teaching writing is never a fixed outcome. In other words, no single course or teacher/professor can or should be expected to produce a "finished" writer. Even so-called "basic" skills of writing are nearly impossible to identify and master at predictable points along formal education.

Who can teach writing? Nearly any educator motivated to teach students as writers and then provided the necessary support to become a writing teacher. Who should teach writing? See above.

As a writer and teacher primarily focused on teaching writing, I am in the process of both and daily aware that writing and teaching writing are always a process of becoming. Few human endeavors are as complex and important as being a writer or being a teacher of writing, and thus, asking who *can* and who *should* teach writing remains just as complex.

## ENDNOTES

1. Smagorinsky, P. (Ed.). (2006). *Research on composition.* New York: Teachers College.
2. Weaver, C. (1996). *Teaching grammar in context.* Portsmouth, NH: Heinemann.

## CHAPTER 8

# WRITING, UNTEACHABLE OR MISTAUGHT?

"Let's not tell them what to write."

Lou LaBrant, The (1936)[1]

Kurt Vonnegut was a genre-bending writer and a freethinker, a lonely pond fed by the twin tributaries of atheism and agnosticism. So it is a many-layered and problematic claim by Vonnegut, also a writing teacher, that writing is "unteachable," but "something God lets you do or declines to let you do."[2] This nod to the authority of God, I think, is more than a typical Vonnegut joke (the agnostic/atheist writer citing God) as it speaks to a seemingly endless debate over the five-paragraph essay, which resurfaces without fail among English teachers and teachers of writing.

To investigate the use of the five-paragraph template as well as prompted writing as dominant practices for teaching writing in formal schooling to all children, I want to begin by exploring my own recent experience co-writing a chapter with a colleague and also couch the entire discussion in a caution raised by Johnson, Smagorinsky, Thompson, and Fry: "Just as we hope that teachers do not oversimplify issues of form, we hope that critics do not oversimplify intentions of the legions of teachers who take this approach" (p. 171).[3]

*Teaching Writing as Journey, Not Destination:*
*Essays Exploring What "Teaching Writing" Means*, pp. 31–35
Copyright © 2019 by Information Age Publishing

## Writers and People Who Write

My colleague Mike Svec and I co-authored a chapter in a volume examining our work as teacher educators who have working-class backgrounds. Mike is an academic who occasionally writes. I am a writer who happens to be an academic. And therein lies a problem for our work as co-writers. Mike spends a great deal of time mulling, reading, planning, and fretting (my word) before committing anything to the virtual page. I write as part of my brainstorming, and fill up the virtual page so I will have something to wrestle with, revise, reshape, and even abandon. Filling up virtual paper is Mike's late stage. Filling up virtual paper is my first stage.

This experience has highlighted for me two important points:

1. Most people (students and academics/teachers included) are not writers, but people who occasionally write (and then, that occasion is often under some compelling requirement and not the "choice" of the person writing).
2. Especially people who occasionally write, and then most often under a compelling reason or situation, suffer from an inordinate sense of paralysis (I am going to argue further below) because they have been *mistaught* how to write (predominantly by template and prompt).

Since most teachers of English/English Language Arts (ELA) and any discipline in which the teacher must teach writing are themselves not writers, the default approach to writing is at least informed by if not couched in Mike's view of writing—one that has been fostered by template and prompted writing instruction (the authoritarian nod in Vonnegut invoking God above). And this is my big picture philosophical and pedagogical problem with depending on the five-paragraph essay as the primary way in which we teach students to write: Visual art classes that aim to teach students to paint do not use paint-by-numbers to prepare novices to be artists, and I would argue, that is because those teachers are themselves artists (not teachers who occasionally paint). However, most teachers of writing in all disciplines are themselves not writers, but teachers who occasionally (or in the past occasionally) write (wrote).

## Why Scripts, Templates, and Prompts Fail Students and Writing

In a graduate summer course for English/ELA teachers, I had the students read a commentary by Mike Royko (syndicated columnist) on flag burning.[4] I asked them to mark the parts of the essay and underline the thesis as they read. And these students who were also teachers dutifully did so. Royko's piece in most ways does not conform to the five-paragraph essay, but the teachers marked and labeled an introduction, body, and conclusion—underlining a sentence as the thesis. They immediately imposed onto the essay the script they taught their students (the script they were taught).

When we shared, they noticed differences in their labeling and marking. Most notable was the thesis: Royko's piece is a snarky, sarcastic commentary that *directly states support for flag burning laws* but in fact rejects flag burning laws by sarcastic implication. As a consequence, no direct thesis exists—although we can fairly infer one. I continue to use examples such as this with first-year students to investigate and challenge templates for essays they have been taught (for example, essays by Barbara Kingsolver) in order to work toward what Johns calls "genre awareness" instead of "genre acquisition."[5]

Yes, essays have openings that tend to focus the reader, but most openings are primarily concerned with grabbing and maintaining the reader's interest. And openings are typically far more than one paragraph (essays have paragraphs of many different lengths as well, some as brief as one word or sentence). Essays then proceed in many different ways—although guided by concepts such as cohesion and purpose. And then, essays end some way, a way I would argue that is not "restate your introduction in different words" (writers such as Kingsolver often use framing through an image, for example, that is established in the opening and repeated in the closing). *Ultimately, the five-paragraph essay allows both teachers and students to avoid the messy and complicated business that is writing—many dozens of choices with purpose and intent.*

Scripts, templates, and prompts do most of the work *for* student—leaving them almost no opportunities to experiment with the *writer's craft*, whether that be in the service of history, science, or any other discipline. Without deliberate practice in the business of writing (making purposeful decisions while implementing the writer's genre awareness against the constraints of the writing expectations), students (and even academics) are often left in some degree of paralysis when asked to perform authentically as writers. As a Zach Weinersmith's comic succinctly illustrates, the five-paragraph template/script and writing prompt serve greater ease in *assigning* and *grading* writing (absolving the writing teacher of having expertise and experience as a writer, in fact), but as the student in the comic declares: "Suddenly I hate writing." And Jennifer Gray notes:

> [M]any of [the students] checked out of the writing process and merely performed for the teacher. Their descriptions about their writing lack enthusiasm and engagement; instead, they reflect obedience and resignation. That

is not the kind of writer I want in my classes; I want to see students actively engaged with their work, finding value and importance in the work.[6]

•

As much as I love Vonnegut, I disagree about writing being unteachable. And Vonnegut's own role as mainly a writer who occasionally taught writing presents another lesson:

> Nothing is known about helping real writers to write better. I have discovered almost nothing about it during the past two years. I now make to my successor at Iowa a gift of the one rule that seemed to work for me: Leave real writers alone.

Well, yes, we do know quite a great deal about teaching writing—and we have for many decades. So if "leave them alone" means do not use artificial scripts, I am all in, but certainly developing writers of all ages can be fostered directly by the teacher.

*Love*

I am left to worry, then, that the main problem we have with teaching writing is that for too long, we have *mistaught* it as people who occasionally write, and not as writers *and* as teachers. This is a herculean ask, of course, that we be writers *and* teachers. But for the many who do not now consider themselves writers but must teach writing, it is the opportunity to begin the journey to being a writer *with* students by committing to genre awareness instead of genre acquisition.

Awareness comes from investigating the form you wish to produce (not imposing a template onto a form or genre). Investigate poetry in order to write poetry; investigate essays in order to write essays. But set artificial and simplistic templates and scripts aside so that you and your students can see the form you wish to write.

Ultimately, Barbara Kingsolver's warning about child rearing also serves us well as teachers lured by the Siren's song of the five-paragraph essay: "Be careful what you give children, or don't, for sooner or later you will always get it back."[8]

## ENDNOTES

1. LaBrant, L. (1936). The psychological basis for creative writing. *English Journal, 25*(4), 292–301.
2. Vonnegut, K. (1967, August 6). Teaching the unteachable. *The New York Times*. Retrieved from http://www.nytimes.com/1967/08/06/books/vonnegut-teaching.html

3. Johnson, T. S., Smagorinsky, P., Thompson, L., & Fry, P. G. (2003). Learning to teach the five-paragraph theme. *Research in the Teaching of English, 38*(2), 136-176.

4. Royko, M. (1995, July 19). Why should we stop at mere flag burning? *The Baltimore Sun*. Retrieved from http://articles. baltimoresun.com/1995-07-19/news/1995200159_1_flag-burning-jewish-flag-dumb-laws

5. Johns, A.M. (2008). Genre awareness for the novice academic student: An on-going quest. *Language Teaching, 41*(2), 237-252.

6. https://www.smbc-comics.com/index.php?id=3749

7. Gray, J.P. (2015, May 26). What do students think about the five-paragraph essay? [Web log]. *Teachers, Profs, Parents: Writers Who Care*. Retrieved from https://writerswhocare.wordpress.com/2015/05/26/what-do-students-think-about-the-five-paragraph-essay/

8. Kingsolver, B. (1992, February 9). Everybody's somebody's baby. The New York Times. Retrieved from http://movies2.nytimes.com/books/98/10/18/specials/kingsolver-hers.html

CHAPTER 9

# WHAT DOES "TEACHING WRITING" MEAN?

Over the past decade, my home university has adopted and implemented a new curriculum that is, in part, built on shifting to a first-year seminar (FYS) concept (instead of the traditional first-year composition model commonly known as ENG 101 and 102). For three years, I chaired the First Year Seminar Faculty Oversight Committee and was temporarily Faculty Director, First Year Seminars—all of which led to my role on a Task Force to consider how to revise our commitment to two first-year seminars with one being writing intensive (FYW).

While the university sought to address a number of curricular issues related to the FYS program, a central concern involved the *teaching of writing* in the FYW—specifically issues related to direct writing instruction (including direct instruction on scholarly citation) and the consistency of the writing-intensive element across all FYWs. Several elements impacted these issues and possible resolutions: (1) the university did not have a formal writing center/institute during the process, (2) the university doesn't have an explicit or formal writing program or stated goals/commitments, and (3) the commitment to the FYS program included the assumption that *all* faculty across *all disciplines* are equipped to teach writing.

I have been teaching writing and researching what that means for over thirty years—the first 18 as a high school English teacher and then at the undergraduate and graduate levels over much of those years, including teaching future teachers of English to teach writing. A number of my

*Teaching Writing as Journey, Not Destination:*
*Essays Exploring What "Teaching Writing" Means*, pp. 37–41
Copyright © 2019 by Information Age Publishing
All rights of reproduction in any form reserved.

scholarly articles, chapters, and books also address teaching writing. And while I learned how to teach writing painstakingly over those wonderful and challenging two decades of teaching high school, I cannot overemphasize what I have learned about the challenges of supporting quality writing instruction more recently—highlighted, I think, by coming against the range of *insufficient* to *misguided* understanding of what we mean when we call for *teaching writing*.

## What Does "Teaching Writing" Mean?

At the risk of oversimplifying, I can answer this question by how I address students who want to learn to write poetry, a wonderful and impossible task that is a subset of the wonderful and impossible task of teaching writing (again with a nod to Vonnegut). Step one, I explain, is read, read, read poetry—preferably immersing yourself into entire volumes by poets you enjoy and want to emulate. Step two, I add, is to write, write, write poetry. And then, step three is to share those drafts with a poet/teacher who can give you substantive feedback—wherein we find ourselves at "teaching writing." If those students follow my guidelines, and then send me poems for my feedback, what do I do?

Central to teaching writing, I must stress, is both the authority of the teacher as well as the attitude of that teacher about writing, which I proposed for the Task Force as follows:

- Faculty who recognize that all aspects of writing are a process and that *undergraduate students continue to struggle with and need guided practice with formal written expression* (including the conventions of the disciplines, citation, and grammar/mechanics).

To teach writing, then, you *must not be caught in the trap* of thinking anyone can be finished learning to write and the concurrent trap of thinking that direct writing instruction is some sort of remediation (since that implies a lockstep sequence of skills that must be acquired).

For example, one challenge we faced at my university was brought to my attention by a librarian who works with FYS/W faculty and receives student referrals from the Academic Discipline Committee. She noted that a number of students were being labeled academically dishonest because they lacked the background in proper citation and that faculty were not teaching citation, but simply marking it incorrect. This issue with citation, again, is a subset of not understanding that teaching writing is ongoing for all students (and any writers)—not something to master at a set point during formal education.

The teaching of writing includes, as I note above about teaching poetry, creating the conditions within which a student can learn to write and then managing the sort of feedback and opportunities to revise/draft that leads to growth as a writer. *Creating conditions* includes reading and examining a wide variety of texts by genre, mode, and media—and that examination must be not only traditional literary analysis but *reading like a writer*. Reading like a writer entails close consideration of *what* a text says and *how*, while navigating the purposeful relationship between the genre and form the writer has chosen for expression and then how the writer has and has not conformed to the conventions of those genres/forms.

Students and the teacher read an Op-Ed from *The New York Times* in order to confront what Op-Eds and argument tend to do as texts and how in order to determine if the claims in the Op-Ed are sound and how successful the piece ultimately is, for example. These conditions also include that students always use reading like a writer as a foundation for drafting original writing. Feedback, then, becomes the element of teaching writing that is both often *only* what people think of as teaching writing and then the most misunderstood phase. The primary problematic view of responding to student writing is "correcting," which overemphasizes and misunderstands the role of conventions in writing (grammar, mechanics, usage).

What many think of as "correcting," I would argue is editing, and thus, its priority in the teaching of writing is after we have addressed much more important aspects of text, as Lou LaBrant argued:

> As a teacher of English, I am not willing to teach the polishing and adornment of irresponsible, unimportant writing.... I would place as the first aim of teaching students to write the development of full responsibility for what they say. (p. 123)[1]

And it is at this implication by LaBrant—responsible and important writing—that I think we must focus on what it means to teach writing.

As teachers of writing, we must give substantive feedback that encourages awareness and purpose in our students as well as prompts them in concrete ways to revise. That feedback must address the following:

- The relationship between the genre/form students have chosen for their writing and then how effective the piece is within (or against) those conventions.
- Purposefulness of sentence, paragraph, and form/mode creation.
- Appropriateness and effectiveness of diction (word choice), tone, and readability (in the context of the designated audience).
- Weight and clarity of *claims* (notably in the context of disciplinary, genre, and mode conventions). [As a note: novice writers tend to

Criteria

be claim-machines, overwhelming the reader with too many and often overstated claims, and almost no evidence or elaboration.]

- Credibility and weight of evidence (again, tempered by the conventions of the disciplines and thus the expectations for citation).
- Effectiveness and weight of *elaboration*—achieving *cohesion* through rhetorical and content strategies (such as detailed examples or narrative) that support the reader's need for clarity, subordination/coordination of ideas, transition, and one or more unifying motifs/theses.

Teaching writing, then, is a *monumental task*, one that may rightly be called impossible; however, we who are tasked with teaching writing should understand the first directive above—learning to write is a process that no one can ever finish—and find solace in Henry David Thoreau (excusing the sexism of his language): "A man has not everything to do, but something; and because he cannot do everything, it is not necessary that he should do something wrong."[2]

No single writing-intensive class or individual teacher should be expected to accomplish any prescribed outcome for students as writers. Instead, the teaching of writing must be guided by the basic concepts I outlined above for teaching a student to write poetry—creating the conditions within which writing can be explored, conditions that include reading like a writer, drafting original writing, and receiving substantive feedback from a mentor. Teaching writing has a long history of being a challenge, one recognized by LaBrant in 1953:

> It ought to be unnecessary to say that writing is learned by writing; unfortunately there is need. Again and again teachers or schools are accused of failing to teach students to write decent English, and again and again investigations show that students have been taught about punctuation, the function of a paragraph, parts of speech, selection of "vivid" words, spelling—that students have done everything but the writing of many complete papers. Again and again college freshmen report that never in either high school or grammar school have they been asked to select a topic for writing, and write their own ideas about that subject. Some have been given topics for writing; others have been asked to summarize what someone else has said; numbers have been given work on revising sentences, filling in blanks, punctuating sentences, and analyzing what others have written.... Knowing facts about language does not necessarily result in ability to use it. (p. 417)[3]

Any student taking a seat in our classes deserves the patience and time necessary for teaching writing, something extremely difficult to do but possible if we can embrace its complexity and offer students, as LaBrant argues, ample opportunities to practice being writers.

## ENDNOTES

1. LaBrant, L. (1946). Teaching high-school students to write. *English Journal, 35*(3), 123–128.
2. Thoreau, H.D. (1849). Civil disobedience. Retrieved from http://xroads. virginia.edu/~hyper2/thoreau/civil.html
3. LaBrant, L. (1953). Writing is learned by writing. *Elementary English, 30*(7), 417–420.

# SECTION III

**BEING A WRITER**

CHAPTER 10

# A PORTRAIT OF THE ARTIST AS ACTIVIST

## "In the Sunlit Prison of the American Dream"

Standing in Starbucks just a couple weeks after I discovered honey in the sweetener and creamer station, I was peeling open a packet of honey when three lines came to me:

> we rape the bees
> because they are sweet
> because we can

My poet-self writes this way; lines *come to me*, and I usually type them into Notes on my iPhone and e-mail that to myself to work on when I have time.

Driving to my university office, I rehearsed those lines over and over, priming myself for the rest of the poem to appear—to reveal itself to me. As a poet, I am often asking myself and the lines that come: What is this about?

I have preferred honey over processed sugar as a sweetener for about three decades, but over the last year, I discovered that among vegans, eating honey is a serious debate; many vegans do not eat honey. It is a

*Teaching Writing as Journey, Not Destination:*
*Essays Exploring What "Teaching Writing" Means*, pp. 45–49
Copyright © 2019 by Information Age Publishing

matter of consent. And while some find veganism an easy target of ridicule, I see such commitments as powerful contexts of living one's ethical and political beliefs.

Bees and honey, then, were buzzing in my unconsciousness as a political and ethical dilemma—one further complicated by my own sense that I wanted to write about *worker* bees as a metaphor for workers in the time of Trump. The tension, however, became how to write a poem that remained a poem while it seemed to call out to be a political statement.

My foundational poetic muse is e.e. cummings, but my single poetic standard is Gwendolyn Brooks's "We Real Cool," a magical diamond of a poem. Concision and precision, undeniable as a paper cut (like William Carlos Williams in "The Red Wheelbarrow" and "This Is Just To Say").

The final version of "we rape the bees (because we can),"* I hope, fulfilled that goal by focusing on sound (I chose the soft "s" as a whisper to the hard "z" associated with bees), wordplay ("trump," "unjust desserts"), essential but vivid images ("golden lips and sticky fingers"), and the briefest of allusions ( only "enslaved" as I resisted how to pack the poem with both slavery and the Japanese Internment).

A good poem, I think, even if it demands to be a political poem, becomes good by all that the poet chooses to leave out as the poet strips the billowing ideas down to the least possible words.

#

"*Uncle Tom's Cabin* is a very bad novel," wrote James Baldwin in "Everybody's Protest Novel," "having, in its self-righteous, virtuous sentimentality, much in common with *Little Women*" (p. 14).[1] Baldwin engages in this essay that tension between art and politics/activism, arguing, "It is this power of revelation which is the business of the novelist, this journey toward a more vast reality which must take precedence over all other claims" (p. 15). Choosing fidelity to art over politics and activism, Baldwin rejects the protest novel:

> But unless one's ideal of society is a race of neatly analyzed, hard-working ciphers, one can hardly claim for the protest novels the lofty purpose they claim for themselves or share the present optimism concerning them. They emerge for what they are: a mirror of our confusion, dishonesty, panic, trapped and immobilized in the sunlit prison of the American dream.
> (p. 19)

The missionary zeal of activism erases both the core values of the artist and the intent of that zeal—and then Baldwin reminds us:

It must be remembered that the oppressed and the oppressor are bound together within the same society; they accept the same criteria, they share the same beliefs, they both alike depend on the same reality. (p. 21)

Turning at the end to Richard Wright's *Native Son*, Baldwin concludes:

The failure of the protest novel lies in its rejection of life, the human being, the denial of his beauty, dread, power, in its insistence that it is his categorization alone which is real and which cannot be transcended. (p. 23)

#

"'Beauty is truth, truth beauty,—that is all/Ye know on earth, and all ye need to know'" ("Ode on a Grecian Urn," John Keats)

#

"In the latter half of the twentieth century, two visionary books cast their shadows over our futures," explains Margaret Atwood,[2] whose *The Handmaid's Tale* has been rejuvenated with the rise of Trump. While strongly associated with George Orwell, see her essays on "Writing Utopia" and "George Orwell: Some Personal Connections,"[3] Atwood turns from Orwell's *Nineteen Eighty-Four* to another classic dystopian work:

The other was Aldous Huxley's *Brave New World* (1932), which proposed a different and softer form of totalitarianism—one of conformity achieved through engineered, bottle-grown babies and hypnotic persuasion rather than through brutality; of boundless consumption that keeps the wheels of production turning and of officially enforced promiscuity that does away with sexual frustration; of a pre-ordained caste system ranging from a highly intelligent managerial class to a subgroup of dim-witted serfs programmed to love their menial work; and of soma, a drug that confers instant bliss with no side effects.

Then she adds, "Which template would win, we wondered?... Would it be possible for both of these futures—the hard and the soft—to exist at the same time, in the same place? And what would that be like?"

Unlike the protest novel, could we find in dystopian science fiction a satisfying merging of art and politics/activism?

While Milan Kundera's novels, notably *The Unbearable Lightness of Being*, seek to dramatize the philosophical and the political, Atwood's dystopian works—from *The Handmaid's Tale* to her MaddAddam Trilogy—are grounded in, as Atwood explains, history, not what she fabricates but what has already happened. Atwood's fiction is fiction in that she reconstructs human behavior while also infusing her dystopias with speculation, the logical extrapolations of actual human behavior. "It was Huxley's genius to present us to ourselves in all our ambiguity," Atwood understands: "Alone among the animals, we suffer from the future perfect tense."

#

The artist is a human driven to create, that urge welling up inside like a fresh batch of honey never aware of any intensions toward sweetness.
This, I think, we must not deny, for if we do, we deny ourselves.

* we rape the bees (because we can)

> "I was carried to Ohio in a swarm of bees"
> "Bloodbuzz Ohio," The National

> "O brave new world,/That has such people in't!"
> Miranda, *The Tempest*, William Shakespeare

we rape the bees
since seized honey is sweet

*because we can*

brute force for unjust desserts
tiny humming workers enslaved

*because we can*

golden lips and sticky fingers
trump the frailty of small things

*because we can*

we rape the bees
since seized honey is sweet

*because we can*

## ENDNOTES

1. Baldwin, J. (2012). *Notes of a native son.* Boston, MA: Beacon Press.
2. Huxley, A. (2014). *Brave new world*: Special 3D edition. New York, NY: Vintage Classics. Retrieved from https://www.penguin.co.uk/articles/find-your-next-read/extracts/2017/feb/margaret-atwood-introduces-a-brand-new-world/
3. Atwood, M. (2006). *Writing with intent: Essays, reviews, personal prose: 1983-2005.* New York, NY: Basic Books.

CHAPTER 11

# TEACHING, WRITING AS ACTIVISM?

> To the extent that I become clearer about my choices and
> my dreams, which are substantively political and attributively
> pedagogical, and to the extent that I recognize that though an
> educator I am also a political agent, I can better understand why
> I fear and realize how far we still have to go to improve our democracy. I
> also understand that as we put into practice an education that critically
> provokes the learner's consciousness, we are necessarily working
> against the myths that deform us. As we confront such myths, we also face
> the dominant power because those myths are nothing but the expression
> of this power, of its ideology.

> Paulo Freire, *Teachers as Cultural Workers*[1]

> Thus, proponents of critical pedagogy understand that
> every dimension of schooling and every form of educational
> practice are politically contested spaces. Shaped by history
> and challenged by a wide range of interest groups,
> educational practice is a fuzzy concept as it
> takes place in numerous settings, is shaped by
> a plethora of often-invisible forces, and can operate
> even in the name of democracy and justice to be
> totalitarian and oppressive.

> Joe Kincheloe, *Critical Pedagogy Primer*[2]

*Teaching Writing as Journey, Not Destination:*
*Essays Exploring What "Teaching Writing" Means*, pp. 51–54
Copyright © 2019 by Information Age Publishing

Low self-esteem and doubt are evil, tiny demons, and both have plagued me lately with a question: Are teaching and writing activism? During racial upheaval, for example, from Ferguson to Bree Newsome's removing the Confederate battle flag from statehouse grounds in South Carolina (SC), the public in the U.S. has had to confront the power and tensions with activism. The activism connected with race and racism across the nation also prompted for me a question about what exactly counts as activism as well as what are our moral obligations when faced with bigotry, racism, sexism, homophobia, and all forms of oppression.

To do nothing, to strike the "I'm not political" pose, we must admit, is itself a political act, one that tacitly reinforces the status quo of oppression and inequity. To proclaim "I don't see race" is to be complicit in the very racism those who claim not to see race pretend to be above. Activism broadly is taking action for change, and despite the cultural pressure that teachers somehow stand above activism and politics, despite the perception that writing is not action, both teaching and writing are types of activism—although each of us who are teachers and writers has decisions about how that looks in our own careers and lives.

For me, the urge to teach and write is grounded in confronting a world that is incomplete, inadequate, and then calling for a world that could be. More than a decade after I began teaching high school English, I discovered critical pedagogy and social reconstructionism during my doctoral program—and was able to place my muddled and naive efforts at *teaching-as-activism* into a purposeful context. As a K–12 teacher, I always held tight to the autonomy of my classroom to do what was right by my students—usually against the grain of the school and the community, and often in ways that were threatening to my career.

The curriculum we offer our students and the pedagogy we practice are *activism* if we embrace that call. Instead of the prescribed textbook and reading list, I augmented what my students read and pushed each year to change, to expand the required reading lists to include women and writers of color. My first quarter of American literature began with Howard Zinn's reconsideration of the Columbus discovering America myth and then built on adding Margaret Fuller to the traditional examination of Ralph Waldo Emerson and Henry David Thoreau.

The second half of that first quarter focused on Gandhi's nonviolent noncooperation as well as an expanded subunit of Black thought—including Marcus Garvey, Booker T. Washington, W.E.B. Du Bois, Malcolm X, and Martin Luther King Jr. (MLK). We considered whose voice matters, and why, along with complicating the often oversimplified presentation of MLK as the only Black voice in U.S. history.

In the 1980s and 1990s of rural upstate SC, these texts and conversations were rare and hard for my students, resisted and rejected by the community (my birth town), and challenging for me as a *becoming*-teacher. And much of this I did badly despite my best intentions. Beyond my classroom, as department chair, I worked to de-track our English classes as much as possible (reducing the levels from 4 to 3), but also ended the practice of multiple texts per grade level that in effect labeled our students walking down the hallways. I also had the department stop issuing grammar and vocabulary texts to all students, moving those texts to resources for teachers who wished to use them.

Then, I did not think of that teaching as activism, however.

So I share all this not to pat myself on the back, but to acknowledge now how our teaching can—and I would argue *must*—be activism. To detail what teaching-as-activism looks like in the day to day. I share also to note that when working within the system as it is handed to us, we are being political in that we are complicit when we passively work as agents of practices that are a disservice to our students, and ourselves. Activism is teaching for that which we want to be and thus against that which we witness as wrong. None of this is easy or comfortable, and I recognize in hindsight, to work against the system has real costs, even if we do not lose our jobs, which of course serves no one well.

My journey to embrace writing as activism was much slower developing, but along the way I have shifted much of my energy toward public work because I believe that also to be activism—raising a voice in the pursuit of change, putting ones *name* behind words that challenge. But it is the writing as activism that gives me greater pause because writing is a solitary and often isolated thing (although teaching is also a profession in which we are isolated from each other, and fail in teaching in solidarity because of that dynamic).

My dual vocations as teacher/writer are significantly impacted by my privilege as well as the perceptions that teaching is not/should not be political and that writing is not really putting one *bodily* into the fray. Thus, my vigilance lies in setting aside paternalistic urges, working beside and not for, and seeking ways in which my unearned privilege can be used in the service of others who are burdened by inequity. As teachers and writers, are we activists, then?

I say that we can be, that we must be. But how that looks is ours to decide; grand and small, our impact on the world is in our daily actions, our daily words. And I am always, always anchored in my high school classroom, where my efforts to open the world to my students, to foster in them a belief that the world can be different, the world can be better were often subtly taped to my wall—the words of Henry David Thoreau:

Any fool can make a rule, and any fool will mind it.
A man has not everything to do, but something; and because he cannot do everything, it is not necessary that he should do something wrong.

I think to be a teacher is to confront our doubts, to break through the stigma we may feel about our desire to make a difference, to change the world, to be activists. These doubts and these callings are shared by writers as well, I believe. Yes, teaching and writing *are* activism, activism we should be proud to own.

## ENDNOTES

1. Freire, P. (2005). *Teachers as cultural workers: Letters to those who dare teach.* Boulder, CO: Westview Press.
2. Kincheloe, J. L. (2005). *Critical pedagogy primer* (2nd ed.). New York, NY: Peter Lang.

CHAPTER 12

# THREE EYES

## Writer, Editor, Teacher

This is the story of one narrator with three eyes: writer, editor, teacher. No, not three physical eyes, but ways of seeing writing. It starts (the story, not the chronology of what actually happened) in a bookstore.

I must admit (shame on me) that I order a great deal of books online. I am still a hard-copy sort who loves the cover and texture and weight of books—although I recognize the possible need to shift into the virtual world. I also must add that my book fetish overrides my concern about big online sellers and chain bookstores. Somehow my moral compass is skewed enough to forgive almost anything as long as the sanctity of the book is honored. (I hasten to add, not much here in my soul to respect, by the way; no delusions on my end about that—although I do love children quite deeply and genuinely because I hold out a tiny speck of hope for the future inside a very dark cloud of certainty it's not going to happen.)

So I was at the chain bookstore to grab a few Haruki Murakami volumes, I hoped. I had plowed through in about a year all his English-language novels, but had yet to venture into his short stories and nonfiction. I expected a chain store had at least some of what I didn't yet own, and although I had promised myself not to buy any more books until after I received Neil Gaiman's *The Ocean at the End of the Lane*, and read that, I was jonesing for some Murakami and I gave in like a heroine addict—or worse, like someone who loves to read.

*Teaching Writing as Journey, Not Destination:*
*Essays Exploring What "Teaching Writing" Means*, pp. 55–58
Copyright © 2019 by Information Age Publishing

I pulled two collections of Murakami short stories off the shelf and touched the covers, testing their weight, and felt suddenly happier than normal. The store was well air conditioned, and I had spent most of the day doing a somewhat hellish bicycling ride with four friends—75 miles into the North Carolina mountains during a warm, almost-summer day in South Carolina. The bookstore and holding two new books had brought me some calm so I just began to look around, touching and holding books I'd never read, glancing over displays of "Summer Reading" (mostly the sorts of books we cram down children's throats in school) and noticing that I had read just about all of them.

Then I saw this:

My first thought was how beautiful the cover is, followed quickly by: *This is not the cover of the copy I own*. I reached for it, touched the cover, tested the weight, and then noticed: "*American Gods*, author's preferred text."

The comic book industry discovered that powerful nerd instinct (something akin to OCD, or simply OCD) that compels some of us to own multiple versions of the same thing. An episode of *The Big Bang Theory*, "The 21-Second Excitation," centers on a new cut of *Raiders of the Lost Ark* containing, yep, 21 more seconds. I understand this because I was a comic book collector throughout adolescence, I still hoard some comics and many books, and I own the DVD of the multiple versions of *Blade Runner*—noting to a friend recently when lending him the set that he should watch only the Final Cut.

Thus, I slipped this version of Gaiman's novel into my hand with the two Murakamis, but this was more than the careless hoarding of a nerd. This story is about Gaiman's "A Note on the Text":

> The book you're holding is slightly different from the version of the book that was previously published....
>
> As they told me about the wonderful treats they had planned for the limited edition—something they planned to be a miracle of the bookmaker's art—I began to feel more and more uncomfortable with the text that they would be using.
>
> Would they, I inquired rather diffidently, be willing to use my original, untrimmed text? (p. xiii)[1]

Now the story loops backward in time. Maybe a couple of months before this and then a few weeks before this (at the time this was originally written).

I have been teaching writing in a variety of ways (high school students, graduate students, undergraduate students) for more than 30 years now. I have been a writer (or better phrased, I should note the amount of time that has passed since I realized I am a writer) since a spring day in 1980 when I sat in my third-story dorm room writing what I consider "my first poem," an e.e. cummings homage about throwing a Frisbee. And I have been an editor of columns and books for several years now, almost two decades.

As a scholar, I often submit work and have essentially the same sorts of responses from the editors in charge of my work, responses that rise above the essential and welcomed editing that all writing needs and deserves. Often, the editor doesn't want my work; the editor wants the piece they would have written.

Now back to Gaiman's "author's preferred text." I looked at that marvelous blue cover, and thought, *What? Neil Gaiman had a text published that he didn't quite want?* So buying this edition of *American Gods*, first, was to appease my own psychoses. Next, it was a political act to honor Gaiman's "preferred text," a political act from a not-really-very-important writer (but a damned loyal reader) to a real-honest-to-god writer. A deposit in the intersection of karmas among writers, readers, lovers of art. But all of this leaves me sad ultimately, sad in a way that will from this moment on inform me as a writer, editor, and teacher.

When I was younger (not much) and couldn't get anyone to publish my work, I dutifully worked through the nearly-all-red track changes of edited submissions. Like the mother's boy I am, I wanted so badly to please— and be published. Over the last several years, however, I have gained the luxury of being well published, and despite my eternal quest to be *wanted*, to have others say my writing matters, I have now pulled scholarly pieces from projects after the editors and I spent a great deal of time revising my initial pieces.

And sitting there with Gaiman's "preferred text" beside the computer, I was working toward being at peace with this idea: Once a piece of my writing stops being mine, and starts being yours, I have to say with all due respect that maybe you should just write the piece yourself.

Although I am not completely sure this is true, I used to share with students that Ernest Hemingway wrote *The Sun Also Rises* to show he could write a better *The Great Gatsby*. (And he did, I think.) All in all, seems the right thing to do. We are the richer for it, and what a shame if one had simply edited the other into writing only the one book? And since I have ignored all conventions of chronology here, let me slip again to a moment when I had to make that decision.

An editor (a kind and careful soul) had heavily edited a piece, moving large sections of text, and then noting (and this will seem quite trivial) that she had changed my final subhead to "Conclusion." The straw that broke the camel's back—I couldn't allow a piece published with my name have a subhead I have been urging my students and works under my editorship to avoid. *Conclusion*? Is there anything more lifeless than that? Anything that tells the reader that this writer doesn't really have anything to offer? That this writer is just getting on with it, getting this thing over?

Writing is collaboration, and so is reading.

As writer, editor, and teacher, however, I must respect the piece the writer wants to share, lest we all sit alone talking to ourselves. The story ended there. I had to work on a poem about lavender silk monkeys and continued to avoid working on three chapters due for scholarly books in a few months.

## ENDNOTE

1. Gaiman, N. (2013). *American Gods: Author's preferred text* (10th anniversary ed.). New York, NY: William Morrow Paperback.

# CHAPTER 13

# WRITING VERSUS BEING A WRITER

It is a key distinction, but one we often ignore in daily life—that between choice and recognition. At lunch, we *choose* the meal we prefer, or while shopping, we *choose* the outfit in the color that appeals to us. And it is there that we are a bit careless about words and concepts; those *choices* are actually about *recognition*. After about 20+ years of choosing not to eat beef, several years ago, I returned to steak on occasion. I order steaks medium-rare because I recognize that a wide variety of qualities of taste and texture appeal to me in aesthetic/palpable ways in a medium-rare steak.

As clumsy as all this may seem, after having been a teacher of writing for over 30 years and a so-called serious writer for a handful of years longer than that, I believe people fall into two camps related to writing: those who need to or are required to write and those who are writers, the first being somewhat in the arena of choice and the second, a recognition of Self. Both those who choose (or are compelled) to write and those who are writers can be taught to write well, I am convinced, but I think in much different ways and with a much different attitude by the teacher (notably, recognizing that one is not better than the other, simply different).

•

As the fall semester of 2014 ended, which included two classes of first year writing, and as I continued to teach and write simultaneously, I

*Teaching Writing as Journey, Not Destination:*
*Essays Exploring What "Teaching Writing" Means,* pp. 59–62

watched the documentary *Regarding Susan Sontag* and read *James Baldwin: The Last Interview* along with Susan Cheever's *e. e. cummings: A Life*.

"I suppose finally the most important thing was that I am a writer," Baldwin explained to Studs Terkel in a 1961 interview, adding:

> That sounds grandiloquent, but the truth is that I don't think that, seriously speaking, anybody in his right mind would want to be a writer. But you do discover that you are a writer and then you haven't got any choice. You live that life or you won't live any. (p. 20)[1]

In Cheever's examination of poet e.e. cummings, the life of the writer is highlighted:

> Cummings seems like a man with an enviably successful career; but like many American writers he had years of anxiety and hardship, of being sniped at and attacked, of struggling to make a living, to buy food and pay the rent. This kind of rejection is part of being a writer. Men and women who are somehow constituted to get energy from rejection—no matter how painful that might be—are the ones who survive as writers. (p. 114)[2]

And here I stress that being a writer is a recognition, some could argue a compulsion, that certainly can and should be fostered, but is not likely something that can be instilled in others. Sontag, cummings, and Baldwin, it seems to me, had little choice in the matter, but also mostly embraced that inevitable of who they saw themselves to be.

## Teaching Poetry as Teaching Writing

As a writer and a writing teacher, I often come back to the power of teaching poetry (reading and wrestling with poetry) and asking students to write poetry, fully aware that most people are not poets. This, I think, is a powerful subset of what it means to teach writing broadly: We are not creating writers, necessarily, and it is not our calling as teachers of writing to treat all students as writers. So let me offer just a brief consideration of teaching writing to those who choose (or who are compelled) to write as that stands against teaching writing to those who are writers (who recognize "[y]ou live that life or you won't live any," as Baldwin implores).

At its essence, writing is about producing an artifact, and understanding that *the written thing itself is static*, although the meaning (think Louise Rosenblatt's interaction of reader, writer, text) is organic. Many other forms of text (film, visual art, etc.) fall under this same quality, but writing is a static thing restricted to the *word* and both the conventional and unconventional units made up of words.

To write poetry, then, is to confront that poetry shares with prose the conventional "word => phrase => clause => sentence" grammar of written language. However, poetry is distinguished from prose by the construction of purposeful lines and stanzas (prose tends to remain within sentence/paragraph boundaries, and thus, not conscious of how those words form on the visual page; prose poetry remains poetry because it is a purposeful rejection of conventional lines and stanzas).

For example, William Carlos Williams writes, "so much depends upon a red wheelbarrow glazed with rain water beside the white chickens"—a grammatical sentence crafted into poetry by the transition into lines and stanzas that impact the reader visually. Or consider "our happiness" by Eileen Myles—a poem remaining fully grammatical but raised to poetry by the *craft* of lines and stanzas.

To sit down and write poetry, then, the writer must consider the essentials of all effective writing, a complex web of choices that ultimately result in an artifact that is paradoxically both static (a visual construction of words) and organic (reader, writer, text). Those essentials include the following:

- *Form, medium, and genre—conventions.* To construct a poem is to face conventions (writers must either conform to those conventions or reject those conventions, purposefully) about form (lines, stanzas, rhyme, meter, etc.—for poetry), medium (print or visual text), and genre (broadly imaginative [fiction] or factual [nonfiction]; and then, narrowly, realism, fantasy, etc.). Writing is not the inverse of reading, but the product of synthetic discourse of being a reader: The more sophisticated the reader, the more craft the writer. For those choosing or compelled to write, this can be overwhelming; for writers, there is pain in this process for sure, but it is both necessary and never-ending.

- *Purposefulness.* Although any writer may certainly begin writing without a clear purpose, the final artifact of writing must be shaped with both the awareness noted above and then the guiding purpose intact. Since poems tend to be brief, writing poetry is an ideal avenue to understanding, recognizing, and maintaining purpose in a piece of original writing. In different contexts and types of writing, we call this "thesis" or "focus," but ultimately, writing is about making purposeful decisions *mechanical, aesthetic, expressive,* and *transmissional.* If we turn back to cummings, Cheever notes that many who responded negatively to cummings raised concerns about whether or not he sought in any way to communicate with readers; for a writer, few charges could be more damning.

- *Audience.* When I conference with students, I ask questions: What is this thing you are writing (see first bullet)? What are you trying to say (second bullet)? And then, who is this for, and why would anyone read this (thus, audience)? If we again return to Rosenblatt, and consider trees falling in the woods with no one around, that static thing called a poem (or essay, or novel) spawned out of a writer's purpose ultimately seeks an audience in order (again, Rosenblatt) to achieve meaning (the organic and difficult thing possibly most mistreated by formal education). For those choosing to write or compelled to write, the audience is often imposed, mechanical—a key reason prompted and formal school writing is so miserably lifeless. Writers, however, are nothing without an audience, a love/hate relationship not unlike being in a family.

- *Coherence*. And finally, as a static thing, all writing achieves coherence—something or some *things* designed by the writer to hold it all together. Writing is cobbling, crafting, synthesizing, shaping— especially the poem. In those conferences, we talk about framing a piece of writing, organization, and how the student-as-writer has decided to move the reader from here to there and there and then ultimately *there*.

So let me end with some offerings.

During one semester teaching first-year writing, we read "Gate A-4" by poet Naomi Shihab Nye. My students loved the piece, and we approached it as an essay, but I have seen it called a short story and a poem (so, what is it?). What mattered most to me, however, is that my students were eager to say that it was clearly written by a *poet*, and that means to me, although they are far from finished in most ways as writers, they somehow *get it*. Few compliments could be higher for a piece, for a writer.

## ENDNOTES

1. Baldwin, J. (2014). *The last interview and other conversations*. New York, NY: Melville House Publishing.
2. Cheever, S. (2014). *E.E. Cummings: A life*. New York, NY: Pantheon Books.

# SECTION IV

## CHOICE

# CHAPTER 14

# STUDENT CHOICE, ENGAGEMENT KEYS TO HIGHER QUALITY WRITING

As a teacher of writing, I immediately connected "Nine Ways to Improve Class Discussions"[1] with George Hillocks's *Teaching Writing as Reflective Practice*.[2] Not to oversimplify, but Hillocks's work emphasizes several key points about effective writing instruction, captured well in a chart at the end of the volume (see graphic on next page).

Hillocks revealed that many so-called traditional approaches to writing instruction were far less effective than many of the practices at the core of writing workshop—notably that *direct, isolated grammar instruction* has a *negative* impact on student writing while *free writing* (without direct instruction) correlates with *improved* student writing.

At all grade levels, then, if our goals of instruction include improving students as writers, we must acknowledge and then implement practices that honor first student choice and engagement. There exists a historical research base as well as a more complex research base that all elements of student writing are improved (grammar/mechanics, content, organization, claims/evidence) if students *choose* the topics they write about and the forms/genres their writing takes—especially when that choice is grounded in classroom activities that engage them in the topics before they compose (see Hillocks, 1995).

*Teaching Writing as Journey, Not Destination:*
*Essays Exploring What "Teaching Writing" Means*, pp. 65–67
Copyright © 2019 by Information Age Publishing

## Figure A.1  Mode of Instruction: Experimental/Control Effects

Figure A.1  Mode of Instruction: Experimental/Control Effects

## Figure A.2  Focus of Instruction: Experimental/Control Effects

Figure A.2  Focus of Instruction: Experimental/Control Effects

Assigning students a literary analysis essay on *The Scarlet Letter* after weeks in which the students are guided through the novel has two potential outcomes that are both problematic: (1) students write horrible essays or (2) students produce clone essays. The problem with (1) is that we typically place the blame for the horrible essays on the students although the source of those horrible essays is mostly the assignment. The problem with (2) is that these clone essays probably reflect compliance, not high quality writing abilities. Our students need and deserve the time and space to become writers through *choice* and *engagement*—not by parroting what we tell them text is about, not by filling in the templates we provide.

Our students need and deserve rich reading experiences in which they begin to gather mentor texts that inform the choices they make, how they engage in forming words about the topics that matter to them. As writing teachers, then, we must design classroom discussions *that put students at the center through choice and engagement* as a powerful way to increase the quality of student writing.

## ENDNOTES

1. Weimer, M. (2015, September 30). Nine ways to improve class discussions. *Faculty Focus*. Retrieved from https://www.facultyfocus.com/articles/teaching-professor-blog/nine-ways-to-improve-class-discussions/
2. Hillocks, G., Jr. (1995). *Teaching writing as reflective practice*. New York, NY: Teachers College Press.

# SECTION V

## CITATION AND RESEARCH PAPERS

# CHAPTER 15

---

# ON CITATION AND
# THE RESEARCH PAPER

---

Like its cousin the five-paragraph essay, the research paper* shares a serious flaw: they are both artificial forms found mostly in formal schooling (and primarily in K–12) that teach more about compliance than about writing. A related problem with the middle and high school research paper assignment is "teaching MLA." One fall, after several weeks of investigating how my first-year students had been taught to write and cite, one student fumed uncontrollably in class that her high school teacher had demanded they learn MLA "because everyone uses MLA in college."

If, then, we begin to view the teaching of writing throughout K–12, into undergraduate and graduate school, and then into the so-called real world, we as teachers of writing must embrace more authentic concepts of writing as well as citation—while also providing students with writing experiences that prepare them for both disciplinary writing throughout college and any writing as scholars or writers they may choose beyond their formal schooling.

Therefore, just as we must set aside the five-paragraph essay, a false template that does not translate into authentic forms or inspire students to write (see Section XI: Five-Paragraph Essay, Chapters 28, 29, 30), we must stop assigning the research paper and demanding that students memorize MLA citation format. Instead, students need *numerous experiences as writers over years* in which they investigate how writers write in many different situations and for many different purposes, including academic

---

*Teaching Writing as Journey, Not Destination:*
*Essays Exploring What "Teaching Writing" Means*, pp. 71–74
Copyright © 2019 by Information Age Publishing

and scholarly writing that is discipline-specific (see Section IX: Disciplinary Writing, Chapters 22, 23, 24, 25). And as teachers, we should focus on authentic forms as well as on the concepts that guide writing. Consider the following guiding concerns for the shift:

- Just as teachers too often teach writing modes (narration, persuasion, description, exposition) as if they are types of essays (they are not), to suggest that anyone writes "research papers" is flipping the role of research. For example, in my first-year writing seminar I assign four essays and then require that one includes both a formal style for citation (APA) and a sophisticated used of a wide range of high-quality sources (a requirement of all our first-year writing seminars). However, my students discover after submitting and conferencing with me about their essays that as they rewrite, sources and citation become essential to virtually *all their writing*. To write well and credibly, then, is to study, *to research;* and to be a credible and ethical writer is to give proper credit to the sources of new-found knowledge.
- "Research" also becomes jumbled in how "research papers" are traditionally taught. Students need to gain a better and more nuanced understanding of what *original research* is as compared to young and established scholars seeking out and then both studying and synthesizing other people's work (typically what K–12 and undergraduate students are asked to do as "research papers"). Conducting an original study and then writing about that process and findings is a quite different and important thing versus generating a literature review and/or seeking out substantial evidence to give an essay greater credibility in the academic/scholarly world.
- Citation and its evil twin plagiarism are also greatly cheated by focusing on students acquiring a specific citation format. Students must understand powerful and complex aspects of finding, evaluating, and then incorporating other people's ideas and works into their own original writing. Citation, however, like essay writing, is discipline- and context-specific. For example, before I ask first-year students to write an essay using a scholarly citation format, I have them write an online piece (modeled on blog posts or online journalism) that depends on *hyperlinks for citations*. This process forces students to step back from MLA and consider the ethics as well as stylistic choices of citation—finding and using only credible sources, thinking about the aesthetics of citation (how many words and where to place the hyperlink), and investigating how the threshold for proper citation and plagiarism shifts for different

disciplines and different types of essays writing (journalism versus high school literary analysis essays using MLA, for example).

- Even more broadly, students must be exposed to the big picture reality that writing is an ethical endeavor—and the parameters of what is or is not ethical shifts subtly as writers navigate different writing environments and purposes.

When and how students incorporate primary and secondary sources into their own original essays must be a continual experiment contextualized by the students' purposes. Therefore, citation and citation styles must be within the teaching of disciplinary conventions. An early and important lesson for students is that multiple formal citation styles exist because of legitimate demands of different disciplines—not because teachers have rules and enjoy torturing students.

Early in my first-year seminar, we discuss the differences in English and history when compared to the social and hard sciences as disciplines. Literary and historical analysis are often grounded in *individual text analysis*; therefore, *quoting* is often necessary in that analysis. But the social and hard sciences tend to incorporate original research, requiring students and scholars to represent accurately a body of research (not one study); thus, writing in those disciplines typically shun quoting and expect *synthesis* (not rote paraphrasing of individual studies, but accurate representations of patterns found in the body of research). Literary and historical writing forefronts *titles* of works and recognizable *names* of those producing written artifacts; but the social and hard sciences are more concerned with findings and conclusions along with the *when* of those studies so parenthetical *dates* and footnote/endnotes support what matters in those disciplines. As a consequence of disciplinary needs—the purposes of writing—many in the humanities embrace MLA or Chicago Manual of Style while the social sciences may prefer APA or a variety of footnote/endnote formats.

Further, students must be introduced to the ultimate purpose of citation formats—publication. While school-based writing seems to suggest MLA, APA, et al., are created for students, these formats are publication manuals—leading to the authentic skill we should be teaching: how to follow a format regardless of the format and navigating the conventions of any discipline. *Students need to understand disciplinary conventions and then the why's and how's of following whatever conventions are appropriate for any writing purpose.*

The "research paper" and "teaching MLA" at the middle and high school levels fail our students in the same ways that the five-paragraph essay fails them. The teaching of writing needs a renaissance that honors both the authentic nature of writing and writing forms as well as the goal of fostering writers, not students who comply to assignments.

\* For this chapter, when I refer to the "research paper," I am confronting the traditional research paper *assignment* found in most high school English classes in which students are walked through a *highly structured process* in order to produce a prompted essay using MLA format. Grades are often highly affected by students complying with (or not) the process and conforming to MLA. Instead, I am suggesting authentic writing assignments that include students participating in and then implementing research because that is necessary for the type of essay written or the disciplinary expectations of the writing; I also believe we need to move toward larger concepts of citation and encouraging students to understand how to navigate *any* citation form as required by different writing purposes. As with the "5-paragraph essay" and confusing modes (narration, description, exposition, and argumentation) for types of essays, calling a writing assignment a "research paper" is overly reductive and inauthentic.

CHAPTER 16

# TECHNOLOGY FAILS PLAGIARISM, CITATION TESTS

My home university took yet another step in our quest to provide our students more effective and intentional first-year and sustained writing instruction during their time at our liberal arts institution. Once we moved away from the traditional English Department-based approach to first-year composition and committed to a first-year seminar format, we opened the door to having professors in any department teach first-year writing. Next came re-thinking the first-year seminar model, but we also took steps to support better professors who have content expertise in the disciplines, experience as researchers and writers, but little or no formal background in teaching writing or composition research. We also began a year-long faculty seminar on teaching writing.

Coincidentally, on the day we were scheduled to address plagiarism and citation, a session I led, I came across in my Twitter feed Carl Straumsheim's "What Is Detected?":

> Plagiarism detection software from vendors such as Turnitin is often criticized for labeling clumsy student writing as plagiarism. Now a set of new tests suggests the software lets too many students get away with it.
>
> The data come from Susan E. Schorn, a writing coordinator at the University of Texas at Austin. Schorn first ran a test to determine Turnitin's efficacy back in 2007, when the university was considering paying for an institution wide license. Her results initially dissuaded the university from paying a five-figure sum to license the software, she said. A follow-up test, conducted this March, produced similar results.[1]

*Teaching Writing as Journey, Not Destination:*
*Essays Exploring What "Teaching Writing" Means*, pp. 75–78
Copyright © 2019 by Information Age Publishing
All rights of reproduction in any form reserved.

I have been resisting the use of Turnitin, or any plagiarism detection software, but my university and many professors remain committed to the technology. The growing body of research discrediting the software suggests, Straumsheim notes:

> "We say that we're using this software in order to teach students about academic dishonesty, but we're using software we know doesn't work," Schorn said. "In effect, we're trying to teach them about academic dishonesty by lying to them."

My general skepticism about technology was confirmed years ago when I was serving on my university Academic Discipline Committee where faculty often debated about whether or not students flagged for plagiarism by Turnitin had actually plagiarized.[2] That debate turned on many issues being raised by the failure of plagiarism detection software, as highlighted at the University of Texas-Austin based on Schorn's research:

- Despite industry claims to the contrary, most plagiarism detection software fails to accurately detect plagiarism.
- The Conference on College Composition and Communication and the Council of Writing Program Administrators do not endorse plagiarism detection software and have issued statements warning of its limitations.
- Plagiarism detection software can have substantial unintended effects on student learning. It perpetuates a very narrow definition of originality and does little to teach students about the complex interplay of voices required in dialogic academic writing.
- Plagiarism detection software transfers the responsibility for identifying plagiarism from a human reader to a nonhuman process. This runs counter to the Writing Flag's concern for "careful reading and analysis of the writing of others" as part of the learning process.
- Plagiarism detection software raises potential legal and ethical concerns, such as the use of student writing to construct databases that earn a profit for software companies, the lack of appeals processes, and potential violations of student privacy and FERPA (Family Educational Rights and Privacy Act) protections.
- Plagiarism detection software does not, by itself, provide sufficient evidence to prove academic dishonesty; it should not serve as the sole grounds for cases filed with Student Judicial Services.
- Instructors who choose to use plagiarism detection software should include a syllabus statement about the software and its use, establish appeals processes, and plan for potential technological failures.[3]

The fourth bullet above—where the authority for both teaching cita-tion and detecting plagiarism is shifted from the professor/teacher to the technology—is the core problem for me because of two key issues: (1) many professors/teachers resist recognizing or practicing that teaching citation (and all aspects of writing) is an ongoing process—not a one-shot act, and (2) focusing on warning students about plagiarism and suspecting all stu-dents as potential plagiarizers (teaching plagiarism, a negative, instead of citation, a positive) are part of a larger and corrupt deficit view of scholar-ship, students, and human nature.

While plagiarism detection software is being unmasked as not as effec-tive as using browser search engines (a free resource), we must admit that even if software or technology works as advertised, best practice always dictates that professors/teachers and students recognize that technology is only one tool in a larger obligation to teaching and/or scholarship. Another related example of the essential folly of placing too much faith in tech-nology when seeking ways to teach students scholarly citation is citation software such as NoodleBib, and Apps such as Cite This For Me.

Despite, once again, many universities (typically through the library services) encouraging uncritically students to use citation software, I dis-courage the practice because almost always the generated bibliographies my students submit are incorrect—in part due to some of the harder aspects of APA for the software to address (capitalization/lower-case issues, for example) and in part due to students' lack of oversight after generating the bibliographies. Ultimately, then, if we think of citation software as a tool, and if students can be taught to *review and edit* generated bibliographies, the technology has promise (setting aside that some citation software embeds formatting that can be problematic once inserted into a document also).

Both plagiarism detection and citation software are harbingers of the dangers of seeking shortcuts for teaching students any aspect of writing; spending school or university funds on these inadequate technologies, I think, is hard to defend, but the greater pedagogical problem is how technology often serves to impede, not strengthen our roles as educators—especially as teachers of writing. Some lessons from these failures of technology include the following:

1. Be skeptical of technology, especially if there are significant costs in-volved. Are there free or cheaper alternatives, and can that funding be better spent in the name of teaching and learning?
2. Be vigilant about teacher agency, notably resisting abdicating that agency to technology instead of incorporating technology into en-hancing teacher agency.

3. Recognize that teaching writing and subsets such as citation are ongoing and developmental commitments that take years and years of intentional instruction.
4. Resist deficit thinking about students/humans (do not address primarily plagiarism, but citation).

Straumsheim draws a key conclusion from Schorn's research: "In addition to the issues of false negatives and positives, plagiarism detection software fits into a larger ethical debate about how to teach writing." The ethics of teaching writing, I believe, demand we set aside technology misserving our teaching and our students—setting technology aside and returning to our own obligations as teachers.

## ENDNOTES

1. Straumsheim, C. (2015, July 14). What is detected? *Inside Higher Ed.* Retrieved from https://www.insidehighered.com/news/2015/07/14/turnitin-faces-new-questions-about-efficacy-plagiarism-detection-software
2. Thomas, P.L. (2007, May). Of flattery and thievery: Reconsidering plagiarism in a time of virtual information. *English Journal, 96*(5), 81–84.
3. Statement on Plagiarism Detection Software. University of Texas at Austin. Retrieved from https://ugs.utexas.edu/flags/faculty-resources/teaching/plagiarism-statement

# CHAPTER 17

# REAL-WORLD CITATION VERSUS THE DRUDGERY OF ACADEMIC WRITING

Throughout my 34-plus years as a teacher, my life as a writer has powerfully informed my work as a writing teacher. Often, however, my teaching of writing has lagged just behind my writer self. For example, my two most distinct writer selves are as a poet and (for lack of better labels) as a scholar/public scholar. Despite my early urge to write short fiction and novels, my career as a writer took a much different turn once I completed my doctorate and moved to higher education.

I have a robust publishing record as an academic and blog as well as publish public work as a regular part of my daily writing life. As a first-year writing professor, I remain deeply committed to teach more effectively writing to students, and one aspect of that has been inviting students to write online essays that use hyperlinks for citation and as a scaffolding process for their submitting a traditionally cited essay using APA and sources anchored with high-quality peer-reviewed journal articles.

So when I found David Theriault's "The Missing Link In Student Writing,"[1] I was inspired to examine here more fully both my process and reasoning for teaching citation, and to address my own use of hyperlinks in my poetry, much as the student assignment in Theriault's post.

*Teaching Writing as Journey, Not Destination:*
*Essays Exploring What "Teaching Writing" Means,* pp. 79–82

## Citation as a Concept and Real-World Essays

Currently, I ask first-year college students to produce four multi-draft essays over a semester. That requirement includes a first full submission of the essay (with evidence of drafting), a conference with me after I provide written feedback (using Word, track changes, and comments), and then at least one revision (students are allowed to revise as often as they like until the final portfolio).

The four essay are broadly scaffolded: the first grounded in personal narrative and coming to rethink what the essay form is; the second, an online essay that incorporates hyperlinks for citation and images/video; the third, a scholarly essay using APA citation and format guidelines, and then the fourth, a choice essay that helps me see what students have learned about the essay form, writer choices, and audience. Let me focus here on Essay 2, the online essay.

Students, I find, come to college with a distorted concept of the essay as a form (usually something akin to the five-paragraph essay and mostly an act driven by a prompt and limited to literary analysis). Students also tend to see MLA as a universal, not discipline-based, approach to citation and essay formatting. Online essays using hyperlinks as citation help expand students' awareness of form and purpose, but it also forces students to become better at evaluating online sources, which too often are simply banned in many classrooms. Requiring students to incorporate images or video also addresses copyright, fair use, and what counts as "text" in communication.

This online essay assignment allows students to focus on choosing and incorporating support and evidence without the tedium of scholarly citation formats that govern in-text citations and bibliographies. The unique and important aspects of hyperlinking, however, offer something scholarly citing does not: stylistic concerns about what words to hyperlink (and how hyperlinking actually emphasizes words for effect) and writing in a way that assumes readers do not click the links (links are essential as evidence but the writer must write in a way that readers do not need to click the link). The online essay continues my emphasis on openings and closings begun in the first essay and then transitions the students on their journey to so-called academic citation and library-based research for scholarly support of their own original writing.

As well, the online essay assignment affords students a wide and engaging range of *mentor texts* that help build their form awareness about what sorts of essays people write: movie, book, and music reviews; analyses of current events; Op-Eds and commentary; personal essays and thought pieces; examination *for the public* of research from many different disciplines, and so forth. One interesting aspect of my process is that many students choose to do an online essay for their fourth, choice essay.

Another important element of hyperlinking and asking students to focus on the unique formatting requirements of online text (single spacing, block paragraphing [no indents], etc.) is fostering students' word processor skills, something they sorely lack (see Theriault's post, which guides students through hyperlinking in a Word document). In both the online and then the formal APA essay, students in my class are *required to use Word effectively* (margins, spacing, block quoting, paragraphing, font style and size, etc.) as well as learning how to navigate track changes and comments when they revise.

And while students often find all formatting requirements drudgery, the online essay and formal scholarly essay assignments help them develop their own care for submitting work as required and understanding that formatting is context-based (my samples for them are my online and scholarly submission files, for example).

## Poetry and Hyperlinks

The process above reflects my own journey *as a writer* who teaches writing and how that has informed my teaching writing since I do much more public and online writing than traditional scholarship. Further, Theriault's lesson asking students to incorporate hyperlinks in original poetry also overlaps with my own work as a poet. While I mostly abandoned my pursuits as a fiction writer, I have been an active poet for over thirty years, publishing occasionally, but focusing primarily, as with my public writing, on posting my poetry through a blog (https://plthomasselectedpoetry.wordpress.com/).

One experiment because of that online medium has been incorporating hyperlinks into my poetry. A recent poem, "'Merica (Charles Manson is dead),"[2] shows how hyperlinks can weave in current events and literary/ historical allusions. I also often use hyperlinks in opening quotes from music, essays, and poetry as well. The use of *hyperlinks as a craft element*, then, as Theriault argues, is both a powerful and real-world aspect of writing that all students should have incorporated into their journeys as writers, and thinkers.

With any luck, hyperlinking—more elegant and immediate—will soon replace the drudgery and mind-numbing variety that academic citation poses for even the most seasoned scholar.

## ENDNOTES

1. Theriault, D. (2017, November 26). The missing link in student writing [Web log]. *The Readiness Is All.* Retrieved from https://thereadinessisall.com/2017/11/26/the-missing-link-in-student-writing/
2. https://plthomasselectedpoetry.wordpress.com/2017/11/21/merica-charles-manson-is-dead/

# SECTION VI

## CREATIVE WRITING

# CHAPTER 18

# ON WRITING WORKSHOP, COGNITIVE OVERLOAD, AND CREATIVE WRITING

"The cause for my wrath is not new or single," wrote Lou LaBrant in 1931, targeting how too often the project method engaged students in activities other than literacy (p. 245).[1] This sharp critique by LaBrant has always resonated with me because even though I am now a teacher educator and have been a teacher for well over thirty years, I have always balked at pedagogy, instructional practices of any kind but especially those driven by technocratic zeal.

As one example, literature circles as an instructional structure represents the essential problems confronted by LaBrant about nine decades ago: the instructional practice itself requires time to teach students how to do the practice properly, and thus, "doing literature circles" becomes a goal unto itself and as a consequence subsumes and/or replaces the authentic literacy goals it claims to seek. Further, many instructional practices border on being gimmicky because they are constructed in such a way to facilitate that anyone (regardless of expertise and experience) can implement them in the role of "teacher."

For a while now, I have been contemplating the tension within teaching writing (composition) between those who teach writing *as teachers* and those who teach writing *as writers.* I certainly default to the latter, and am drawn often to John Warner's public examinations of his teaching of writing (see below) because he also teaches writing as a writer. Warner's pieces about grading contracts and de-grading his first-year writing course came when I was beginning my English/ELA methods seminar and wading into how my candidate must navigate ways to seek authentic practices in the context of the real world of teaching that often models for her teaching writing as a teacher, as a *technocrat*.

Here, then, I want to pull together a few concepts that I think are at their core related to LaBrant's "wrath" and my rejecting of technocratic instruction—writing workshop, cognitive overload, and creative writing. Warner in blog posts and on Twitter[2] questions his commitment to writing workshop, and offered that he has abandoned the term "workshop" for "laboratory."[3] In one response, I mused that this all depends on what we mean by "writing workshop."

Teaching about and practicing writing workshop for me have always been grounded in Nancie Atwell's use of Giacobbe[4]—that writing workshop incorporates time, ownership, and response. Of course, writing workshop also typically involves peer and teacher-student conferencing as well as a number of other strategies such as read alouds and examining model texts. So, although I do not wish to put words in Warner's mouth, I believe he and I share a skepticism about writing workshop when "doing workshop" becomes so time consuming and complex that the pursuit of workshop replaces students actually doing the very messy and unpredictable task of writing, composing. This is again the technocratic trap of instructional strategies of all kinds.

For the teaching of writing, this trap is more common than not, particularly because teachers are often under-prepared as teachers of writing and teachers *who are not writers* (most ELA/English teachers, I would suspect) dominate who is charged with teaching writing. As a result, technocrats have ruined concepts such as the writing process, conferencing, and workshop by scripting and work-sheeting them into practices anyone can implement.

The teaching of writing requires teacher expertise and a high level of teaching as a craft—but fastidious attention to doing workshop or intricate peer-conferencing or mandating students demonstrate the writing process or essay templates ultimately fails fostering young writers. Concurrent with the problems inherent in technocratic pedagogy is failing to consider the importance of *cognitive overload* when students are developing complex behaviors such as writing or reading.

Each of us has a limited amount of cognition we can devote to behaviors. When something becomes "second nature," we then free cognition space. For me, returning to mountain biking exposed this dynamic since road cycling had become "natural" to me, but mountain biking demanded so much purposeful thinking, I was constantly bumbling and frustrated. Few truisms mean more to me as a teacher of writing than paying attention to (thus, avoiding) cognitive overload when your main instructional goal is fostering students as writers.

For example, if the topic or writing form is too demanding for students, they will often devote less or nearly no energy to writing itself. Many of us as teachers have read garbled essays by students, blaming the students instead of recognizing that we have asked them to do more than they were capable of doing concurrently. For this reason, I stress the need to use personal narrative (because the content of the writing is an area of student expertise) as one foundational way to help students focus on craft and authentic writing forms.

K–12 students and first-year undergraduates, I think, need some careful consideration of cognitive overload as they acquire writing craft, and for first-year undergraduates, as they become more adept at the nuances of disciplinary writing in academia. *Avoiding technocratic pedagogy and cognitive overload, then, share the need for the teacher to keep primary the goals of learning; if we are fostering writers, we need to be sure time and effort are mostly spent on writing—not doing a pet instructional practice, not acquiring some disciplinary knowledge.*

Finally, as I discussed avoiding cognitive overload with my ELA/English methods student, I had her reconsider her plan to have students write short stories as the composition element in her short story unit that spring. Just as I balk at technocratic pedagogy, I struggle with asking K–12 students to write fiction and poetry—primarily because these are very demanding forms of writing that encroach on my concern about cognitive overload; students must have both high levels of writing craft and the ability to fabricate narratives in order, for example, to write short stories.

As a high school English teacher, I found that students often reached for derivatives of derivative fiction in order to have something for characters and plot in their original short stories; for example, a student would write about an ER doctor as a main character (he or she always committed suicide at the end), drawing from almost entirely what the student knew about ERs from the TV show *ER*. I made my case about cognitive overload, and then, she and I brainstormed what to have students write instead of their own short stories during her short story unit.

First, I asked her to reconsider her definition of "creative writing" being limited to fiction and poetry. I prefer LaBrant's definition:

> For in truth every new sentence is a creation, a very intricate and remarkable product. By the term "creative writing" we are, however, emphasizing the degree to which an individual has contributed his personal feeling or thinking to the sentence or paragraph. This emphasis has been necessary because too frequently the school has set up a series of directions, to this extent limiting what we may think of as the creative contribution: the teacher names the topic, determines the length of the paper, and even

sometimes assigns the form. For the purposes of this paper I shall, perhaps arbitrarily, use the term "creative writing" to include only that written composition for which the writer has determined his own subject, the form in which he presents it, and the length of the product. (p. 293)[5]

This pulls us back to honoring the broad concepts of writing workshop above, focusing here on "creative" being linked to *student choice* (ownership) over what students write about and what form that writing takes. Next, we brainstormed the possibility of asking students to write personal narratives while also emphasizing that their original personal narratives would have in common with the short stories they are studying—*craft elements*. Students could focus on organizational techniques in narratives, for example, while reading fiction, and then, incorporate that craft in their own personal narratives.

I have examined here ways to rethink writing workshop, cognitive overload, and creative writing so that we forefront our *writing goals* when teaching writing and guard against technocratic and reductive instructional strategies that can mask our own expertise and experience as writers. From LaBrant to Warner, we can unpack that teachers of writing are often working from places of fear—fear about losing control, fear of not being adequately prepared to teach writing, fear students will not write if given choice and freedom. However, "I have heard many teachers argue that, given a free hand, pupils will write very little," LaBrant explained. "I can only say that has not been my observation nor my teaching experience ..." (p. 299). And then Warner: "With the de-graded contract, students are writing more, and more importantly feel free to take risks in their writing."

Our antidote to these fears is trust, and then the willingness to honor for ourselves and our students the value in risk. Teaching writing *like writing itself* is fraught with fits and starts as well as failure. Trying to control those realities results in either masking them or destroying the greater goal of fostering writers.

## ENDNOTES

1. LaBrant, L. (1931, March). Masquerading. *The English Journal, 20*(3), 244–246.
2. https://twitter.com/biblioracle/status/818825596507721730
3. https://twitter.com/biblioracle/status/818832097037012993
4. Atwell, N. (2014). *In the middle: A lifetime of learning about writing, reading, and adolescents.* Third ed. Portsmouth, NH: Heinemann.
5. LaBrant, L. (1936, April). The psychological basis for creative writing. *The English Journal, 25*(4), 292–301.

6. Warner, J. (2017, January 9). Grading contract journey part II: Fiction writing [Web log]. Just Visiting. *Inside Higher Ed.* Retrieved from https://www.insidehighered.com/blogs/just-visiting/grading-contract-journey-part-ii-fiction-writing

CHAPTER 19

# APPRECIATING THE UNTEACHABLE

## Creative Writing in Formal Schooling

Benjamin Bloom's eponymous taxonomy has been bastardized, oversimplified, and misunderstood for as long as it has been a staple of teaching. My major professor for my doctoral work, Lorin Anderson, was a student of Benjamin Bloom, and Anderson has also spent a great deal of scholarship revising Bloom's taxonomy as well as refuting the ways it is typically misused.[1] In the revised taxonomy, noting that seeing the taxonomy as linear and sequential is distorting, the earlier elements of "synthesis" and "evaluation" (often interpreted as evaluation being the highest) have been revised to "evaluating" and "creating," again with the implication often being that "creating" is the highest.

I would argue that some elements of the taxonomy are more complicated but not necessarily qualitatively better, but it does seem credible to suggest that creating is an advanced act by anyone, especially a student, since it involves synthesis—the drawing together into a new whole parts that may or may not have previously been considered related. And here we come to art, the hard-to-define product of synthesis, purpose, and expression.

Written art, fiction writing, has now been examined by neuroscience,[2] revealing as Carl Zimmer explains:

*Teaching Writing as Journey, Not Destination:*
*Essays Exploring What "Teaching Writing" Means*, pp. 91–93
Copyright © 2019 by Information Age Publishing
All rights of reproduction in any form reserved.

Some regions of the brain became active only during the creative process, but not while copying, the researchers found. During the brainstorming sessions, some vision-processing regions of volunteers became active. It's possible that they were, in effect, seeing the scenes they wanted to write.

Other regions became active when the volunteers started jotting down their stories. Dr. Lotze suspects that one of them, the hippocampus, was retrieving factual information that the volunteers could use.

One region near the front of the brain, known to be crucial for holding several pieces of information in mind at once, became active as well. Juggling several characters and plot lines may put special demands on it.[3]

For teachers, especially English/ELA teachers or all teachers who teach their students to write, this study, although limited, should help push them away from traditional template and prompted writing assignments and toward a redefinition of "creative writing" that Lou LaBrant called for in her 1936 piece, "The Psychological Basis for Creative Writing."

Consider these excerpts from LaBrant, urging teachers to foster authentic, and thus creative, writing by students:

Although teachers of English should be an especially discriminating group when verbal products are concerned, unfortunately we have been as guilty as other educators in devising equivocal phrases and vague statements. We have talked about "tool writing," "mechanics of reading," "creative writing," and "functional grammar." We have suggested a knowledge as to where grammar ceases to be functional and becomes formal, although grammarians have assured us that all formal grammar is derived from speech. We have verbally separated good usage from grammar, reading skills from reading, and implied other such distinctions. "Creative writing" is probably another one of these vague inventions of our lips. (pp. 292–293)

Before continuing I should make it clear that in discussing creative writing and its basis in child need, I am not suggesting that this is the total writing program. There is no necessity for deciding that formal, carefully organized papers have no place in the high-school student's writing; but neither is there need to conclude that the necessity for writing assigned and limited history papers precludes the possibility of creative work. In my own classes both needs are recognized. (p. 294)

The foregoing are the chief reasons I see for a program of creative writing. Such a program as here outlined is not easy to direct nor is it a thing to be accepted without careful thought. It demands a recognition of each pupil as an individual; a belief in the real force of creative, active intelligence; a willingness to accept pupil participation in the program planning. I have heard many teachers argue that, given a free hand, pupils will write very little. I can only say that has not been my observation nor my teaching experience.... (p. 299)

Let's not tell them what to write. (p. 301)

When Vonnegut declared fiction writing was unteachable, and although we may disagree with him about his broad claim, his implication remains important: Teaching creative writing is extremely complex because creative writing itself is extremely complex. But let's also acknowledge that having students write creatively ("that written composition for which the writer has determined his own subject, the form in which he presents it, and the length of the product," as LaBarnt defined; see Chapter 18) must not be reserved for gifted students only, but something every student deserves to explore. Redefining creative writing in school (rejecting template and prompted essays) and inviting *all* students to write creatively raise expectations while also insuring equity.

## ENDNOTES

1. Anderson, L.W. (2012). What every teacher should know: Reflections on "Educating the developing mind." *Educational Psychology Review, 24,* 13–18.
2. Erhard, K., Kessler, F., Neumann, N., Ortheil, H.-J., & Lotze, M. (2014, October 15). Professional training in creative writing is associated with enhanced fronto-striatal activity in a literary text continuation task. *NeuroImage, 100,* 15–23.
3. Zimmer, C. (2014, June 20). This is your brain on writing. *The New York Times.* Retrieved from https://www.nytimes.com/2014/06/19/science/researching-the-brain-of-writers.html

# SECTION VII

## DIAGRAMMING SENTENCES

# CHAPTER 20

# DIAGRAMMING SENTENCES AND THE ART OF MISGUIDED NOSTALGIA

Having been a serious competitive and recreational cyclist (not "biker") for all but a handful of years over three decades, I cringe and must bite my tongue every time people refer to their bicycle "seat" (it is a "saddle"). During those years committed to cycling, I have also become well acquainted with the history of the professional sport and a fairly accomplished bicycle mechanic. I can take apart and assemble a high-end road bicycle, and I know the proper names for all the parts.

All of that knowledge and skill, however, have not made me a better cyclist. And since I have spent those same approximate years also pursuing careers as a writer and teacher (mainly of English, specifically writing), I remain baffled at both recurring arguments found in Juana Summer's NPR piece and the public responses to it:

> When you think about a sentence, you usually think about words—not lines. But sentence diagramming brings geometry into grammar.
>
> If you weren't taught to diagram a sentence, this might sound a little zany. But the practice has a long—and controversial—history in U.S. schools.
>
> And while it was once commonplace, many people today don't even know what it is....
>
> But does it deserve a place in English class today? (The Common Core doesn't mention it.)[1]

---

*Teaching Writing as Journey, Not Destination:*
*Essays Exploring What "Teaching Writing" Means,* pp. 97–101
97

I found this article through Facebook, where the original posting was praising sentence diagramming and many who commented followed suit. Oddly—although not surprising—when I weighed in with a century of research refuting the effectiveness of sentence diagramming for teaching writing, my comments were brushed off as a "viewpoint" and one person even boldly stated that no one could convince her that sentence diagramming wasn't effective.

During a teaching career—mostly in English—that spanned over six decades and included a term as president of the National Council of Teachers of English (NCTE), Lou LaBrant confronted the grammar debate, including sentence diagramming, in 1952:

> Let us admit that in thousands of schoolrooms our teaching of punctuation has concerned sentences no child ever made, errors which adults and publishing houses provided, books which we have spent hours trying to "motivate," and corrections of so-called "errors" which are approved forms everywhere except in our classrooms. We have wasted hours on diagramming dull sentences when what a sentence calls for is not to be drawn but to be understood. Who understands "Thou shalt not steal" the better for having written not on a slanting line under shalt steal? Our first step is clearing away busy work, meaningless matters, and getting at the problems of speaking about something worth saying and writing with sincerity and zest. Reading is not to be "something I had"; it should be "something I do." (pp. 346-347)[2]

Six years previous, LaBrant identified the research base examining isolated direct grammar instruction and teaching writing: "We have some hundreds of studies now which demonstrate that there is little correlation (whatever that may cover) between exercises in punctuation and sentence structure and the tendency to use the principles illustrated in independent writing" (p. 127).[3] In 1953, although there is a danger in her simple phrasing, LaBrant offered an eloquent argument about the job of teaching writing:

> It ought to be unnecessary to say that writing is learned by writing; unfortunately there is need. Again and again teachers or schools are accused of failing to teach students to write decent English, and again and again investigations show that students have been taught about punctuation, the function of a paragraph, parts of speech, selection of "vivid" words, spelling – that students have done everything but the writing of many complete papers. Again and again college freshmen report that never in either high school or grammar school have they been asked to select a topic for writing, and write their own ideas about that subject. Some have been given topics for writing; others have been asked to summarize what someone else has said; numbers have been given work on revising sentences, filling in

blanks, punctuating sentences, and analyzing what others have written....
Knowing facts about language does not necessarily result in ability to use it.
(p. 417)[4]

And thus, we come to LaBrant's most powerful metaphor for teaching
writing:

> Knowing about writing and its parts does not bring it about, just as owning
> a blueprint does not give you a house.... The end has all along been writ-
> ing, but somewhere along the way we have thought to substitute mechani-
> cal plans and parts for the total. We have ceased to build the house and
> have contented ourselves with blueprints. Whatever the cost in time (and
> that is great), and whatever the effort, our students must be taught to write,
> to rewrite, to have the full experience of translating ideas into the written
> word. This is a deep and full experience, one to which each in his own way
> has a right. (p. 256)[5]

At mid-20th century, then, LaBrant expressed *evidence-based positions on
teaching writing* (and the ineffectiveness of isolated direct grammar instruction and sentence diagramming) that have been replicated by numerous
teachers and scholars for decades—notably the work of Connie Weaver[6]
and George Hillocks. Hillocks, for example, has shown that isolated direct
grammar instruction has negative consequences on students as writers.[7]

NCTE has catalogued the same debates, misunderstandings, and
research base: Guideline on Some Questions and Answers about Grammar[8]
and Resolution on Grammar Exercises to Teach Speaking and Writing.[9]
And despite a cumulative and clear recognition of the effective and ineffective approaches to teaching children to write (see *Writing Next*[10]), we find
articles such as the NPR piece above and the responses I witnessed on Facebook. And while I don't suffer the delusion that I can stem the grammar/
sentence diagramming debates, I want to offer here some framing clarifica-
tions that I think may help both teachers and the public better understand
the issues:

- Isolated direct grammar instruction (including sentence diagramming) is ineffective in general for *fostering students as writers*. If our
  goal, however, is to teach grammar, then isolated grammar instruction could be justifiable.

- And thus, isolated direct grammar instruction fails writing instruction because (1) it too often replaces time better spent reading
  and writing by students, (2) it requires a great deal of instruction
  related to terminology and systems that (a) does not transfer to
  composition and (b) again consumes huge amounts of classroom
  time, and (3) formal and isolated grammar instruction remains

*decontextualized* for students since grammar (like algebra) requires abstract reasoning by children and teens who may have not yet reached the level of brain development necessary to navigate or understand the system at the explicit level.

- However, the two key points here include the following: we are discussing *writing instruction* as the primary goal and we are confronting *isolated direct grammar instruction*. So let me be very clear: No one in literacy suggests *not* teaching grammar; the question is not *if,* but *how* and *when.* Thus, once students are required and allowed to have rich and extended experiences reading and writing by choice, direct instruction is very effective *after* those experiences and when anchored in those students' own demonstrations of language acquisition, misunderstanding, or gaps.

- Connected to the context and *when* of direct grammar instruction is the importance of balanced literacy,[11] which calls for literacy teachers to incorporate any practice (including sentence diagramming, including grammar exercises) that helps individual students (even when that practice rubs against *generalizations* found in the research base).

- And finally, many people have a distorted nostalgia about why they have learned so-called standard English. While people are quick to ascribe harsh and traditional grammar instruction as effective in their own learning, that doesn't make it so. In fact, many people grew as readers and writers *in spite of* traditional practices—or what is often the case, they can't recognize their existing facility for language (often brought from home), which made them good at direct grammar exercises and sentence diagramming, as the actual cause of that success.

So I return to LaBrant, and her plea that teaching young people to write is about goals and weighing what truly matters:

There are many ways of writing English, and the teacher of composition must know, before he thinks of means for teaching, what kind of writing he thinks important to teach. He may be content if the writing is composed of sentences with correct structure, with periods neatly placed, verbs correctly ended, pronouns in the right case, and all attractively placed on the page. I have heard teachers say that if their pupils do all this, and spell with reasonable correctness, they (the teachers) are content. I am willing to admit that a conventional paper, such as is just described, tempts one to be satisfied; but I am not willing to admit that it represents a worth-while aim. As a teacher of English, I am not willing to teach the polishing and adornment of irresponsible, unimportant writing.... I would place as the first aim of teaching students to write the development of full responsibility for what they say. (p. 123)[12]

If we seek to teach young people to write, and thus to think, in complex and original ways, we remain confronted by the need to see that writing is learned by writing—just as I have honed my skills as a cyclist by riding a bicycle about 5000 to 10,000 miles annually for most of the last thirty years. Naming correctly the parts of the bicycle, taking apart and putting together a bicycle—these have not made me a better cyclist. For students as writers, blueprints, still, are not houses, diagramming is not composing.

Simply stated, then: The effective writing classroom must never be absent the direct teaching of grammar (again, not *if*, but *when* and *how*), *but* the grammar-based classroom has often been and continues to be absent writing by students—and therein is the failure.

## ENDNOTES

1. Summers, J. (2014, August 22). A picture of language: The fading art of diagramming sentences. *NPR*. Retrieved from https://www.npr.org/sections/ed/2014/08/22/341898975/a-picture-of-language-the-fading-art-of-diagramming-sentences
2. LaBrant, L. (1952, September). New bottles for new wine. *The English Journal, 41*(7), 341-347.
3. LaBrant, L. (1946). Teaching high-school students to write. *English Journal, 35*(3), 123–128.
4. LaBrant, L. (1953). Writing is learned by writing. *Elementary English, 30*(7), 417-420.
5. LaBrant, L. (1957). Writing is more than structure. *English Journal, 46*(5), 252–256, 293.
6. Weaver. C. (1996). *Teaching grammar in context*. Portsmouth, NH: Heinemann.
7. Hillocks (1995).
8. http://www2.ncte.org/statement/qandaaboutgrammar/
9. http://www2.ncte.org/statement/grammarexercises/
10. Graham, S., & Perin, D. (2007). *Writing next: Effective strategies to improve writing of adolescents in middle and high schools—A report to Carnegie Corporation of New York*. Washington, DC: Alliance for Excellent Education.
11. Spiegel, D. L. (1998, October). Silver bullets, babies, and bath water: Literature response groups in a balanced literacy program. *The Reading Teacher, 52*(2), 114-124.
12. LaBrant (1946).

# SECTION VII

## DIRECT INSTRUCTION

CHAPTER 21

# RECLAIMING "DIRECT INSTRUCTION"

After I posted two blogs on authentic literacy instruction, several readers tripped over my use of the term "direct instruction." Before examining the value in that term (and what it means), let me offer a couple of anecdotes.

While I was teaching high school English, a colleague teaching math had a classroom directly across from my room, separated by a court yard. With, I think, equal parts joking and judgment, that teacher used to say often, "I wish I could teach while sitting at *my* desk." Not unimportant here is the distinct pedagogical differences among math and English teachers—one that I believe we can fairly say is a tension between math teachers being teacher-centered and sequential while English teachers can lean more often toward student-centered and workshop approaches (although my caveat here is that English teachers can be some of the most traditional teachers I have ever met).

In my story above, the math teacher's comment is an excellent example of the confusion over "direct instruction." Yes, many people see direct instruction as lecture—thus, mostly if not exclusively teacher-centered with students relatively passive. For this colleague, my students working in a writing workshop with me responding to drafts, conferencing, and the other *purposeful* elements of workshopping did not meet her definition of "teaching."

Another illustrative story involves my daughter.

Her second grade teacher was a colleague of my wife, who teaches physical education at the primary school. One day in passing my daughter's second grade teacher told my wife that my daughter had been doing extremely well on her spelling tests *until she began intensive and direct phonics instruction*. Since then, she noted, my daughter's spelling grades had suffered significantly. This second example represents the ultimate failure of a narrow view of teaching having to be a certain limited type of direct instruction.

Now, when I use the term "direct instruction," as one person perfectly commented about my blog post, I am addressing *purposeful and structured or organized instruction*, but I am *not* using the term as only teacher-centered practices. To be direct, or purposeful, then, I see teaching as an act with several goals: curricular (including standards and high-stakes tests addressing those standards), disciplinary, and student-centered.

In any given class, teachers must address all three, but pedagogically, teachers often have some degree of autonomy over *how* to address these goals. As I champion "direct instruction," I am cautioning against placing curriculum and discipline (content) above student, but I am also calling for building all instruction on some evidence of *need*. Curriculum guides and standards justify a need; the discipline (ELA as literacy, literature, and composition) justifies a need; and students come to all courses with needs. "Direct instruction," then, is purposeful and organized teaching targeting one or all of these needs.

As a critical constructivist, I maintain that *we must start with allowing students to produce artifacts demonstrating what they know, what they don't know, and what they are confused about in the context of our curricular and disciplinary obligations*. Direct instruction is simply teaching with purpose to address those needs. A failed view of direct instruction is grounded in covering the curriculum or the obligations of the discipline regardless of the students in the course.

Teaching algebra sequentially, likely with the textbook determining the structure, in order to document that you taught algebra; teaching a phonics program, again, in order to document that you taught reading—this is the failure of a narrow view of "direct instruction" that supplants the needs of the students with the needs of curriculum and the discipline. If and when a child is spelling and decoding well, to go over phonics is a waste of time, but also very likely harmful—just as many studies of isolated grammar instruction show students becoming more apt to make "errors" after the instruction.

So here we can begin to unpack that the problem is not with "direct," but with "isolated." The problem is with teaching the discipline, teaching a program, teaching to the standards and/or high-stakes tests *instead of teaching students*. I am advocating for direct instruction built primarily on student needs—purposeful and structured lessons designed after gathering evidence of student strengths, weaknesses, and confusions.

And I must stress that my argument here is wonderfully confronted and unpacked by Lisa Delpit, who came to this debate because she recognized the other side of the coin I haven't addressed yet: so-called student-centered practices that cheat students (mostly our vulnerable populations of students) by misunderstanding the role of direct instruction, by misreading progressive and critical practices as "naturalistic" or unstructured. Writing and reading workshop are not about giving students free time to read and write; workshops are about time, ownership, and response that is purposeful and structured. Student-centered practices are not about letting children do whatever the hell they want. As Delpit has addressed, that isn't teaching, and it certainly cheats students in similar ways that bullheaded and narrow uses of teacher-centered practices harm students.

If a teacher isn't guided by needs and grounding class time in purpose, that teacher isn't teaching. But until you have a real breathing student in front of you, *you cannot predict what that direct (purposeful) instruction will (should) look like*. Ultimately, I believe narrow uses of the term "direct instruction" are designed to shame student-centered and critical educators.

I refuse to play that game because I am directly (purposefully) teaching when I place the needs of my students *before but not exclusive of* the needs of the curriculum and the discipline. And, yes, while I also hope someday more teachers can teach while sitting at their desks, I am more concerned about how we can come to embrace teaching as purposeful and structured without reducing it to a technocratic nightmare for both teachers and students.

# SECTION IX

## DISCIPLINARY WRITING

CHAPTER 22

# WRITING AS A DISCIPLINE AND IN THE DISCIPLINES

On the now defunct NCTE Connected Community, a student teacher asked about teaching students to integrate quotes and evidence into their writing. Although a direct and specific question, there is a great deal to unpack here. First, my 18-year career as a high school English teacher as well as my continuing 16+ years as an English educator and first-year writing professor has revealed to me that most teachers of high school ELA have much better preparation for teaching literature than for teaching writing. Next, my first-year writing students show me the consequences of how writing is taught at the high school level, primarily as the responsibility of ELA teachers. In order, then, to answer this question from a student teacher, we need to explore writing *as a discipline* and writing *in the disciplines*.

Problem 1 embedded in this question is that direct instruction of writing remains primarily the responsibility of English/ELA teachers, who also have disciplinary responsibilities as teachers. This means ELA teachers must address *literacy skills* (reading and writing as well as speaking and listening) while also covering *literature content*. And thus, problem 2 with the question is that it reveals how problem 1 creates muddled teaching and learning for students in high school ELA classes, a failure to distinguish between writing as a discipline and writing in the disciplines.

As a first-year writing professor, I have to *unteach* the muddled learning that my students bring to college from high school—misconceptions student have about citation (from learning MLA instead of broad and

*Teaching Writing as Journey, Not Destination:*
*Essays Exploring What "Teaching Writing" Means,* pp. 111–114
Copyright © 2019 by Information Age Publishing
All rights of reproduction in any form reserved.

discipline-based concepts about finding and using sources) as well as about writing essays (grounded in disproportionately having written literary analysis and being bound to templates such as the five-paragraph essay). What, then, should high school ELA teachers do in the context of the student teacher's question?

Start by being more explicit with students about both the broad qualities of effective writing paired with the narrow conventions of effective writing bound by form and disciplinary expectations. At the high school and college levels, most writing instruction and assignments are grounded in non-fiction essays, and disciplinary essay writing involves making claims along with providing evidence to support those claims. Writing assignments, then, at the high school level are far more effective for fostering students as writers and preparing them for college when those assignments are discipline-based, and not merely prompts fitted into templates.

Teaching writing in high school must include a wide range of writing opportunities (not just literary analysis) that help students learn broad concepts of effective writing. But high school ELA teachers also must continue to teach their discipline—how scholars both read and write about literature. This means that before we can teach students how to integrate quotes into their writing, we must address *in what contexts* quotes are appropriate types of evidence.

A writing lesson and assignment addressing disciplinary writing begins by examining the conventions of the disciplines. When do writers use direct quotes? For students, essays that require quotes to support claims may be common in English and history, for example, when the topic of the essay includes textual analysis of both *what the text expresses* and *how* the ideas are constructed in the primary text. A literary analysis of color imagery in a poem requires a writer to quote from the poem to show both the use of color imagery and how that technique creates some meaning for the reader.

However, in the social sciences, essays often are not about primary texts but about ideas, research findings, and students, like scholars, are tasked with showing that the claims of the essay are supported by a substantial number of sources. Quoting from a single source is not a powerful approach, but synthesizing ideas from several credible sources is.

In both situations, claims are supported by evidence, but the type of essay and the discipline within which the essay is constructed drive how students would choose evidence and then incorporate that evidence into their original essay. This sort of discipline-based approach to how we assign and teach writing should inform lessons on citation also; MLA or APA use is a question of discipline, not something assigned (arbitrarily) by a teacher. Once students are aware of the conventions of essays forms and disciplines, we can then address the narrow concerns of the student teacher—the grammatical and stylistic concerns associated with integrating quotes and other forms of evidence into essays.

In the writing text I wrote and used with my high school students, I highlighted some key concerns about integrating quotes:

- When quoting or paraphrasing/synthesizing from sources, writers have an *ethical obligation* to represent *accurately and fairly* the original texts; avoid cherry picking and manipulating quotes/ideas to fit an agenda or claim.

- Quotes must be integrated while maintaining traditional grammatical and syntactical structures; therefore, using ellipsis, brackets, or other mechanics to shape the quote to match grammatically a sentence is necessary and appropriate if those structures do not change the meaning of the original text.

- Cut-and-paste quoting—and overuse of block quotes—should be avoided since these are typical of underdeveloped or immature writing.

- Weaving smaller portions of quoted material into original sentences is typically more effective and reflects a more mature writing style.

- Using source author/primary text author names with quoted material can be a feature of some disciplinary writing. Care must be taken with those attributions, however. The author of fiction, drama, or poetry may be *inappropriate* as a tag if a character/speaker is being quoted (Polonius, not Shakespeare, pontificates on brevity and wit); if quoting from a nonfiction essay, then the writer as a tag is appropriate. In the social sciences, the names of the researchers and the titles of the research are typically *not* addressed in the flow of the essay since the findings of the research are more important than who wrote it.

And with this last point, we come back to how we can better address writing as a discipline and writing in the disciplines.

My college students typically have a one-size-fits-all approach to writing (thinking as students but not as writers or scholars) grounded in MLA and literary analysis; therefore, when they write, for example, in an education course using APA, they struggle with announcing every source in the flow of the essay (not typical in the social sciences) and tend to plod through each source one at a time without a sense of synthesizing the key findings in a *body* of research. These symptoms reflect a lack of understanding about writing in the disciplines.

Finally, let me end here with a few additional thoughts. Preservice and in-service teachers of ELA/English deserve much better preparation and support as teachers of writing, and laying all or most of the responsibility for teaching writing at the feet of ELA/English teachers is a tremendous disservice to them and students. We all must work to address those problems, but in the meantime, teaching writing as a discipline and writing in the disciplines can be handled with much more care and nuance so that students are served well as developing writers and thinkers while also being better prepared for the expectations of college.

# CHAPTER 23

# READING LIKE A WRITER (SCHOLAR)

## Kingsolver's "Making Peace"

Just a few weeks into the fall semester of college, a first-year student of mine revealed her exasperation about the inordinate amount of time and energy she had spent in high school "learning MLA" because her teachers claimed "everyone in college uses MLA." This moment in class captures perfectly the great divide that exists between the mostly rote and significantly flawed approaches to teaching writing in K–12 settings governed by high-stakes accountability and the disciplinary writing that students must demonstrate in college and then (possibly) as writers or scholars themselves.

In my writing intensive first-year seminars, we seek to unpack what students have been taught about writing before college, and then begin a journey in which we read authentic texts (both popular and disciplinary essays) like writers and scholars. I have adopted over my career as a writer and writing teacher a philosophy that begins with the broad (literary essays by writers) and then couches the narrow (disciplinary essays by scholars) within that.

Below, I walk through Barbara Kingsolver's "Making Peace," from *High Tide in Tucson*,[1] as an example of how reading like a writer (scholar)—asking what a writer is doing, how (style, literary/rhetorical technique,

*Teaching Writing as Journey, Not Destination:*
*Essays Exploring What "Teaching Writing" Means*, pp. 115–118
Copyright © 2019 by Information Age Publishing

grammar, and mechanics) the writer is accomplishing it, and why it works or doesn't—repeated often and throughout a semester, and even an entire college career, can instill genre awareness so that students can cast off their roles as *students* to become writers and scholars.

## From Literary Essays to Disciplinary Writing

"When I left downtown Tucson to make my home in the desert," Kingsolver confesses in her opening sentence, "I went, like Thoreau, 'to live deliberately'" (p. 23). When my students and I explore this essay by Kingsolver, we have already done an activity on openings—in which we look at just the first paragraphs of several of Kingsolver's essays in order to begin to challenge the introduction/thesis paradigm and move toward a wide range of strategies for engaging and focusing the reader. Again the purpose here is to pull back to the broad conventions of essays (literary essays for a mostly lay audience) in order to nest disciplinary writing in those conventions (acknowledging that many disciplines do conform to a functional [but not aesthetic] template: introduction with overt thesis, body, and conclusion).

In that first sentence—and then throughout the essay with references to Preston Adams, Joseph Campbell, Friedrich Engels, Karl Marx, Charles Darwin, Lewis Henry Morgan, and Kafka—Kingsolver reveals both her awareness of and her speaking to a targeted audience, well-educated and literate readers.* As well, the entire opening paragraph is highly detailed (images) and humorous, and thus, engaging and interesting. For literary essays, then, we note that instead of offering an overt thesis, reader engagement is primary. In fact, while Kingsolver has a very clear focus (thesis), it isn't revealed until several pages in: "Ownership is an entirely human construct" (p. 26).

Kingsolver's confrontation of ownership becomes much more direct and even scholarly toward the end when she notes: "Life is easier since I abdicated the throne. What a relief, to relinquish ownership of unownable things"—which is reinforced by quoting Engels (p. 33). Throughout, our reading this essay like writers (scholars), we begin to note the conventional differences between a literary essay and disciplinary writing, highlighting Kingsolver's own direct and subtle nods to the disciplines (literature, economics, anthropology, religion, botany, and biology). And so we begin to frame this essay against disciplinary conventions:

- While Kingsolver highlights narrative and literary constructions, disciplinary writing tends toward exposition.

- Kingsolver's citations are sparse—names, quotes—but disciplinary writing has a much more stringent threshold for identifying references and quotations.

- Organization and structure are more aesthetic, including Kingsolver's use of graphic breaks to show transitions (the publisher uses a wave image), but disciplinary writing tends toward subheads and more overt structural devices as well as more direct statements of claims.

- In both Kingsolver's essay and disciplinary writing, however, diction, style, grammar, and mechanics must match the purpose of the essay as well as the targeted audience; in other words, these matters are about *appropriateness and purpose, not correctness.* There are no universally right words, there are no rules of grammar.

Just as I focus on openings, I also highlight endings. Kingsolver's "Making Peace" builds to a two-sentence final paragraph: "*So what,* they all declare with glittering eyes. This is their party, and I wasn't exactly invited" (p. 34). Here, I emphasize that just as Kingsolver eschews the mechanical introduction/thesis, she also avoids the conclusion as *restatement of the introduction.* Instead, literary essays often *frame* the body paragraphs; in this essay, Kingsolver returns to the *party/not invited* motif from the end of the first paragraph. *Framing* is an aesthetic approach that many disciplines ignore, especially if the disciplinary writing is primarily functional, such as transmitting new or synthesized information.

For students as emerging writers and scholars, the lessons of reading like a writer (scholar) are about appropriateness in the context of conventions and purposefulness within the writer's/scholar's awareness of their audience.

## From Reading Like a Writer (Scholar) to Drafting to Conferencing

My goals and process for first-year seminar students in a writing intensive course include exploring *What is an essay?* and then *What is a disciplinary essay?* In those explorations, I am seeking ways in which students can become autonomous, ways in which students can rise above being students in order to embrace their autonomy as writers and/or scholars. Reading like a writer (scholar) is foundational to those goals so students begin to ask what writers are doing, how writers are achieving their purposes, and in what genres and conventions writers (scholars) are working.

The walk-through above is within a process that asks students to craft and submit a personal narrative followed by an online essay (using hyperlinks for citation) and then a disciplinary essay using a discipline-specific citation style sheet. Students also submit a fourth essay, but that is determined by their needs after completing the first three. Vital to that process and anchored by reading like a writer are professor/student conferences after the initial submission of each essay. Reading like a writer practices help inform what students need to consider, but also provide concrete references during the conferences.

For example, I begin conferences by asking who the primary/intended audience is as well as what the purpose of the essay is: to inform that audience or to call that audience to some action or behavior. From there, we begin to investigate the essay draft against what we have discussed with authentic essays and reading like a writer (scholar): we consider the effectiveness of the opening, the scope and amount of claims, the authority of the student in the context of those claims and the topic(s), the use (or lack) of evidence, and the framing of the essay. These investigations of the first draft become revision strategies for the student, with a premium placed on the agency of the student as a writer (scholar).

Just as reading like a writer replaces the narrow high school focus on literary analysis (the literary technique hunt and parroting back to the teacher what they said about the text), we replace the mechanical essay template of high school with a developing genre awareness of students as becoming-writers (scholars) who write with an awareness of audience and conventions (both popular and disciplinary) that demonstrates purposefulness, and not mere rote compliance. My exasperated student shaking her head about the misguided focus on MLA prompted many other students to express the same sort of frustration. But more troubling is that very bright students with outstanding potential are often nearly frozen with uncertainty when faced with authentic expectations of essay writing.

The essay, however, is a vibrant and beautiful thing, rendered like students into a lifeless state by formal schooling. Reading like a writer (scholar) helps breath life back into reading as well as writing, opening the door for students to become the writers (scholars) they can be.

*In Kingsolver's "Creation Stories," for example, she begins with "June is the cruelest month in Tucson," as allusion aimed at a literate audience indeed.

## ENDNOTE

1. Kingsolver, B. (1995). *High tide in Tucson: Essays from now or never*. New York, NY: HarperCollins.

CHAPTER 24

# INTERSECTIONS AND DISJUNCTURES

## Scholars, Teachers, and Writers

Discussing scholars as writers, Michael C. Munger explains, "We train people in methods, and theory, but we don't tell them that writing is something you have to practice."[1] And that practice, Munger argues, must be "like you exercise: at least a little bit, most days.... Furthermore, writing makes you a more focused and attentive reader of other works. When you are writing, you read to interrogate that author about a particular point."

This interview about the intersection of scholars (academics, professors) and writing wades into a fascinating and troubling phenomenon that I expose first-year writing students to in their seminar midterm. I ask them to choose a professor on campus in a discipline they are considering for their major, and then to interview that professor about writing as a necessary aspect of being a scholar. My students discover, and are *surprised* to discover, that most of the professors openly share that they *dislike* writing, *struggle* with writing, and/or simply tolerate having to write in order to have their research published.

A parallel reality exists in K–12 education. During one of my graduate courses in literacy, I asked how many of the 11 students had ever been participants in a writing workshop; none of them raised a hand. Taken

*Teaching Writing as Journey, Not Destination:*
*Essays Exploring What "Teaching Writing" Means,* pp. 119–122
Copyright © 2019 by Information Age Publishing

together, we are faced with an important hurdle in the teaching writing: *at all levels of formal education, writing is taught by scholars/academics and teachers who themselves are not writers, who have had no or very little direct instruction in being writers* (as noted by Munger above).

Some of the questions we must investigate, then, include the following:

- Must anyone who teaches writing *be a writer*?
- What are the most effective ways to foster the teaching of writing among those who are not writers, who struggle as writers, and who see writing as a necessary evil?
- How can and should we support those who write by necessity but never feel compelled as writers (a reality that comprises most students and many scholars and teachers)?

Having been a writer and a teacher for about the same amount of time and since my primary focus as a teacher has been the teaching of writing, I often wrestle with the questions above, but during the last decade-plus while I have been teaching first-year writing at the university level and also providing faculty development for professors teaching writing, I have come to understand better that *there are more disjunctures than intersections among scholars, teachers, and writers*.

As a high school English teacher, I had to fight for time to write; my life as a writer, in fact, intruded on my work as a teacher in direct and indirect ways (about the latter, I suffered subtle and not-so-subtle antagonism from some colleagues for publishing). When I moved to higher education, writing became something valued as part of my work, my schedule allowed ample time for me to do as Munger suggests and write daily, and the expectations for being a professor (teaching, scholarship, and service) included *explicitly* scholarly publication.

However, lest you believe higher ed to be some sort of writer's Shangri-la, being a productive writer and writing for the public have also created tensions for me in academia, where a very narrow expectation for being a writer persists (being prolific viewed with skepticism, hints that one cannot write that much without sacrificing something such as teaching; public writing viewed as frivolous use of a scholar's time and too political). As noted above, though, what links my K–12 and higher education experiences is that most teachers/professors charged with teaching writing are not themselves writers—although most professors are more likely than K–12 teachers to write by necessity.

Here is a lesson I now see more clearly: We have failed, mostly, to confront directly that *writing is typically taught by those who aren't writers*, but we have *implicitly* addressed that disjuncture by attempting to make the teaching of writing teacher-proof. To teacher-proof writing instruction, we have chosen, as Johns examines, *genre acquisition* over *genre awareness*.[2] Briefly, that means in-school writing instruction tends to assign writing in template form (five-paragraph essay and its cousins) and to reduce all writing to that artificial form (in terms of what "essay" means to students as both writers and readers). In effect, teacher-proofing writing instruction removes most of the instructional decisions from teachers and almost all of the writing decisions from the students-as-writers. As well, both writing instructors and students-as-writers are primarily complying with directives that are artificial (or as Johns notes, "'staged'").

To foster the most effective writing teachers—and thus to foster students-as-writers—a few key approaches are warranted:

- Couch calls for writing instructors to be writers in the acknowledgement that most are not, and may not feel compelled to be writers.
- *Be aware of and avoid shaming* writing instructors who are not writers or who see writing as merely functional to other pursuits.
- Provide all writing instructors with authentic experiences in direct writing instruction themselves; teachers of writing need to have had experiences *as writers and students* in the instructional practices they should use with their students.
- Reject the traditional efforts to teacher-proof writing instruction and begin to build for teachers and students a broad range of experiences with *genre awareness* grounded in the disciplines (see Chapter 22) and so-called real-world writing.
- Revitalize reading and text experiences in formal schooling from K–12 to college so that students experience powerful models for the ways in which writing occurs, both within and against a manageable toolbox of conventions linked to the disciplines and published writing.
- Include for all teachers/professors, K–12 and college, *expectations* for writing, *professional rewards* for writing, and then the sort of *time* and *administrative support* needed to fulfill writing obligations without impinging on primary obligations to teach.

The irony, I believe, is that the road to effective and empowered writing teachers is as nuanced and complex as the sorts of lessons we need to teach about writing, a many-headed beast that is often hard to wrangle, much less understand.

We can and must admit that more disjunctures than intersections exist among scholars, teachers, and writers. Bridging those gaps is a daunting challenge, but traditional teacher-proof approaches fail both teachers and their students. Writing instruction and how writing is viewed by teachers/ professors and students require that we step away from many reductive and ineffective assumptions so that we can start again for the first time more honestly and newly committed to teaching and writing as valuable but complex endeavors.

## Suggested

"The Age of the Essay," Paul Graham[3]

### ENDNOTES

1. Toor, R. (2017, June 18). Scholars talk writing: Michael C. Munger. *The Chronicle of Higher Education*. Retrieved from https://www.chronicle.com/ article/Scholars-Talk-Writing-Michael/240354
2. Johns (2008).
3. http://www.paulgraham.com/essay.html

CHAPTER 25

# HELPING STUDENTS NAVIGATE DISCIPLINARY WRITING

## The Quote Problem

As a semester ended, I had been leading classroom discussions with my first-year writing and education foundations students about the elements of writing we had explored over the past few months. Most, if not all, academic writing at the college level requires students to ground their claims in credible evidence. This last point is something I allow my students to discover over the semester in first-year writing, but as the final drafts of essays loomed in their not-so-distant futures with the submission of their final writing portfolio, I stressed to them some guiding concepts to carry throughout their undergraduate and graduate experiences: Identify and check all claims made in writing, and then provide strong evidence those claims are valid.

Since satire is often more incisive than the drudgery of writing or grammar texts, I shared with students two pieces, one from McSweeney's and one from *The Onion*: "Student Essay Checklist"[1] and "Since The Beginning of Time, Mankind Has Discussed What It Did on Summer Vacation."[2] The former includes two brilliant—and accurate—jokes about student writing:

*Teaching Writing as Journey, Not Destination:*
*Essays Exploring What "Teaching Writing" Means*, pp. 123–128
Copyright © 2019 by Information Age Publishing

Misattribution of quotation: "As Abraham Lincoln said, 'Do unto others as you would have them do unto you.'"

Broad declaration about the characteristics of all people: "Everyone loves pizza!" "No one likes Minnesota!"

And the latter, broadly, parodies that second habit above in the introduction:

For as far back as historians can go, summer vacations have been celebrated by people everywhere as a time for rest and relaxation. Many advancements have been made in summer breaks since these early times, but it is also true that many different traditions have lived on and continue to remain with us today. This is why, since the beginning of time, mankind has discussed what it did on its summer vacation.

Despite my best efforts, college students are drawn to making huge indefensible claims, and then they fail those claims in two ways—the absence of any proof (I assume they believe these claims are so obvious, no proof is needed), or the most rudimentary and inadequate efforts at providing proof (almost always providing *one* quote from *one* source). Here I want to focus on the quote problem and how we can better foster the use of evidence in student writing.

## The Quote Problem

In 2017, the president of the United States spurred a national concern for fake news, often directly stirring that debate through his reckless use of Twitter. After the president Tweeted a *discredited* video slurring Muslims,[3] White House press secretary Sarah Sanders offered this response:

"It's important to talk about national security and national security threats," Sanders said. "The president sees different things to be a national security threat and he sees having strong borders as being one of the things that helps protect people in this country from some real threats we face."

"Whether it's a real video, the threat is real and that is what the president is talking about, that's what the president is focused on, is dealing with those real threats and those are real no matter how you're looking at it," she said.[4]

For those of us who teach students to write in ethical and credible ways, we witness in this exchange many of the elements parodied above: overstated claims and the careless use of evidence.

While it seems fruitless to confront this habit with President Trump and his staff, I believe there are some important ways we can better address the use of evidence, and the quote problem, without students at all grade levels. Similar to the example about the bogus video used to push a baseless ideology, students are in fact often driven to a similar strategy through what they are taught directly and by implication. Simply put, students learn to quote simply to quote.

Consider as one example, Thomas Newkirk in 2005 confronting the problems with the writing section in the SAT:

> When I first read this essay, I imagined some free spirit, some rebel, flaunting the ethics of composition and inventing evidence to the point of parody. But when I shared this letter with a teacher from Texas, she assured me that **students were coached to invent evidence** [bold added] if they were stuck. In my most cynical moment, I hadn't expected that cause. And what is to stop these coached students from doing the same on the SAT writing prompt? Who would know? (p. 22)[5]

This corruption of writing linked to high-stakes testing is extreme, but *students also are routinely taught in subtler ways that quoting is somehow the goal itself when writing in school*. It is that dynamic I want to confront, and suggest ways around.

The problem is that students tend to write throughout K–12 schooling in English, and by middle and high school, they are mostly writing text-based (literary or historical analysis) essays that require them to quote extensively from the primary text(s) being examined. As a result, students extrapolate narrow disciplinary conventions of English and history to generic rules for all school-based writing.

## Disciplinary Writing: The Solution

I teach first-year writing as a transition from high school to the more complex and demanding expectations of the disciplines. One technique for that transition is helping students recognize citation and style sheets (MLA, APA, Chicago, etc.) as discipline-based systems that serve different and purposeful conventions of the disciplines; in other words, none of those guidelines is universally sacred, and thus, not to be memorized, but applied as appropriate. But a more powerful technique is helping students step back from their quote problem (Just quote it!) in order to reconsider both the claims they make and how they support those claims with evidence.

First, we discuss why they are so obsessed with quoting by unpacking the conventions of text-based analysis common in the fields of English and history. In those contexts, the exact wording and the content of those passages are often equally important to the analysis in writing. Literary analysis tends to address writer technique *and* message, how they interact. And when a historian claims Thomas Jefferson held certain beliefs in private, quoting extensively from his letters is not only effective but also essential to the credibility of the claims.

Concurrent with students becoming fixated on quotes, students also learn the importance of paraphrasing when many are required to write cited essays using MLA and then grounding their work primarily in published literary analysis, secondary sources. In both student experiences with literary analysis on the Advanced Placement Literature exam and then writing research papers on literary texts, students have extremely narrow views of evidence as either *quoting or paraphrasing one source at a time*. Again, these conventions of writing may often serve students well in English, history, or philosophy at the college level, but the same strategies are ineffective in the hard and social sciences.

Since my field is education, I ask my students in first-year writing to use APA citation and style while also guiding them through disciplinary writing outside of the humanities because students as scholars are likely throughout college not ever again to write a literary analysis—are likely to write mostly in disciplines with conventions unlike English and history. Throughout the semester, I take care to emphasize that any conventions we use must be appropriate to the purpose of the writing, the audience, and the discipline within which the work is framed. We eschew seeing anything as a universal rule.

Our students, then, would be better served at all grade levels in K-12 and then in college if we grounded our teaching of writing in disciplinary conventions beyond the humanities and, for English teachers, beyond literary analysis and MLA citation and style. Here, then, are some ways to do just that:

- Foster in students a nuanced awareness of making claims in writing. As the parodies above suggest, we must purposefully help students avoid making grand and often unsupportable claims based on what they believe is true—and seek to make claims based on studying and researching *before developing their claims* in writing. (Having students draft as discovery instead of requiring students provide introductions with a thesis statement before drafting is also recommended.)
- Expand student awareness of evidence to include three levels that are driven by disciplinary conventions: quoting, paraphrasing, and synthesizing. Quotes are important if the how (craft) is as important as the what (content) of the passage, but quoting also must be credible and a valid representation of the generalization being

made (in other words, students must evaluate the source quality and insure the passage is not an outlier). Paraphrasing serves as evidence in disciplines that value the use of individual *secondary* sources (when the what is important but the craft of passage isn't relevant), such as published literary analysis. However, a tremendous array of disciplinary writing in the hard and social sciences prefers synthesis over quoting or paraphrasing; synthesis requires that students express ideas found in several sources that are credible and valid.*

- Guide students through the different discipline-based expectations for incorporating sources in original writing. Direct references to authors and titles in the flow of discussion are common in literary analysis, but a synthesis of ideas from multiple peer-reviewed studies in psychology places references in parentheses or foot/endnotes, *without announcing* any author names or titles of those published studies.*

Teachers of writing, then, will serve our students better if we pull back from literary analysis, MLA, and demanding students quote in order to foster in them a more sophisticated sense of making claims and providing evidence within the conventions appropriate to the topic and discipline. Especially high school English teachers must acknowledge that the majority of our students who attend college will never write another literary analysis and will likely use a citation style other than MLA. Grounding writing instruction in disciplinary conventions helps our students avoid the quote problem, and if we are effective, become better equipped to make credible claims and offer valid evidence in ways that our political leaders seem unable to accomplish.

* In both cases, two sections from a scholarly essay[6] using APA serve as good examples of synthesis versus paraphrasing:

> For this volume on comic books, then, interrogating the medium in the context of race is extremely complex because comic books are a significant subset of popular culture (increasingly so with the rise of superhero films based on comic books throughout the late twentieth and into the early twenty-first centuries), which necessarily both reflects and perpetuates all aspects of the culture it serves—including bigotries such as sexism, racism, classism, jingoism, and homophobia (McWilliams, 2009; Rhoades, 2008a, 2008b; Singer, 2002; Thomas, 2010; Wright, 2001).

And:

From the 1980s (a hot decade for rebooting origins, highlighted by Frank Miller's Batman) and into the early 2000s, Captain America's origin continued to be reshaped. Notable for a consideration of race is Truth: Red, White and Black from 2003, which details a remarkable alternate origin as a medical experiment on black men (echoing Tuskegee), resulting in Isaiah Bradley ascension as the actual first Captain America (Connors, 2013; Hack, 2009; McWilliams, 2009; Nama, 2011).

## ENDNOTES

1. https://www.mcsweeneys.net/articles/student-essay-checklist
2. https://www.theonion.com/since-the-beginning-of-time-mankind-has-discussed-what-1819584687
3. Fact check: Retweeted Anti-Muslim videos misrepresent what happened. (2017, November 29). *CBS Los Angeles*. Retrieved from http://losangeles.cbslocal.com/2017/11/29/fact-check-retweeted-anti-muslim-videos-misrepresent-what-happened/
4. Stracqualursi, V., Travers, K., & Phelps, J. (2017, November 30). White House defends Trump's retweets of far-right group. *ABC News*. Retrieved from http://abcnews.go.com/Politics/trump-retweets-british-nationalist-anti-muslim-videos/story?id=51455324
5. Newkirk (2005).
6. Thomas, P.L. (2017). Can superhero comics defeat racism?: Black superheroes "torn between sci-fi fantasy and cultural reality." In C. A. Hill (Ed.), *Teaching comics through multiple lenses: Critical perspectives* (pp. 132–146). New York, NY: Routledge.

# SECTION X

**FIRST-YEAR COMPOSITION**

CHAPTER 26

# YOU DON'T KNOW NOTHING

## U.S. Has Always Shunned the Expert

My redneck past includes a childhood steeped, like the family formula for making sweet tea, in a demand that children respect authority—authority-for-authority's sake, the status of authority despite the credibility of the person in that status. And is typical in the South, these lessons were punctuated with refrains such as the one my mother launched at us often: "He's a know-it-all that don't know nothing." But the best laid plans of parents often go awry, and they certainly did for me because this aspect of my redneck past backfired big time, resulting in a life-long skepticism of authority as well as my own pursuit of expertise trumping status.

Among my most irritating qualities, I suspect, is I work very hard not to hold forth until I am well informed, but when I do hold forth, I am passionate and that passion often comes off as arrogance. I have little patience with debating when the other side lacks credibility, and I also balk at the silliest of all—"We will agree to disagree, then."

*Well, no, since your position has no credibility.*

So I am particularly fascinated with what I consider a parallel interest currently with fake news and post-truth, what Tom Nichols calls "The Death of Expertise."[1] Nichols and his argument, coming from his conservative perspective, represent, I think, why expertise currently and historically has been marginalized in the U.S. Pop culture, in fact, has documented well how the so-called average American finds expertise and being educated mockable—think Fonzie on *Happy Days* and Ross on *Friends*. Uneducated Fonzie is always smarter than the educated, and Ross is a laughing stock among his friends, notably often one-upped by the very anti-intellectual Phoebe and Joey.

Nichols and I share a concern about how little expertise matters in political and public discourse as well as policy, but while he and I share some elements of being experts, we are divided by our essential ideologies. This presents a paradox: The U.S. rejects a cartoonish and monolithic "expert class," but most fields/disciplines have a fairly wide spectrum of stances within them (in other words, the "expert class" rejected by the U.S. simply doesn't exist). But even that is oversimplified. Let me return to my redneck past.

In the South specifically, rejecting expertise is often about traditional views of respecting authority, best captured, I think, in how Huck Finn's father shames Huck for his book learning. Huck even confesses: "I didn't want to go to school much, before, but I reckoned I'd go now to spite papa" (p. 17).[2] One of my former colleagues recounted often that his own father identified sending my friend to college was the worst mistake his father ever made. Perversely, many see being informed, knowledgeable as rudeness, disrespectful.

A better recent confrontation of expertise than Nichols's, I think, is Freddie deBoer's "What Is Aleppo?," focusing on Gary Johnson, Libertarian Party presidential candidate in 2016:

> I would like to nominate Gary Johnson's infamous "What is Aleppo?" gaffe as the moment which, for me, most typifies 2016, at least as far as our intellectual culture goes.
>
> Predictably, and deservedly, Johnson was raked over the coals for this. A major presidential candidate — one who had far more electoral impact than Jill Stein, for instance — not knowing about this important foreign policy issue was disturbing. But it's essential to recognize what he actually got in trouble for. Johnson's great failure, what actually fed his public humiliation, was not a lack of knowledge. It was a lack of knowingness.[3]

deBoer argues: "Ours is a culture of cleverness, not of knowledge, one that is far more comfortable in assessing wit than in assessing evidence."

And here we may have a more accurate window into why someone who is not really an expert, such as Donald Trump, but is smug and cavalier about *being smart*, is more compelling in the U.S. than actual experts. Trump passes deBoer's test:

> That kind of thing: obviously smart but not, like, all tryhard about it. You are expected to work out relentlessly to train your body and to show everyone that effort, but your intelligence must be effortless, even accidental.

This is a very high-school popularity kind of dynamic in which bravado trumps credibility; again, think Fonzie's allure in pop culture: "See, the drop-out is smarter than all those teachers!"

My own career as an educator has highlighted these exact patterns. As a teacher of English, I am not credible in the field of English because I am *just a teacher* with an undergraduate, master's, and doctorate in education (not English). However, to politicians and the public, I am routinely rejected in debates about education *because* my experience and expertise lie in education.

As a prelude to the rise of Trump, consider Arne Duncan, who has no degree in education and who has only experience in education as a political appointee. Who do you think has more public and political influence on education—Duncan because of his statuses of authority or me with 30-plus years in education, an advanced degree, and a substantial publication history?

That question is nearly laughable in the United States.

Let me end with a couple examples that are useful for a more nuanced consideration of the role of experts, grounded, I think, in deBoer's discussion. First, consider Joseph R. Teller's "Are We Teaching Composition All Wrong?"[4] and Doug Hesse's "We Know What Works in Teaching Composition,"[5] both published in *The Chronicle of Higher Education*. I immediately wrote a rebuttal to Teller (see Chapter 27), and discovered through responses to my concerns that Teller has greater expertise in literature than composition (which I suspected). Hesse's rebuttal is grounded in his *expertise in composition*, his status of authority (president of NCTE), and his appeal to disciplinary authority (citing ample research that accurately reflects the field of composition).

None the less, Teller's piece speaks to both an uniformed public and a click-bait culture, and it is likely, as John Warner speculated on Twitter,[6] that Hesse's *better piece* will not garner as many views or as much commentary as Teller's. This debate between experts serves to highlight, again, the failure of media in terms of honoring expertise, but it also demonstrates that expertise is often narrow and that disciplines are more often contentious than monolithic (although there are some things that are essentially settled and no longer debatable).

Bluntly, we must admit that simplistic resonates more than complex—and expertise is not only narrow but also complex. So we are faced with a historical and immediate problem, one that could be solved if we reconsidered our cultural antagonism toward expertise and embraced a greater appreciation for informed stances, the realm of the expert. As a critical pedagogue, I appease my skepticism about authority and quest for expertise by honoring being authoritative over authoritarian. It is ours to resist extremes, neither ignoring experts nor abdicating all authority to experts.

As cumbersome as it may seem, democracy that honors all voices works well only when we start with the most informed voices and then allow "all voices" to occur in an educated space. Currently, we are prisoners to bravado drowning out expertise, and in that echo chamber, freedom cannot survive.

## ENDNOTES

1. Nichols, T. (2014, January 17). The death of expertise. *The Federalist*. Retrieved from http://thefederalist.com/2014/01/17/the-death-of-expertise/
2. Twain, M. (1994). *Adventures of Huckleberry Finn*. Mineola, NY: Dover Publications.
3. DeBoer, F. (2016, December 30). What is Aleppo? *Jacobin*. Retrieved from https://www.jacobinmag.com/2016/12/gary-johnson-aleppo-meritocracy-intelligence-politics/
4. Teller, J.R. (2016, October 3). Are we teaching composition all wrong? *The Chronicle of Higher Education*. Retrieved from https://www.chronicle.com/article/Are-We-Teaching-Composition/237969
5. Hesse, D. (2017, January 3). We know what works in teaching composition. *The Chronicle of Higher Education*. Retrieved from https://www.chronicle.com/article/We-Know-What-Works-in-Teaching/238792
6. https://twitter.com/biblioracle/status/816668197961265152

# CHAPTER 27

# IS JOSEPH R. TELLER TEACHING COMPOSITION ALL WRONG?

While provocative in ways I suspect he never intended, Teller's "Are We Teaching Composition All Wrong?" (discussed in Chapter 26) proves to be an essay that should, ironically, be significantly revised after conferencing with someone well versed in teaching composition. Broadly, Teller's essay makes a common first-year composition mistake by significantly misrepresenting "teaching composition" and then proceeding to attack the misrepresentations. However, late in the piece, Teller wanders into some important conclusions that actually are warranted composition practices (see Chapter 28)—despite his suggesting these are somehow alternatives to endorsed practice.

Teller opens by claiming that "compositionists have been enamored of a pedagogical orthodoxy" he briefly details in three bullet points. In my first-year seminar, here would be the primary area for conferencing and revision: how does the writer justify the condescending "enamored" (it appears Teller has a literaturist's low opinion of the compositionist lurking underneath the real reason for this essay; maybe a bit of professional distress over having to teach first-year composition instead of upper-level literature?); and where is any evidence that the claim and three points are credible?

After failing to include evidence for his central claim, however, Teller declares composition "pedagogical orthodoxy" a failure—a pretty hasty and damning conclusion. To detail those failures, Teller launches into revision

---

*Teaching Writing as Journey, Not Destination:*
*Essays Exploring What "Teaching Writing" Means*, pp. 135–138
Copyright © 2019 by Information Age Publishing
135

and a jumbled criticism of "workshop," highlighting a central failure of this essay and a grounding lesson that must be addressed in first-year composition classes: defining terms (a bedrock of disciplinary writing). Before examining Teller's concerns about students not revising, I must highlight that Teller appears to reduce "workshop" to "peer editing/conferencing" since the only aspect of workshop he addresses is peer conferencing.

It is without a doubt that a critical unpacking of the effectiveness of peer editing/conferencing is warranted; many writing teachers struggle with that. But writing workshop is significantly more than peer conferencing. None the less, over a semester of 40+ class sessions, I devote 4 class periods in part to peer conferencing with about triple that amount of class time devoted to other aspects of workshop: brainstorming, discussion, reading, drafting, exploring evidence, and so forth.

Now, about revision: my students revise essays significantly or they do not receive credit for the essay, and thus, cannot receive credit for the course. Revision strategies and minimum expectations for revising are addressed and detailed in conferences, and then, my students do revise, and typically are eager to do so. Effective for me has been not to grade essays, but to have minimum elements for credit in the course that include drafting essays, conferencing, and revising/rewriting essays. I don't want to make the mistake also suffered by Teller—assuming anecdotes prove credible generalizations—but I am reasonably sure many composition professors have students revise, and revise well—and those strategies are in fact aspects of warranted writing pedagogy.

Next, Teller complains: "Even when students engage complex issues from readings in their papers, they do not use the basic argumentative structures they need in order to give their ideas voice, cohesion, and support." Here is a key moment when Teller's essay is doubly problematic since he identifies good practice as if it isn't already good practice. The suggestion that composition as a field somehow now rejects direct teaching of "argumentative structures" or "voice, cohesion, and support" is misleading, and frankly, baffling.

Teller appears to link, next, this lack of instruction he manufactures with demands for composition teachers "that 'critical reading' should be as integral to a writing course as the teaching of argumentation, structure, paragraphs, and sentences." Again, Teller is drifting toward a powerful concern among composition teacher: how to balance disciplinary content (the *stuff* we write about) with composition content (the *stuff* Teller has falsely suggested composition is "enamored" with ignoring). Too much and too complex disciplinary content can and often does overwhelm first-year students, leaving them unable or unwilling to focus on developing as writers, but composition courses cannot and must not be free of disciplinary content.

The compromise embraced within the field of composition is shifting away from the sort of "close reading" that is common and essential in disciplinary courses and toward reading like a writer (see Chapter 54)—unpacking the readings in a course for the what and how of the text to highlight the role of rhetorical strategies, modes, and writer's craft in making and sharing meaning. Although significantly misleading and jumbled, Teller builds to a final set of bullet points, again presented as if they are counter to warranted writing pedagogy but are in fact mostly well within warranted writing pedagogy.

Responding to student essays early, often, and intentionally? Well, of course. Also, "frequent essays, frequent feedback"? Again, absolutely. His third point confronts and challenges a somewhat idealized view of peer conferencing, and I agree peer conferencing has limitations—thus, Teller's caveats seem solid, and worth greater examination.

Next, "process serves product" proves hard to dispute, but his assertion about a hypothetical "bright" student potentially producing writing that doesn't need revision is a bit odd since he seems to use this point to reinforce a larger challenge to focusing on process and drafting in first-year composition. Professional writers and scholars nearly universally revise, and almost always benefit from feedback, time for the piece to breath, and revision. In a composition course, then, novice writers should revise—because "an excellent essay in one draft," well, that Bigfoot doesn't exist. And I base this on 30+ years of teaching writing that has included a number of bright students who all benefitted from drafting even their best work.

Teller's fifth bullet—"Sometimes it's better to ditch an essay and move forward"—may be the best example of the jumbled nature of his argument because *abandonment* is an essential aspect of essay drafting. In other words, to embrace abandoning a draft is not an argument against requiring drafts by students, as Teller suggests. When I conduct the required conference after the first submission of each essay, the first question we address is whether or not the student wishes to continue with the current essay; *starting over, significantly recasting, or modestly revising or editing the current essay is the foundational set of questions of the drafting process.*

At Teller's final bullet, I want to emphasize how effective workshop and conferencing can be because if this were a first-year student's essay, I would note that his final point is the heart of a much better new essay confronting the proper place of disciplinary content and extensive reading requirements in a composition course. This concern by Teller remains a vibrant and difficult debate in the field of composition and among professors, worthy then of an essay. As is often the case when responding to student essays, in fact, I find the kernel of an essay late in what the student believes is a final essay—again demonstrating the value of time, ownership, and response (the central elements of workshop Teller fails to identify or explain).

While there is much potential in Teller's final bullets, the last two paragraphs return to misrepresentation and more than a hint at the potential motivation for his essay. Composition as a field is not "enamored" with pedagogy, and certainly does not "fetishize" the writing process. These are belittling swipes at a cartoon version of writing best practice. And thus, the last two paragraphs remind me too much of what is often wrong with first-year essays—turning personal angst into careless and lazy grand pronouncements.

Teller's argument needs to be better informed, more tightly focused, and much more fully supported—likely recast as an interrogation of only one of his points (the reading and disciplinary content issue). And as fate would hate it, these could all be addressed in a proper writing workshop and a few careful passes at guided revision.

# SECTION XI

## FIVE-PARAGRAPH ESSAY

CHAPTER 28

# HOW THE FIVE-PARAGRAPH ESSAY FAILS AS WARRANTED PRACTICE

At the core of John Dewey's pragmatism and progressivism is Dewey's contrarian view of "scientific"—the warranted assertion.* For Dewey, and in the context of teaching and learning, a warranted practice would be based on a substantial, diverse, and appropriate *body* of evidence, including how theory looks in the *unpredictable* real world. Although the term "best practice" is much sullied, the rightful use of that term certainly approaches Dewey's vision for education—how we practice in daily teaching what we are able to know from a range of evidence from experimental/quasi-experimental quantitative research to classroom-based action research.

However, Dewey's faith in scientific education as warranted practice suffered from his own skepticism about prescriptions, templates, and mandates; Dewey viewed education as a perpetual experiment and refused to dictate for any classroom what he discovered as warranted for *his* classroom. As a result, in the early 20th century and throughout the history of universal public education, progressivism has been rarely practiced but often vilified and misunderstood.[1] Even during the accountability era when prescriptions and mandates have become the norm, some have sought ways to promote "best practice" in the Dewey tradition of warranted practices—offering what teachers should *increase* and *decrease* in their practice.

But probably the best example of Dewey's warranted practice emerged in the 1970s and 1980s with the rise of the National Writing Project (NWP) and the call to teach writing authentically, to merge the practical experiences of writing with writing instruction.

As a true progressive, former NCTE president Lou LaBrant argued in the 1930s for choice and authentic writing pedagogy—about four decades before the rise of the NWP and workshop approaches to writing instruction. Not to be hyperbolic, but no one listened to LaBrant, and despite a brief bit of momentum by the NWP, the accountability era effectively killed authentic writing instruction. Thus, the five-paragraph essay, writing templates, prompted writing, and scoring rubrics have mostly dominated writing instruction in the U.S. for about a century.

Throughout, however, a substantial body of evidence from researchers, scholars, and practitioners has concluded that the five-paragraph essay approach to teaching writing remains *efficient* but *corrosive* to writing goals in the following two ways:

1. The five-paragraph essay approach to teaching writing produces bad writing and (even worse) bad (and lazy) thinking—the entire world of expression and thought reduced to making grand claims supported by three points.
2. And despite advocates' claims that the five-paragraph essay is an entry point or foundation for authentic writing, the evidence shows most students *never* make the transition.

Ironically, Dewey's resistance to templates and prescriptions resulted in his being mostly ignored but also was a harbinger for the enduring allure and negative consequences of templates and prescriptions.

Many English teachers are not writers themselves, and have had little or no experiences as students in writing workshops or authentic writing experiences. The five-paragraph essay approach to teaching writing, then, is *efficient* and lends itself well to assigning writing, responding to writing, and grading writing—all of which have supplanted both authentic writing goals and Dewey's call for warranted practice.

During the accountability era, teachers are under enormous and ridiculous pressure to have students score well on very bad tests, and are increasingly placed in classroom environments that do not allow authentic practice. Often, when teachers embrace efficiency over authentic, warranted practice, we should not blame the teachers as much as the larger contexts within which they work with little to no professional autonomy. As a public school teacher throughout the 1980s and 1990s in South Carolina where we embraced accountability, standards, and tests early and with missionary zeal, I taught in and struggled under these reduced circumstances.

But I also contend that we can commit to warranted practice; we *must* commit to warranted practice—and the consequences will be positive for students and likely even within the reductive world of standardized test scores.

Instead of templates and prompts, I invite students to investigate and interrogate a wide variety of texts, to read like writers. With each text, we try to determine the *type of writing*, developing *genre awareness* and building a toolbox of names for types of writing. Next, we identify the *conventions* that define that type of writing before asking how the writer both conforms to and also writes against those conventions. We stress that writing is about *purposeful decisions*—not rules, or templates.

We begin to highlight what *modes* (narration, description, exposition, persuasion) the writer incorporates, where and why. We also identify the *focus* of the piece (I do not use "thesis") and explore how the writer's *craft* accomplishes that. Instead of introduction, body, and conclusion, we analyze *openings* and *closings* as well as *claims, evidence, elaboration* (explanation, synthesis/connection, transition). And again, we are building the students' writer's toolbox—but I do not do the writer's work *for the student* in the reductive ways the five-paragraph essay does.

Ultimately, the five-paragraph essay fails as warranted practice because templates eradicate all the decisions writer make, and students are simply practicing how to be compliant—not to be writers. The practitioner's voice calling for authentic writing instruction reaches back a century, and we remain in a contentious battle between traditional and efficient practice versus authentic and warranted practice. Today, those of us calling for the long overdue end to the five-paragraph essay and arguing instead for warranted practice are echoing LaBrant from 1947, lamenting:

> A brief consideration will indicate reasons for the considerable gap between the research currently available and the utilization of that research in school programs and methods. (p. 87)
>
> This is not the time for the teacher of any language to follow the line of least resistance, to teach without the fullest possible knowledge of the implications of his medium.... [L]et us spend some time with the best scholars in the various fields of language study to discover what they know, what they believe uncertain and in need of study. Let us go to the best sources, and study the answers thoughtfully. (p. 94)[2]

* See from "Dewey's Epistemology: An Argument for Warranted Assertions, Knowing, and Meaningful Classroom Practice," Deron R. Boyles:

> In place of such a traditional account, Dewey crafts a new version of epistemology—one that has as a key element the notion of warranted assertibility.

Warranted assertions replace justification in the traditional syllogism while at the same time imploding the syllogism itself. Where justification served a correspondence theory of truth in the traditional account of knowledge, warranted assertions merge truth and inquiry together in such a way that correspondence to an external world is no longer the point. The point, instead, is the interdependency of truths and the processes of inquiry: the temporal satisfaction of solved problems in a world that is not set apart from the knower's use(s) of the world or place(s) in that world. In this way, idealists and realists are misguided when they describe epistemology as way of determining knowledge. "Knowledge" is not the focal point of epistemology for Dewey: "knowing" is. "Knowledge" represents the end of inquiry but, according to Dewey, it is also often supposed to have a meaning of its own—disconnected from inquiry. The result is that inquiry is subordinated to the fixed end called "knowledge." By "knowing" Dewey means inquiry in a world that is not static. He means inquiry into things "lived" by people. He means experimenting with solving problems such that the action entailed in the solving of problems is inquiry itself and warranted in the assertions made about the solved problem when it is solved (where "solved" is understood as temporal and a portal to further inquiry). Accordingly, in the "living" of life, problems will be faced and solved—often in serendipitous ways—such that achieving "justified true belief" (as traditional epistemology expects) is not useful. As Dewey put it:

> [Warranted assertion] is preferred to the terms belief and knowledge [because] it is free from the ambiguity of these latter terms, and it involves reference to inquiry as that which warrants assertion. When knowledge is taken as a general abstract term related to inquiry in the abstract, it means "warranted assertibility." The use of a term that designates potentiality rather than an actuality involves recognition that all special conclusions of special inquiries are parts of enterprise that is continually renewed, or is a going concern. (pp. 7–8)[3]

## ENDNOTES

1. Kohn, A. (2008, Spring). Progressive education: Why it's hard to beat, but also hard to find. *Independent School*. Retrieved from https://www.alfiekohn.org/article/progressive-education/
2. LaBrant, L. (1947, January). Research in language. *Elementary English, 24*(1), 86–94.
3. Boyles, D. R. (2006). Dewey's epistemology: An argument for warranted assertions, knowing, and meaningful classroom practice. *Educational Policy Studies Faculty Publications.* Paper 7. Retrieved from http://scholarworks.gsu.edu/eps_facpub/7

CHAPTER 29

# JOHN WARNER SWEARS OFF ESSAYS, AND STUDENTS? (YES, AND SO SHOULD EVERYONE)

John Warner, writer and formerly a visiting instructor of first-year writing, posted the provocatively titled "I'm Never Assigning an Essay Again."[1] And kept the ball rolling on Twitter[2]:

> Thinking this morning that best thing we can do for college students is to ask them to stop seeing themselves as "students."

> To a student, the grade is what matters, no matter how it's achieved, or whether or not it comes coupled with knowledge.

> Studenting is largely viewed as a kind of game to be hacked. This is why cheating isn't seen as wrong. It's a sensible shortcut.

That's right, it appears Warner was swearing off essays and students in his role as a writing instructor for first-year college students.

I immediately pounced on Warner's post and Tweets by sharing a key article I come back to often—especially in my work at a selective liberal arts university: "The Good Student Trap" by Adele Scheele.[3] "The odd thing about life is that we've been taught so many life-less lessons," Scheele laments, and then hits the key point about how school creates the "good student trap":

> We were learning the Formula.
>
> - Find out what's expected.
> - Do it.
> - Wait for a response.
>
> And it worked. We always made the grade. Here's what that process means: You took tests and wrote papers, got passing grades, and then were automatically promoted from one year to the next. That is not only in elementary, junior, and senior high school, but even in undergraduate and graduate school. You never had to compete for promotions, write résumés, or rehearse yourself or even know anyone for this promotion. It happened automatically. And we got used to it.

Until the formula doesn't work, of course. "All that changes once you find that studying history or art or anthropology can be so much more than just jumping through hoops," Scheele explains. "Your academic pursuits can lead to new experiences, contacts, and jobs. *But so much disappointment has resulted from misusing college, treating it as school instead of life* [emphasis added]."

And here is where my work as an educator significantly overlaps with Warner's two assertions: (1) the need to end the template-approach to essays that exists almost exclusively in formal classroom settings, and (2) the inherent failure of training young people in student behaviors, which are like the canned essay, unlike human behaviors in the real world. So in most of my classes, we start by having frank discussions about behaviors of students and how they appear if we step back from them. For incoming first-year students, I typically start with the need to use the restroom during class.

K–12 formal schooling has equated normal human urinary and bowel needs with something just short of a high crime. In K–12 schooling, your restroom needs must be conditioned to the school's schedule, and when that fails, you must raise your hand and ask permission. In college, however, you simply get up and go to the restroom. This transition away from the K–12 dehumanizing of students to normal adult behavior helps my students begin to investigate how we (professor/students) behave in class settings, how they should view their roles in learning (doing assignments instead of "homework," and completing the learning experiences for themselves and not the professor), and what scholarship means instead of "being a student."

I have linked the end of the school essay and the call for my students to drop student behaviors as essential for the sort of education I believe all young people deserve, a liberatory one. These goals merge in my writing-intensive courses in which I ask students to stop behaving as students and to begin to behave as writers (and what that entails is a long process we explore throughout the semester)—so that we can learn to write together in ways that serve their personal, academic, and career wants and needs.

I hope more educators follow Warner's lead—although these sorts of transitions I ask of my students are painful—and that we can all soon come together by swearing off essays and students.

\* See his post from the next day also: "Kill the 5-Paragraph Essay."[4]

## ENDNOTES

1. Warner, J. (2016, February 21). I'm never assigning an essay again [Web log]. Just Visiting. *Inside Higher Ed.* Retrieved from https://www.insidehighered. com/blogs/just-visiting/im-never-assigning-essay-again
2. https://twitter.com/biblioracle/status/701775360854245377
3. Scheele, A. (2004, May 6). The good student trap. *The Washington Post.* Retrieved from http://www.washingtonpost.com/wp-dyn/articles/A50758-2003May13.html
4. https://www.insidehighered.com/blogs/just-visiting/kill-5-paragraph-essay

CHAPTER 30

# SEEING THE ESSAY AGAIN FOR THE FIRST TIME

Teaching writing, like writing itself, is an arduous journey without any hope of a destination fairly called "finished." Both require equal parts confidence and humility as well. Each fall, then, when I wear my writing teacher hat most visibly while teaching two sections of first-year writing, I am as anxious and apprehensive as my students about teaching them to write. One Friday, I responded to their first essay submissions, and then, I posted on their course blog a brief set of common issues we explored during the require conferences before they revised Essay 1, and prepared to draft Essay 2:

I recommend reading these two pieces:

- Too Tired to Go to Heaven?, Aaron Simmons[1]
- *The Economist's* review of my book reveals how White people still refuse to believe Black people about being Black, Edward E Baptist[2]

Here are some common issues you should focus on for rewriting Essay 1:

- Work more diligently and purposefully on your openings and closings. You need to take more care with specifics and details; avoid telling about and show the reader a story instead.

*Teaching Writing as Journey, Not Destination:*
*Essays Exploring What "Teaching Writing" Means*, pp. 149–152

- Establish your focus (thesis) within the first four or so paragraphs and then keep the discussion on that focus throughout the essay.
- Can you explain briefly to someone what your focus is and what organizational plan guides your essay?
- Reconsider your title and subheads (add subheads if you haven't used them). Be interesting and vivid with both.
- While one or two purposeful fragments can be effective even in academic writing, run-on sentences always appear to be "errors." Edit run-ons and take much greater care with sentence formation and sentence variety.
- Huge and formless paragraphs are unappealing and ineffective. Form your paragraphs with purpose and prefer shorter, not longer.
- Integrate quotes with care to both how to punctuate and in connection to the source.
- Add sources where needed and begin citing properly using APA.
- Avoid extreme claims of "all," "none," "most," and so forth.
- Your word choice (diction) determines the tone of your writing, and also creates your authority. Lazy verbs and informal words should be revised.
- Verb tense should be appropriate but also should be purposeful and consistent. **Verb tense shift** (jumping between, among tenses without any clear reason) exposing the writing as careless.

Over my career, I have adopted a process I find most effective (although still lacking): I provide students ample models of the whole authentic artifact I want them to attempt (in this case, the essay), and I ask them to make a genuine attempt with some but not full explicit instructions before that attempt; after I have their work in front of me, I then prepare a more explicit plan for direct instruction (the bullets above). Somewhere long ago, I culled from the work of Howard Gardner that teaching should begin with clearly identifying *what students know*, *what they don't know*, and *what they misunderstand*. I build on what they know, provide them what they don't know, and then wrestle like a priest confronted with Regan in *The Exorcist* to release them from those misunderstandings (a task Gardner admits is nearly impossible).

Over that time as both a writer and a teacher of writing, I have rejected writing templates (see Chapter 60), the tyranny of the thesis sentence, rubrics, and writing to prompts as well as detailed writing assignments that relieve students of any choices as writers and thinkers. However, I remain mostly baffled at what works instead of these traditional approaches—and continue to seek ways to understand better what impedes my students from writing—and thinking—with greater sophistication.

That fall's experience with Essay 1 revealed to me, I think, a bit of an epiphany. While I am never really surprised at any of my students' essay drafts, and I can predict many of the revision needs before I see a set of papers, I do continually read those essays not to uncover my students' deficits, but to rethink *how to teach writing better*. Eventually, I came to recognize something, if not new, that was far more clear to me. In one of our course texts, *Style: Lessons in Clarity and Grace*, the concept of coherence is central—but I have never thought of the importance of that concept as clearly as I do now. The essays I read demonstrated to me that these very smart and genuinely engaged first-year students, admitted to a selective college, had almost no real conceptual understanding of sentence formation (and variety), paragraphing, and worst of all, just what the hell an essay is as a form.

That itself was not anything new, but what was new, for me, was that I could argue very directly that the root of what my students *did not know* and *often badly misunderstood* was the template used to teach students in most K–12 settings. Further, I now believe that teachers using those templates are also misled about their students' concepts of sentence formation, paragraphs, and essays because the template and prescriptions *mask the lack of understanding*. Of course, this may seem obvious, but the path to understanding the essay as a form, and then the academic essay as a discipline-specific form, includes not a linear or sequential but foundational grasp of both sentence formation and paragraphing.

My work as a teacher of writing now includes more aggressively investigating how to address coherence better, how to foster purpose and awareness in my students-as-writers. Rules and prescriptions, I am convinced, impede the development of conceptual understanding of how and why to form sentences and paragraphs in order to achieve an essay—a non-fiction short form with an opening and closing, with claims supported by evidence and elaborations. Again, my students have taught me that our traditional urges to start with parts and build to wholes is flawed; students often need to have the whole in mind so that the parts make sense.

As we worked toward revising those first essays, I was more convinced than ever that we needed to keep our eyes on model essays, asking always: What makes an essay, an essay? Templates and prescriptions may make the journey seem easier, but ultimately, that trip is hollow because students have mastered mostly compliance.

Writing, however, is an act of composing—building something new out of the craft at the writer's disposal. There is no way to make that easy, but there are ways to make it purposeful. That is grounded in conceptual awareness of authentic and whole artifacts; the essay always in pursuit of the essay.

## ENDNOTES

1. https://jaaronsimmons.wordpress.com/2017/09/15/too-tired-to-go-to-heaven/
2. https://www.theguardian.com/commentisfree/2014/sep/07/economist-review-my-book-slavery

# SECTION XII

## GENRE AWARENESS

# CHAPTER 31

# INVESTIGATING ZOMBI(E)S TO FOSTER GENRE AWARENESS

My initiation into the fiction of Roxane Gay was a wonderful moment of disequilibrium when I read her short story "There is No 'E' in Zombi Which Means There Can Be No You Or We."[1] The opening of the story is a staccato tease that sets the stage for even greater disorientation:

**[A Primer]**
**[Things Americans do not know about zombis:]**

They are not dead. They are near death. There's a difference.
They are not imaginary.
They do not eat human flesh.
They cannot eat salt.
They do not walk around with their arms and legs locked stiffly.
They can be saved.

"So what were zombies, originally?" asks Victoria Anderson, Visiting Researcher in Cultural Studies, Cardiff University, explaining:

The answer lies in the Caribbean. They weren't endlessly-reproducing, flesh-eating ghouls. Instead, the zombie was the somewhat tragic figure of a human being maintained in a catatonic state—a soulless body—and forced to labour for whoever cast the spell over him or her. In other words, the zombie is—or was—a slave. I always find it troubling that, somewhere along the line, we forgot or refused to acknowledge this and have replaced the suffering slave with the figure of a mindless carnivore—one that reproduces, virus-like, with a bite.[2]

The zombie narrative has captivated pop culture in the U.S. now for several years, notably the AMC series *The Walking Dead* and the comic book it is based on and novels such as *World War Z*. With the release of *Pride and Prejudice and Zombies*, Anderson expected this popularity to continue—along with the reimagined but mischaracterized zombie conventions.

For the classroom—especially when we are addressing reading and writing—the zombie narrative in its many iterations is an ideal entry point for investigating genre. Zombie narratives are a specialized sub-genre and blending of horror and science fiction. Since zombie narratives in print and film have been in U.S. pop culture for about eight decades, teachers can expect students at all levels to come to class with some existing assumptions about what zombies are and what zombie narratives entail—in other words, the conventions of zombie narratives as a genre.

As a writing teacher, I ascribe to Johns's emphasis on building genre awareness (as opposed to genre acquisition)[3] in developing writers *and* readers. Here, then, I want to outline briefly how to use zombie narratives as part of fostering genre awareness in students.

First, I would have students in small groups identify their own experiences with zombie narratives—naming what they have read or viewed. From that, students would then construct "what we know about zombies." This focus on starting with what conventions students already possess helps generate engagement and context for the larger lesson on genre awareness.

Next, I would ask students to read Gay's short story (or another that is age appropriate since Gay's story is for older readers) as a model text for comparing how that story matches or contrasts with the "what we know about zombies" list each group has created. Finally, I would share Anderson's article above in order to have a discussion about the concept of *conventions*—how expectations for a certain type of writing (or film) are shifting but bound to a time and place. The concept of zombies is much different now than in its origin.

Since superhero films are also all the rage, a companion activity to support helping students investigate the concept of conventions and genre is to allow them to research the many different versions for key superheroes—such as Spider-Man or Batman—that have existed over the 50-70 years of mainstream comic book superheroes. Some key caveats about fostering genre awareness are helpful for designing and implementing many lessons such as the one above:

- Fostering genre awareness as part of the writing and/or reading curriculum is an ongoing process. You can never "finish" that process, and all students at all levels need to be engaged continually with the *questions* of genre, form, and mode. Above, for example, asking: What makes a short story, a short story, or what makes Anderson's essay, an essay, and how might the public piece of hers compare to a scholarly essay on zombies?
- Genre awareness helps students build their own emerging and developing rubrics about how to tackle a writing project or interrogate a text. For example, a student learns to start with "what I know about X," and then while writing or reading to use that to *inform* how she/he proceeds in making meaning through composing or reading.
- Conventions serve communication as fluid frames that texts *conform to or break*; in other words, the structure helps create meaning, but the specifics of that structure are not as important as the structure itself.

"It's a call to memory because the zombie – the actual zombie – reminds us of something very important," Anderson concludes:

It reminds us to remember—who we are, and where we came from, and how we came to be—individually and collectively—especially for those of us whose personal and community histories are caught up in the blanketing fog of cultural amnesia. The zombie reminds us to taste salt.

Anderson's meditation on the shifting conventions of zombies, I think, speaks to the power of conventions themselves since how we construct our genres and what genres we embrace in pop culture are as much about us as about the narratives themselves.

Ultimately fostering genre awareness is about helping students know *who they are* as well as about the world in which they live.

## ENDNOTES

1. Gay, R. (2010, October 1). There is no "E" in zombi which means there can be no you or we. *Guernica*. Retrieved from https://www.guernicamag.com/gay_10_1_10/
2. Anderson, V. (206, February 19). Pride, prejudice and the mutation of zombies from Caribbean slaves to flesh-eaters. *The Conversation*. Retrieved from http://theconversation.com/pride-prejudice-and-the-mutation-of-zombies-from-caribbean-slaves-to-flesh-eaters-54996
3. Johns (2008).

# CHAPTER 32

# O, GENRE,
# WHAT ART THOU?

"What is genre in the first place?" asks novelist Kazuo Ishiguro during a conversation[1] with writer Neil Gaiman, who reviewed Ishiguro's novel, *The Buried Giant*. Ishiguro continues: "Who invented it? Why am I perceived to have crossed a kind of boundary?" Ishiguro then makes an interesting speculation about focusing on genre:

> Is it possible that what we think of as genre boundaries are things that have been invented fairly recently by the publishing industry? I can see there's a case for saying there are certain patterns, and you can divide up stories according to these patterns, perhaps usefully. But I get worried when readers and writers take these boundaries too seriously, and think that something strange happens when you cross them, and that you should think very carefully before doing so.

As I have grown older as both a teacher and a writer, I have become both more interested in genre (as well as medium and form—the distinctions and intersections) and less certain, like Ishiguro, about the utility of the labels.

Over the past several years, in fact, I have stumbled over publishers labeling Haruki Murakami's *1Q84* and Neil Gaiman's *American Gods* as "science fiction." While I love both books and authors, I am hard-pressed

*Teaching Writing as Journey, Not Destination:*
*Essays Exploring What "Teaching Writing" Means,* pp. 159–162
Copyright © 2019 by Information Age Publishing
159

to define either novel as science fiction; in fact, I am like Gaiman confronting Ishiguro's *Giant*:

> Fantasy and historical fiction and myth here run together with the Matter of Britain, in a novel that's easy to admire, to respect and to enjoy, but difficult to love. Still, "The Buried Giant" does what important books do: It remains in the mind long after it has been read, refusing to leave, forcing one to turn it over and over. On a second reading, and on a third, its characters and events and motives are easier to understand, but even so, it guards its secrets and its world close.
>
> Ishiguro is not afraid to tackle huge, personal themes, nor to use myths, history and the fantastic as the tools to do it.

Just as many enduring writers do, Ishiguro, Murakami, Gaiman, Margaret Atwood, and Kurt Vonnegut—just to name a few—weave genre conventions together, working within, against, and beyond the so-called boundaries of genre, medium, and form.

Unfortunately, formal education (and thus students and teachers) tends to remain trapped in the rote, the narrow, and the prescribed—or genre acquisition:

> ... GENRE ACQUISITION [is] a goal that focuses upon the students' ability to reproduce a text type, often from a template, that is organized, or "staged" in a predictable way. The Five Paragraph Essay pedagogies, so common in North America, present a highly structured version of this genre acquisition approach. A much more sophisticated version, introduced in Australia but now popular elsewhere, has been devised by the proponents of Systemic Functional Linguistics (Christie 1991; Martin 1993; Eggins 2004). Using well-established pedagogies, practitioners follow a teaching/learning cycle as students are encouraged to acquire and reproduce a limited number of text types ("genres") that are thought to be basic to the culture (Macken-Horarik 2002).[2]

However, for the skilled writer, genre awareness is part of the craft of writing, but not templates that dictate:

> A quite different goal is GENRE AWARENESS, which is realized in a course designed to assist students in developing the rhetorical flexibility necessary for adapting their socio-cognitive genre knowledge to ever-evolving contexts. Though there are few genre awareness curricula, for a number of reasons (see Freedman 1993), I will argue here that a carefully designed and scaffolded genre awareness program is the ideal for novice students – and for other students, as well.[3]

## Investigating Text as a Writer

For my first-year college students, we start the writing experience by cataloguing everything they have been taught about writing essays in school (concepts about introductions, bodies, conclusions, thesis sentences, and paragraphing, for example), and then we investigate the Prologue to Louise DeSalvo's memoir *Vertigo*. That investigation asks students to consider how this piece of nonfiction compares to what they have been taught about writing in school, but we also examine what the term "memoir" means against other terms such as "autobiography," "biography," and the fiction/nonfiction dichotomy. Next I add this exchange, "How to write a memoir: Jeanette Winterson and Helen Macdonald," that sets as rule one for writing memoir: "Don't try to 'fit' the genre."[4] Learning to write becomes a continual tension between what we think we know about text as that is confirmed and contradicted by what we read—as preparation for what we write.

Being a writer is inseparable from being a reader, but both are *ways of being* that are always evolving, never fixed just as no genre, medium, or form is ever truly fixed. As Gaiman and Ishiguro discuss genre, and Gaiman explains, "I think that there's a huge difference between, for example, a novel with spies in it and a spy novel; or a novel with cowboys in it and a cowboy novel," Ishiguro adding:

> So we have to distinguish between something that's part of the essence of the genre and things that are merely characteristic of it. Gunfights are characteristic of a western, but may not be essential to making the story arresting.

So there is where I am guiding my students as emerging writers and developing readers—to have the sense of purpose and awareness to recognize "essence" versus "characteristic," to attain a level of sophistication that *informs* them in their writing and reading *but doesn't artificially restrain them*. For both the reader and the writer, then, genre is a question, one to ask continually and not a definition or a prescription. And then, we must admit, the ultimate question remains: Was the text satisfying? That, too, becomes the source of even more debate, which, I would add, is the real essence of writing and reading because as long as there are readers the text always lives.

That, of course, if what every writer wants, to live forever:

> **NG** I know that when I create a story, I never know what's going to work. Sometimes I will do something that I think was just a bit of fun, and people will love it and it catches fire, and sometimes I will work very hard on some-

thing that I think people will love, and it just fades: it never quite finds its people.

**KI** Even if something doesn't catch fire at the time, you may find it catches fire further down the line, in 20 years' time, or 30 years' time. That has happened, often.

## ENDNOTES

1. Gaiman, N., & Ishiguro, K. (2015, June 4). "Let's talk about genre": Neil Gaiman and Kazuo Ishiguro in conversation. *New Statesman.* Retrieved from https://www.newstatesman.com/2015/05/neil-gaiman-kazuo-ishiguro-interview-literature-genre-machines-can-toil-they-can-t-imagine
2. Johns (2008).
3. Johns (2008).
4. Cain, S. (2015, June 4). How to write a memoir: Jeanette Winterson and Helen Macdonald. *The Guardian.* Retrieved from https://www.theguardian.com/books/2015/jun/04/how-to-write-a-memoir-jeanette-winterson-and-helen-macdonald

# SECTION XIII

## GRADING

CHAPTER 33

# RETHINKING GRADING AS INSTRUCTION

## Three Ways

### 1. Grades Fail Student Engagement With Learning

Possibly my greatest commitment while teaching public school English in a rural SC high school was listening to my students, and by that, I do not mean listening to them during class discussions or in conferences (I did that also). I mean listening to students *when they didn't know an adult was listening*. Some of those moments that have shaped my teaching include the following:

- **Student comment:** A student walking into class told a friend that she had just failed a pop quiz in the previous class after studying all night, and from then on, she wasn't going to waste her time studying. **My lesson:** Pop quizzes often taught students the exact wrong lessons intended; thus, I very early on never gave pop quizzes (leading eventually to giving no tests, for similar reasons).
- **Student comment:** Two students were leaving my class once at the end of the school day. One asked the other if they had any homework in another class; the friend replied, "No, we just have to read." **My lesson:** Students did not see reading as homework,

*Teaching Writing as Journey, Not Destination:*
*Essays Exploring What "Teaching Writing" Means*, pp. 165–172
Copyright © 2019 by Information Age Publishing
All rights of reproduction in any form reserved.

and after I asked what the students meant, I discovered that students had learned *they did not need to read* since teachers told them everything they needed in class the next day. This profoundly impacted how I invited and required student reading in my classes, including offering adequate time in class for them to read, increasing choice in their reading, and adding an *artifact of reading* (response journals, annotating text, notes to classmates, etc.) to any out-of-school reading expectations.

Some of the listening I did, however, took much more time and required inference on my part. But it is that sort of listening that ultimately shaped my understanding that grades, averaging grades, rubrics, and grading policies contribute significantly to student opportunities to *avoid* being engaged with learning. Let me explain.

Over a long period of time, and while carefully listening and even asking questions, I learned that many students gamed their math classes so that they passed math courses while never passing a single math test or exam. Students had discovered that playing the game of averaging grades and manipulating the impact of nontest assignments (homework, projects, class participation, extra credit) on those averages allowed students to pass the course with a minimum of studying or learning the material for quizzes, tests, and exams. And, yes, the irony here is that students used math to avoid being engaged in actually learning math.

Since students were armed with detailed grading policies, many would keep a running record of their averages, weigh that against the extra credit and nontest grades they could compile, and then maintain cumulative averages just at the passing barrier (often something they learned they could negotiate near the end of the course, as well). This is just one example of "school-only" practices and "student" behaviors that have guided my own teaching policies that seek ways to end both: I don't want my class to be "playing school," and I don't want the young people in my classes to behave as students.

This came to mind as I exchanged e-mails with Peter Smagorinsky, University of Georgia, about a post of mine, "Email to My Students: 'the luxury of being thankful,'" lamenting giving grades at the end of the semester. I want to clarify what I do and why, but also add how I have course policies that delay traditional grading but are driven instead by *minimum requirements for course credit* that support engagement.

First, some may have assumed that my nongrading practices are somehow related to my teaching at a selective university where that is possible. But I must emphasize that *I started de-grading my classes early in my career while teaching in a rural SC public high school, and I did so with all levels of students*. My practices are *not* about idealized students or settings.

Next, de-grading a class is not about being soft, or easy, or asking less of students. De-grading is about demanding more from students, notably more engagement. In my courses (then and now), students had/have to participate fully in all activities and assignments.* To put this in traditional contexts, students are not allowed to "take a zero" on an assignment and then just pass by on the resulting average. There is no, "I just took zeros on my papers last year and still passed English." (And many students told me that when I was teaching public school.)

Again, then and now, when students are required to write four original and drafted essays over a grading period or during a course, that means several minimum requirements: initial submission of each drafted original essay (made *directly observable* during writing workshop in class), required conferences with me after each initial essay submission, and required essay revision meeting minimum expectations of revision (a detailed *revision plan* we created in each conference). Don't fulfill minimum requirements, and you do not receive credit for the grading period or the course (and, yes, I did this during my public school teaching career).

I balance those demands with other important policies: (1) students are allowed to continue revising their work as much as they want and time allows, and (2) late work is not only accepted, but necessary. The de-graded classroom is about engagement in the learning process and artifacts of learning. There is nothing soft or easy about any of this, and these are not practices suitable for only *some* students. And students are not allowed the manipulation of grades and averages that I have witnessed and continue to witness in traditionally grade-driven courses where students focus on the grades or passing and not engaging with learning. Minimum observable requirements for student participation trump significantly traditionally graded and averaged testing in terms of creating genuine student engagement in learning.

I want to emphasize that these are not idealistic practices or claims; I also practice *concessions to the reality of grades in formal schooling*. The "de-" in de-grading of my classes is best framed as "delayed" because I do invite students to discuss the grades their works-in-progress deserve throughout the process and, of course, I do assign grades at the end of each course. While delaying grades, however, I am increasing the *quality and quantity* of feedback my students receive and of student engagement in learning for the sake and advantages of learning.

## 2. Rejecting the Error Hunt and Deficit Practices

As a beginning English teacher, I joined the department of the high school where I had graduated only five years earlier, becoming a colleague with teachers who had taught me. That introduction to the field allowed me behind the curtain, and one of those secrets was being handed a sheet that detailed every grammar and mechanics error students were likely to make in their writing and the amount of points to be deducted from their grade (writing was assigned the traditional content/grammar grade then such as B/D-). One fragment, by the way, was an immediate deduction that resulted in an F on grammar. This was department policy, and my efforts to navigate that system were akin to Sisyphus, his rock, and that damned mountain.

Since then, well over thirty years ago, I have become a nongrader, but I also have investigated and adopted concepts about grading (since we all at some point *must grade*) that I believe are incredibly important in the context of seeing grading (and feedback) *as a part of instruction*—and not something we do to students and their work after we teach.

A teacher asked on a discussion board for ELA teachers about subtracting points for grammar in student writing, and that was an ideal entry point to rethink how grading (especially of writing) sends instructional messages to our students. My first caution is about a serious flaw with traditional grading that is grounded in viewing assessment situations in a deficit model whereby we have students start with an *unearned* 100 points from which we subtract credit by identifying errors. This fosters an atmosphere of risk aversion—which is not a healthy environment for developing literacy. Specifically, when teaching writing, we must abandon the "error hunt."[1]

Therefore, we can send a much healthier message about student performances of learning if we acknowledge that students begin all assessment situations with zero and then *give them credit for what they accomplish*, what the artifact of learning demonstrates—and *not where they fail*. I learned this concept of grading through my Advanced Placement training that encourages viewing writing *holistically* and then reading for what students do, not conducting the "error hunt." Conceptually, then, we must change our language and then couch our grading in a drafting process that gives students the space to *take risks* while receiving ample feedback as they revise and edit their writing.

Our language about writing must stop referring to "mistakes" and "errors," while also not asking students to "correct" their work. Instead, we should *delay addressing if our students are being conventional* (grammar, mechanics, and usage) until late in the drafting process when we can agree a piece of writing is worth editing. The question is not if and how much to deduct for surface features not being conventional, but *when* to consider those issues relevant to the drafting of the piece of writing.

Our feedback during the drafting process is our instruction, and then, most of us at some point must abandon each assignment, requiring that we assign a grade, *an act that also is teaching students lessons*—ones that should match our philosophy of teaching/learning as well as what we want them to embrace about writing and literacy. Here, I recommend that we take a holistic approach (I love the upper-half, lower-half concepts of the AP 9-point scale**), but I also believe we should help students learn that all aspects of writing contribute to that holistic response.

The two categories we should be using to grade writing, I think, are *revision* (if and how students demonstrate content, organization, diction, style) and *editing* (grammar, mechanics, and usage). When I have graded, I weighted those categories *to reflect my main lessons about what makes writing effective* by using a 20-point scale articulated as 10 points for content and organization, 5 points for diction and style, and 5 points for grammar, mechanics, and usage. In all assessment, we should be seeking ways in which grading is both philosophically matched with our instruction and a seamless aspect of our instruction.

If you are teaching students writing quality is holistic and that surface features are less significant to meaning than content, organization, and diction/style, then calculating a grade based on deducting points for errors contradicts (and probably supersedes) your lessons. Therefore, reducing the grading of writing by students to a set of points to be deducted fails as assessment and instruction.

While most teachers have no real option to de-grade the classroom, we can step back from deficit views of student work and grading in order to embrace grading and instructional practices that create positive learning environments (where risk is encouraged) and celebrate what our students accomplish in their journey as readers, writers, and thinkers.

## 3. More Thoughts on Feedback, Grades, and Late Work

My good friend and stellar colleague, Ken Lindblom, posted "Should Students' Grades Be Lowered for Lateness?," spurring a series of Tweets about grading late work. Ken's thoughtful post focuses on these foundational ideas:

As an educator, I try to base my decisions on a principle of authenticity. In other words, I try to make my decisions more on real-world norms than traditional school norms. I try to ensure that I am preparing students for the world beyond school, not for school. As a result, I try to make sure that the ways in which I assess students' work is similar to the ways in which they would be assessed in a professional situation.

There are times when a professional can absolutely not be late: grant applications, proposals for conferences/speaking, ... I'm not sure I can come up with a third example to make a series.

But adults can be late with almost anything else: publication deadlines, job evaluations, doctor's appointments, taxes–even most bills have a grace period.[2]

Here I want to tease out a few ideas related to feedback on student work (artifacts of learning), grades, and late work.

Like Ken's concern for *authenticity*, I tend to work from a personal and professional aversion to *hypocrisy* based on teaching English in a rural South Carolina public high school and then in a selective liberal arts university, also in SC. I have been practicing and refining de-grading and de-testing practices for over 30 years. Let me emphasize, since I have been challenged before, I have implemented—and thus currently advocate for—de-grading and de-testing in many school contexts, including public schools (not just at the university level).

So my path to rejecting grades and tests has many stages and elements. First, I had to confront that calculating grades bound only to averages often distorts grades unfairly for students. Mean, median, and mode are all credible ways to analyze data, and among them, in formal schooling, the mean (average) is both the norm and often the weakest. I show students this simple example; a series of grades: 10, 10, 85, 85, 85, 85, 85, 85, 100, 100 = 730. The average is 73, which most teachers would assign, but the mode is 85, and if we note these grades are sequential and *cumulative* (10 as the first grade in terms of time, and 100 the last grade), a legitimate grade assignment would be the 100. In other words, using the same data, a teacher could assign 73, 85, or 100 to this student, and all can be justified statistically.

My conclusion has been this greatly challenges the value of assigning grades because those who control the rules, control reality. Thus, I do not assign grades to any student artifacts of learning (and I do not give traditional tests). Instead I offer *feedback* that supports students as they revise and resubmit those artifacts. However, I cannot refuse to assign students grades for courses. Therefore, another distinction I have come to appreciate is the difference between grading an assignment and determining a grade for a grading period or course. Therein lies my approach to late work, but first, let's consider adult hypocrisy.

Over my career as an educator at nearly every level possible, I witness daily teachers and professors who fail to meet deadlines (regularly); talk, do other things (grade papers), stare at their computers/smart phones, and so forth, during meetings; and behave in a number of ways that they do not tolerate by students in their classes, behaviors that negatively impact students' grades. I also drive daily with adult motorists who exceed the speed limit without any punishment—as most of us have come to realize a grace zone of staying less than ten mph over that limit. *In other words, the real world of rules is much fuzzier than the rules of formal schooling.* These are the behaviors I see when I am confronted with student late work.

About late work, then, I have some clear policies. First, I would never change a grade assigned to an artifact of learning that distorts the actual quality of that artifact. A "B" essay is a "B" essay regardless of when it is submitted. As an educator, my primary concern is student learning, and I suffer no delusions that *when* that happens is more important than *if* it happens. I also ascribe to Rick Wormeli's dictum that fair isn't always equal; thus, I do not allow very narrow expectations that I treat all students exactly the same override that I am there to serve *each* student as well as *all* students.

Next, I always record "lateness" and then consider that when I assign a grade for a grading period or course. If a student has one or two assignments late (clearly an outlier), I may ignore that when determining the grading period/course grade, but if there is a pattern of lateness, then the grading period/course grade must reflect this. In other words, I believe we must *separate* artifact quality (the basis of assigning period or course grades) from grading period/course grades.

Feedback and grades on artifacts of learning send students clear messages about what they produce (their learning), and then grading period/course grades send a message about the totality of their accomplishments as *students*. So if we return to Ken's context, we can imagine a manager telling a habitually late worker: "Your work here is excellent, but if you aren't here on time, we will have to let you go." Especially in the recent 30-plus years of standards, educators have fallen prey to standardization, and as a result, we have too often abdicated our professional autonomy and allowed technical norms to supplant our much more important goals and obligations, the human dignity and learning of each child assigned to our care.

And because most people have greater regard for medical doctors than teachers (sigh), I'll end with an example my major professor offered in my doctoral program. A patient is admitted to the hospital running a dangerously high fever. After several days, during all of which the nurses record that patient's temperature hourly, the doctor comes in, adds those temperatures, calculates the average, and refuses to release the patient, although the current temperature is 98.6.

Right, no medical doctor would allow the norm of averages to override her/his medical authority. And neither should educators.

## See Also

Missing Assignments–and the Real World, Nancy Flanagan

The Perils of Late Work and How to Make It Count, Starr Stackstein

It's Time to Ditch Our Deadlines, Ellen Boucher[3]

* As an example, here is my minimum requirement statement from a first-year writing seminar:

Minimum Requirements for course credit:

- Submit all essays in MULTIPLE DRAFTS before the last day of the course; initial drafts and subsequent drafts should be submitted with great care, as if each is the final submission, but students are expected to participate in process writing throughout the entire semester as a minimum requirement of this course—including a minimum of ONE conference per major essay.
- Demonstrate adequate understanding of proper documentation and citation of sources through a single well-cited essay or several well-cited essays. A cited essay MUST be included in your final portfolio.

** The process for scoring a written response to an AP Literature prompt includes thinking in terms of a range of scores 9–8, 7–6, 5, 4–3, 2–1. Above 5 is upper half, and below, lower half. As you read, you are constantly monitoring holistically if you believe the essay is upper or lower by focusing on in what ways the student is fulfilling the expectations of the prompt and remaining accurate in the analysis of the literature being discussed. Typically, that process allows the reader to return to the rubric to refine the grade after completing the essay. If you know the response is upper half but only marginally so, then returning to the 7 and 6 rubric descriptors help refine the final score.

## ENDNOTES

1. Weaver (1996); Rosen, L. M. (1987, March). Developing correctness in student writing: Alternatives to the error-hunt. *The English Journal, 76*(3), 62–69.
2. Lindblom, K. (2016, January 11). Should students' grades be lowered for lateness? [Web log]. *Edukention*. Retrieved from https://edukention.wordpress.com/2016/01/11/should-students-grades-be-lowered-for-lateness/
3. http://blogs.edweek.org/teachers/teacher_in_a_strange_land/2016/01/_missing_assignmentsand_the_real_world.html;   http://blogs.edweek.org/teachers/work_in_progress/2016/01/the_perils_of_late_work_and_ho.html; https://www.chronicle.com/article/It-s-Time-to-Ditch-Our/237530

# CHAPTER 34

# NOT HOW TO ENJOY GRADING BUT WHY TO STOP GRADING

The morning I placed copies of the revised edition of *De-testing and De-grading schools: Authentic Alternatives to Accountability and Standardization* in envelopes to mail to chapter authors was a bittersweet task since we lost my co-editor Joe Bower during the process of creating a revised edition. Concurrently as well, I read later that day a post from John Warner, in which he opens with a confession: "Like a lot of college instructors, I have, from time to time, expressed my dislike of grading."[1]

This post by Warner in particular hit home because of my own journey as a teacher of writing and a much less successful life as a writer as well. In my updated chapter of our de-testing and de-grading book, I examine in detail my own reasons for and approaches to not grading student writing, but instead to focus my time and energy on giving ample feedback while students brainstorm and then draft original essays they find compelling. In part, I explain:

> Along with the pedagogical and assessment autonomy I experience as a
> professor (now tenured), the university's transition to first-year seminars
> has influenced greatly my practices and offered ample evidence about how
> de-grading a writing classroom works, and doesn't. In all of my university
> courses, in fact, I refuse to put grades on assignments throughout the se-

*Teaching Writing as Journey, Not Destination:*
*Essays Exploring What "Teaching Writing" Means,* pp. 173–176
Copyright © 2019 by Information Age Publishing

mester. Instead, I have two practices: (1) I provided ample feedback as well as require and allow students to revise most assignments until students are pleased with the work, and (2) I invite and urge students to arrange conferences as often as desired throughout the semester to discuss their grades (what their grades would be if assigned, what they would assign themselves, and what I anticipate they will be assigned at the end of the course).

De-grading the writing class and encouraging a conversation about grades instead of labeling assignments with grades have combined to lift the effectiveness of my writing instruction significantly because these practices reinforce the autonomy and agency of the students and shift the focus of the classes to the quality of the compositions and the growth of the students as writers and away from courses as credentialing.

I want to stress again here that I began de-grading my classroom while still a K-12 teacher without the protection of tenure (I have always worked in a right-to-work state without union protection) so I am not suggesting that de-grading is reserved for the rarified air of higher education.*

I call on *all* teachers of writing, then, to set aside the urge to grade essays, and instead, to embrace a process in which the teacher/professor is a collaborator in helping novice writers grow through drafting their own work as real-world writer do—as Warner details:

> The final assignment is different. It asks them to craft an argument of their own design aimed at an audience of their choosing. They're to use the skills they've practiced earlier, and I am instead reading to discover what they have learned about the subjects they've chosen.
>
> Instead of a teacher, assessing skills, I am a reader, responding to ideas, and in many cases the students are presenting ideas and arguments I wasn't aware existed.

The path to de-grading the classroom is difficult because we face traditional hurdles of teaching being inseparable from evaluating students, and then we must help our student shake off the shackles of being *evaluated students* in order to explore the opportunities afforded being an apprentice.

Teachers/professors too must cast off the shackles of grading. Consider Warner's epiphany that addresses how he has taught and graded essay writing in his first-year courses versus how he has taught and responded to writing in fiction courses:

> By accepting the flaws as inevitable before I begin, my fundamental orientation changes, both in how I read and respond to the work, but more importantly, my own emotional experience when grading. In fact, I've never even called what I do in a fiction class "grading." It is simply reading and responding, which is a lot more fun.

Finally, then, from my chapter in the de-testing and de-grading volume, I want to share here a few "guiding principles for de-grading the writing classroom":

1.  Reductive responses to student writing (grades, rubric scores) fail to enrich the writing process (see Gould, 1996, regarding singular quantification of complex processes[2]). Teacher feedback must be rich, detailed, and targeted to support revision. The most powerful feedback includes identifying key strengths in a student's work ("Do this more often") and questions that help guide students toward revision ("Why are you omitting the actual names of your family members in your personal narrative?"). To share with students the specific and contextualized characteristics that constitute an evaluation (such as an A) provides students as writers the evidence needed to build their own rubrics of expertise for future writing, and learning.
2.  Teacher and student roles in the de-graded writing classroom must be revised—teachers as authoritative, not authoritarian; teacher as teacher/student; and student as student/teacher. [3] The de-graded writing classroom allows a balancing of power that honors the teacher's agency as a master writer and master teacher of writing without reducing the status of the student as beneath her/his agency and autonomy, both of which are necessary for the growth of any writer.
3.  De-grading the writing classroom increases the importance and impact of peer conferencing by removing from the teacher the primary or pervasive role of evaluator. Feedback from peers and from the teacher becomes options for students as they more fully embrace their roles as process writers.

The teaching of writing, in my opinion, is not unique compared to teaching anything—so I am a strong advocate for de-testing and de-grading all education. However, as Warner has discussed so well, the *teaching of writing as authentic practice* is impossible to separate from the corrosive impact of grading on both the teacher/professor and the students. The de-graded writing classroom seeks to honor the sanctity of teaching and mentoring, the autonomy of students as writers-to-be, and the act of writing itself as essential to human liberation.

* Also from my de-testing and de-grading chapter:

> I want to emphasize, also, that these are not idealistic practices or claims;
> I do practice concessions to the reality of grades in formal schooling. The

"de-" in de-grading of my classes is best framed as "delayed" because I do invite students to discuss the grades their works-in-progress deserve throughout the process and, of course, I do assign grades at the end of each course.

While delaying grades, however, I am increasing the quality and quantity of feedback my students receive and of student engagement in learning for the sake and advantages of learning.

## ENDNOTES

1. Warner, J. (2016, May 5). Sometimes I don't hate grading. Why? [Web log]. Just Visiting. *Inside Higher Ed*. Retrieved from https://www.insidehighered.com/blogs/just-visiting/sometimes-i-dont-hate-grading-why
2. Gould, S. J. (1996). *The mismeasure of man*. New York, NY: W. W. Norton and Company.
3. Freire, P. (1993). *Pedagogy of the oppressed*. New York, NY: Continuum.

# CHAPTER 35

# THE NEARLY IMPOSSIBLE

## Teaching Writing in
## a Culture of Grades, Averages

A former student and current English teacher and I have something in common when teaching students to write: A nearly paralyzing frustration with students' resistance to draft and revise their essays. While discussing this problem with the early-career teacher, I was once again reminded of how the traditional culture of grades and averaging makes the teaching of writing nearly impossible, especially for beginning teachers.

I have wrestled with the problems with grades and averaging before and co-edited a volume on de-testing and de-grading education. But the essential problem remains: When teachers of writing are denied professional autonomy in their assessment and feedback practices, their writing pedagogy and the learning of their students are inevitably eroded. As long as students are allowed to play the averaging game (completing assignments rendered irrelevant as long as the math produces a passing grade in the end), authentic learning and holistic outcomes are moot.

To offer an example outside of literacy and the teaching of writing, I noticed while teaching high school that many students in math courses *never passed a single math test*, but passed the course because they accumulated enough extra credit to have a passing final grade (through averaging) for the course. I also had students tell me directly that they had simply

---

*Teaching Writing as Journey, Not Destination:*
*Essays Exploring What "Teaching Writing" Means*, pp. 177–180
Copyright © 2019 by Information Age Publishing

taken zeroes for all their essay assignments the year before my class, but passed English by making high enough grades on vocabulary, grammar, and literature tests.

This teacher—as many of my former students have done once they entered the classroom—has implemented many of my strategies for encouraging students to draft: setting deadlines for drafts, linking participating in drafting to possible final grades on essays, etc. Still, she admitted that students could skip the drafting, or even completing essays at all, and still *because of school and district policies* pass the course—without ever really engaging in the learning processes that the course was intended to address. As is common with young and excellent teachers, she has taken on the bulk of the blame for this problem. "What can I do?" has become her refrain.

First, I want to stress that if and when I have been an effective teacher of writing, much of that success has been grounded in my assessment autonomy at both the secondary and university levels. While teaching high school and as a college professor, I have been afforded the professional support to require that students complete all essays and fulfill the obligation of drafting and revising those essays; if and when students do not meet those minimum requirements, they have failed. I have always made the analogy that a sick patient must follow a doctor's orders, including taking prescribed medicines, in order to heal. If that patient refuses to follow orders, the doctor is not responsible. (The doctor, of course, *is responsible* for a valid diagnosis and prescribing the right medications and treatments.)

Since I cannot magically afford most teachers the sort of autonomy I have enjoyed, I want to consider below some real-world strategies for making the teaching of writing more authentic in the counter-productive culture of grades and averaging:

- *Seek colleague (and department) support for assessment and feedback policies that model the importance of drafting and writing essays.* One aspect of the negative impact of grades and averaging is that students receive a powerful and consistent message across all their teachers and courses that *playing the average game* is not only all right, but what education is. Good writing pedagogy among teachers and within a department is more powerful than when any teacher works as an island.

- *Identify clearly for students, parents, and administrators that* **drafting is a primary instructional goal** *within the larger writing unit.* This is a Sisyphean battle, but teachers of writing must create a culture in which drafting is embraced as an essential part of writing—not that drafting is some sort of option or busy work assigned by the teacher.

- *Design grading scales, assessment weights, rubrics, and assignments so that they all accurately reflect the primary importance of essay writing and drafting in the course.* Yes, I abhor all of those traditional structures, but I also recognize they are often not negotiable for most teachers; and thus, we must manage traditional grading in a way that is least corrosive. The number of grades and the weight of grades in averaging can and should be shifted so that drafting and completing essays is essential for students to pass, or to do well.

- *Resist evaluating good assessment and writing practices by the "100% compliance or failure" formula.* Throughout my career, I have routinely been confronted with the teacher who rejects my proposals for teaching with "Not all of my students will...." No practice need be 100% effective to be the right practice, but what is also puzzling with this argument is that traditional approaches can be dismissed with the same argument.

- *Periodically review teaching and assessment practices against specific writing goals.* Here is a common question I pose to teachers struggling: What is your main instructional goal? Then I ask them to evaluate what they are doing against that goal—and to determine what their threshold is for standing firm on those practices and goals. If drafting is an essential student practice and instructional goal, lessons and assessment practices and policies must reflect that fact.

- *Ultimately all educators must have reasonable expectations for themselves, their students, and their instructional goals.* It is not ours to do everything for every student, and it profits no one for any teacher to be a martyr. While I recognize the power of holistic behaviors and artifacts of learning (and am skeptical of the analysis bias of traditional schooling), I do urge a baby-steps approach to teaching and learning. Patience for the teacher and the student. Literacy broadly and writing more narrowly are journeys, not to be fixed with inoculations.

- *Spend as little psychological energy as possible on policies that are not negotiable.* District and school policies for grading—usually entrenched traditional approaches to testing, assessment, averaging, and grades—certainly deserve critique by teachers of conscience. But that advocacy for change cannot become a constant source of fretting and self-flagellation. I wish more educators would advocate for de-testing and de-grading the classroom, for rejecting averaging grades in favor of portfolios, revision, and effective teacher feedback. But day-to-day teaching must focus on the autonomy that teachers have, not what they are denied. Teaching is necessarily a tremendous psychological drain; we need not spend our energy on that over which we have no immediate control.

While teaching English *and* seeking to foster our students as writers, we must be concerned when students can pass or make Bs/ Cs in our courses while avoiding or refusing to draft or submit essays. But when faced with that dilemma, we must first carefully identify the source of that possibility. A culture of grades and averaging works against us in many schools, and thus, we must then work within the autonomy we do have to make our writing pedagogy and assessment practices more closely aligned—even when we cannot achieve perfect.

# SECTION XIV

## GRAMMAR

CHAPTER 36

# LOST IN TRANSLATION

## More From a Stranger in Academia

Decade four and round two in academia—this time at the university level where, one might assume, things would be easier.

First, a flashback.

I am the English department chair, and the entire faculty is sitting in the high school library for a faculty meeting about standardized test scores for our school. Having entered education in the fall of 1984—the first year of South Carolina's all-in commitment to accountability, standards, and high-stakes testing—I have taught for over 30 years under the weight of test scores. Before the principal and the math department chair shared our students' scores on the test-of-the-moment, the principal offered what he believed was a friendly caveat about the English scores: "Just want you all to remember that we don't teach grammar here," with a nod and a smile in my direction.

Now fast-forward to my current position where I teach two first-year writing seminars, had a now defunct role as Faculty Director of First Year Seminars, and continue to co-facilitate our efforts at offering faculty develop in teaching writing. In our Faculty Writing Fellows sessions, I am routinely addressed whenever someone mentions grammar, notably commas, with a similar caveat—although these don't seem quite as friendly as they are marginalizing.

*Teaching Writing as Journey, Not Destination:*
*Essays Exploring What "Teaching Writing" Means,* pp. 183–185
Copyright © 2019 by Information Age Publishing
All rights of reproduction in any form reserved.

To be committed to critical pedagogy, critical constructivism, de-grading/ de-testing, and authentic writing instruction is to be a stranger in academia. You are tolerated with bemusement, as the mostly harmless weirdo in the room. You aren't credible—although you have worked for over 30 years honing your craft, taking great care as a teacher and writer to teach only warranted practices and to honor above all else the human dignity and autonomy of your students. Nope, you "don't teach grammar"—which is both false and used in the sort of condescending way people in the U.S. say "liberal" or people in the South say "Bless your heart."

My urge to be abrasive always prompts me to say: "Actually I teach grammar the *right way*." But I don't say anything. Mostly I stew—the same way I stew about writing free verse poetry under the judgmental purview of those who think free verse is a lazy person's game. And, I keep at it—doing warranted practice diligently despite the suggestions otherwise. I teach relentlessly that language, its use and the forces that seek to control its use (including those who shout "grammar rules!"), is about *power*—as James Baldwin confronts in his brilliant defense of Black English:

> It goes without saying, then, that language is also a political instrument, means, and proof of power. It is the most vivid and crucial key to identify: It reveals the private identity, and connects one with, or divorces one from, the larger, public, or communal identity. There have been, and are, times, and places, when to speak a certain language could be dangerous, even fatal. Or, one may speak the same language, but in such a way that one's antecedents are revealed, or (one hopes) hidden. This is true in France, and is absolutely true in England: The range (and reign) of accents on that damp little island make England coherent for the English and totally incomprehensible for everyone else. To open your mouth in England is (if I may use black English) to "put your business in the street": You have confessed your parents, your youth, your school, your salary, your self-esteem, and, alas, your future.[1]

I don't teach students grammar, mechanics, and usage *rules*; I guide my students as we interrogate the conventions of language—why they exist, how they have changed, and why each student's own empowerment depends on their being aware and in control of those conventions and their language (see Chapter 38 on the use of "they" as a singular pronoun). And beyond my ethical reasons for approaching language this way, ethical reasons grounded in critical pedagogy, I am motivated by a negative: I don't want to fall into a trap confronted by Lou LaBrant: "On the other hand, we should not, under the guise of developing literary standards, merely pass along adult weariness" (p. 276).[2]

The prescriptive-grammarian-as-teacher, I fear, is harping on pet peeves, setting themselves up for sullying the language and their students' passion for expression—but certainly opening themselves up for losing their own credibility because virtually all users of language are pickers and choosers about strict adherence to the so-called "rules." My stress level is triggered each time I receive e-mails from a prescriptive grammarian who spells my sacred Southernism "ya'll." I am a writer and I teach writing—both of which are at the core of who I am as a person. Ultimately, then, I side with LaBrant: "As a teacher of English, I am not willing to teach the polishing and adornment of irresponsible, unimportant writing" (p. 123).[3]

But, alas, it is this sort of principled approach to teaching, and teaching writing, that pushes me farther and farther afield of academia. And so a stranger in academia, I eye the fire escape, like Tom in *The Glass Menagerie* anxious with the awareness that "the other boys in the warehouse regarded [him] with suspicious hostility."

## ENDNOTES

1. Baldwin, J. (1979, July 29). If Black English isn't a language, then tell me, what is? *The New York Times*. Retrieved from http://www.nytimes.com/books/98/03/29/specials/baldwin-english.html
2. LaBrant, L. (1949, May). Analysis of clichés and abstractions. *English Journal, 38*(5), 275–278.
3. LaBrant (1946).

# CHAPTER 37

# TEACHING LITERACY, NOT LITERACY SKILLS

Through the lens of having been a teacher/professor, published writer, and recreational/competitive cyclist almost all of my adult life, several high school experiences are now illustrative of larger facts about the tension between teaching discrete skills versus fostering holistic performances. In high school, I made As in math and science courses, but typically received Bs in English—and the source of that lower grade was poor scores on vocabulary tests. I balked at studying, found the process laborious and a waste of my time (better spent reading, collecting, and drawing from my comic book collection or reading the science fiction novels discouraged by my English teachers).

Throughout high school, I also worked frantically to be a good athlete, focusing on basketball. I wore ankle weights 24/7, including jumping rope hundreds of times each night with the weights on. Despite my efforts and desire, I made the teams, but sat on the bench throughout high school. Two aspects of that seem important: A track/football coach used to deride my ankle weight efforts by saying, "The only good those will do you is if you are in an ankle weight race"; and I could often be the best or near the best on any of my basketball teams when we had free throw shooting contests in practice.

Today, I feel safe claiming I have an unusually large vocabulary, and my career is deeply driven by advanced literacy. In fact, I routinely teach graduate-level courses in literacy. All of this is gnawing at me because I have

*Teaching Writing as Journey, Not Destination:*
*Essays Exploring What "Teaching Writing" Means*, pp. 187–190
Copyright © 2019 by Information Age Publishing
187

been watching a discussion on a professional community of English teachers about vocabulary instruction. This thread reminds me of the recurring posts about grammar instruction.

During my graduate courses, vocabulary and spelling are nearly a daily topic—along with concerns about "teaching grammar." When I have co-led a Faculty Writing Fellows seminar for college professors who are exploring teaching writing at the university level (most of whom are outside of traditional disciplines for teaching writing), we always spend a great deal of time addressing and discussing the same concern: how to teach grammar.

As someone who *loves* to read and write, who *lives* to read and write—and as a teacher and writer—it makes my soul ache to confront how English teachers and English classes are often the sources of why children and adults loathe reading and writing. But I also know intimately about that dynamic because in many ways that was me; I left high school planning to major in physics, only discovering I am a writer and teacher once I was in college. And to this day I can see that damned vocabulary book we used in high school.

So when I became a high school English teacher, and faced throughout my early years what teachers continue to face today, I was determined that if I *had* to do vocabulary (required by the department and implicit in assigning students tax-payer-funded vocabulary books), I was going to find some way to do it as authentically as possible. From those early years before I abandoned vocabulary instruction entirely and even accomplished as department chair having grammar and vocabulary texts *not* issued to students but provided as classroom sets to teachers who requested them, I recall a really important moment: A student wrote a sentence with the word "pensive" from the week's vocabulary list—"The girl's boyfriend was very pensive when he bought her flowers." The student was going through the motions of completing my inauthentic assignment (writing original sentences from the vocabulary list each week instead of doing the textbook exercises) that I thought was *better* and had simply looked at the one-word definition offered, "thoughtful."

In fact, despite trying to make isolated vocabulary instruction authentic, I spent a great deal of time explaining to students that people didn't use this word or that word the way the student had—although for them, the sentence seemed perfectly credible. So what does all this mean?

Formal literacy instruction from K–5 through middle school into high school and even college is mostly failing our mission because we have fallen victim to an efficiency and analytical model of what literacy is and how to acquire so-called advanced literacy. Two of the best examples of this skills plague are the obsession with prescriptive/isolated grammar instruction and the Queen Mother of literacy scams, the "word gap."

The "word gap" persists despite the inherent flaws in the one research study driving it because most people have been lulled into believing the literacy-skills-equal-literacy hoax. [Think the Great Hooked on Phonics Scam that lures parents into believing that reading aloud is reading.] Reducing literacy to and teaching discrete skills has been embraced in formal education because of the cult of efficiency that won out in the early decades of the education wars. That cult of efficiency was successful because classroom management has always overshadowed pedagogy in public schooling and also because the testing and textbook industries discovered there was gold in them there hills of schools. Textbooks, worksheets, and multiple choice tests are certainly a soma of structure for the teacher and student alike—but they ain't literacy.

Literacy is holistic, and the skills plague kills literacy.

Here, now, I want to make two important points about the skills plague. First, we have made a serious mistake in flipping how people acquire so-called literacy skills such as vocabulary and grammatical dexterity. As Stephen Krashen[1] argued on that teacher discussion thread, while it is true that highly literate people have large vocabularies and often great grammatical dexterity, they have come to those skills by reading and writing a great deal, in authentic ways. But the efficiency cult has taken the fact that highly literate people have large vocabularies, for example, and flipped that to mean that we simply need to fill up students with words (usually arcane) or train them in root words, prefixes, and suffixes to create *presto!* literate humans. Let me stress here that turning the holistic-to-discrete-skills pattern around is not only hogwash but also detrimental hogwash to our goals of literacy.

And so my second point is this: Students continue to spend inordinate amounts of time on harmful skills activities that would be better spent doing the holistic acts of reading and writing—holistic acts that would in fact accomplish the skills growth we claim we are seeking. We know, as well, that students are not writing (for example) nearly enough—neither in amount of essays or length of essays—because teachers and students are overwhelmed with accountability mandates grounded in the efficiency model.

Let me end with one of my graduate courses.

For 24 graduate students, all teachers, who had only reading and written assignments in the course (no tests, worksheets, or textbooks), I responded to over 320 drafts of three written assignments in a four-week period. I highlighted this for the class to note that authentic literacy instruction committed to holistic approaches to literacy is not efficient, but it is incredibly time consuming and difficult. I am in my 50s, and I can see the vocabulary books in high schools that I still loathe—but I don't recall a single word from that experience. I am in my 50s and I still recall the day I sat listening to R.E.M.'s "You Are the Everything," which made me fall in love with the word "eviscerate." I can also picture in my mind the words I highlighted as I read—words I didn't know or also fell in love with as a writer—even when I was nudged to reconsider "decimate" in *World War Z*.

I remain angry and sad that the work we do as English teachers continues to create classrooms in which students have their love for reading and writing eviscerated instead of celebrated.

## ENDNOTES

1. Krashen, S. (1989). We acquire vocabulary and spelling by reading: Additional evidence for input hypothesis. *The Modern Language Journal, 73*(4), 440–463.

# CHAPTER 38

# FOSTERING CONVENTION AWARENESS IN STUDENTS

## Eschewing a Rules-Based View of Language

> The best lack all conviction, while the worst
>
> Are full of passionate intensity.
>
> "The Second Coming," William Butler Yeats

> [W]e should not, under the guise of developing literary standards, merely pass along adult weariness.
>
> "Analysis of Cliches and Abstractions," Lou LaBrant (1949)

> Any fool can make a rule, and any fool will mind it.
>
> Henry David Thoreau

Let us start with two writers from the monuments of "great authors"—Chaucer and Shakespeare (like Prince and Madonna, from the land of one-name people). Both Chaucer and Shakespeare wrote with double negatives and double comparatives/superlatives. In their eras, these constructions were emphatic, not breaking some rule of grammar. Now for

---

*Teaching Writing as Journey, Not Destination:*
*Essays Exploring What "Teaching Writing" Means*, pp. 191–193

context: On an English teacher forum a battle was waged (one rivaling Beowulf versus Grendel) over the use of "they" as a gender-neutral singular pronoun.

That's right, while a presidential election was brewing, we teachers of English were hotly debating pronoun/antecedent agreement. So it is there, I would like to make a stand for descriptive grammar as a compromise for the unrelenting grammar war. How, I can feel you asking, can taking a side be a compromise? Let me try to explain.

My journey to how I teach grammar, mechanics, and usage has been profoundly informed by the history of the English language and linguists—both of which strongly support a descriptive view of language that recognizes and embraces change. As well, I am a writer, one who uses the language in the service of my craft, and thus, one who does not work within rules, but through an awareness of conventional usage. Two key points are worth examining more fully—conventions and awareness.

Language does not function under rules (fixed and prescriptive) but under *conventions* that are both *situational* and *temporal*. Again, read Chaucer or Shakespeare with a keen eye on their usages that became "incorrect," or peruse Nathaniel Hawthorn's writing with Olympic gold medal amounts of commas, many of which in our contemporary time would not be used with absolutely no loss of meaning. Language conventionality, in fact, is a much healthier view of language usage than rules since those conventions are organic, growing out of actual language usage that gravitates toward effective (and even efficient) communication of ideas.

"Why are these homies dissin my girl? Why do they gotta front?" from Weezer reflects the tendency of language to clip—"dissin" for "disrespecting" and "front" for "putting on a front." Again, Rivers Cuomo and Weezer are representing the exact manipulations of language found in Shakespeare, who is nearly the pinnacle of "authors we worship." Next, the key to my argument that a descriptive view of language is a compromise in the grammar war is teaching *convention awareness* instead of rules acquisition.

Taught with a descriptive approach to language (for example, noting that many if not most people *use* "they" as a gender-neutral singular pronoun), convention awareness addresses both that conventions exist, and often with *status marking* consequences (see Weaver[1]), and that some conventions are in *flux* (I was taught a rigid distinction between "shall" and "will," one now defunct with dearly departed "shall," and contemporary students remain confronted with a similar rigid view of "who" and "whom," while poor "whom" is barely breathing and Hospice surely is on the ready). In other words, the descriptive view of language acknowledges the prescriptive view, and ultimately renders the student an agent in their use of the language (see what I did there?). However, the prescriptive rules-based approach to language necessarily ignores or marginalizes the much more historically and linguistically sound descriptive view.

I teach my students that pronoun/antecedent agreement remains a status marking usage convention for many in the academic world—highlighting that while common usage of "they" as a gender-neutral singular pronoun is increasing, many in academia or formal publishing remain committed to "they" as always plural, noting, however, that many in academia also strongly conform to gender-neutral and gender-sensitive usages of language. Ultimately, I want my students to recognize that conventions (and especially viewing language through rules) is about power—who decides what for whom (a few short breaths and chest compressions). For our students to be aware, then, of both descriptive and prescriptive views of language, for those students to gain a recognition that language use is about purpose and choice, bound by situation and audience, is for them to become agents in how their own credibility and authority is viewed.

As a final plea from someone who teaches first-year writing to college students, I want to note that students who have been taught a rules-based view of language are often disillusioned as soon as they see how often professional writers are not conforming to those rules. Like fragments. Those students tend to struggle with gaining their own voices and their own autonomy over language. In other words, a rules-based view of language tends to erode a student's appreciation of the beauty and power of language—while teaching convention awareness fosters in students both the moves for and enjoyment in investigating language usage.

Encouraging students to enthusiastically wrestle with language is a goal of our English classes worth fighting for (wink-wink, nod-nod). So this is my modest proposal, one dedicated to a full and complex appreciation of language usage. It is also a plea for a much healthier approach to language that understands "they" most certainly will be a gender-neutral singular pronoun soon, just as "whom" is about to join "shall" in the great archaic constructions in the sky. All that is sure to remain is the language itself, and it is ours to treat it and our students with the kindness and dignity they deserve.

## ENDNOTE

1. Weaver (1996).

CHAPTER 39

# NOT IF, BUT WHEN

## The Role of
## Direct Instruction in Teaching Writing

In a 1946 piece for *The English Journal*, "Teaching High-School Students to Write," Lou LaBrant addressed the role of drills and direct instruction when teaching students to write:

> The question always arises when such a program as the one described above is proposed as to the role of drill. Here again is a term—"drill"—which may mean many things. *We have some hundreds of studies now which demonstrate that there is little correlation (whatever that may cover) between exercises in punctuation and sentence structure and the tendency to use the principles illustrated in independent writing* [emphasis added]. On the other hand, it is often possible to discuss with a class a problem which appears in many papers and to extend the discussion into a day's work on it. For this study I have found sentences taken from class writing most effective, particularly if I encourage the student who made the error to explain what he was trying to say. *Little is gained from blind drills, that is, from drills prepared in advance by some textbook writer who could, of course, not know the idiosyncrasies of the class* [emphasis added]. (p. 127)[1]

Two points are worth repeating (emphasized above): (1) In 1946, the research base had "hundreds of studies" showing that isolated, direct instruction of grammar was not effective as writing pedagogy, and (2) front-loaded direct instruction was also ineffective for teaching writing.

While teaching high school English, I focused primarily on teaching my students to write. Although I was always a skeptic of direct grammar instruction as useful to teaching writing, I was an eager and masterful front-loader of direct instruction on writing. I spent much of my planning and lots of my class time yammering away about this or that before allowing students to write. And then the epiphany—one captured perfectly by LaBrant at the end of her essay:

> Sufficient discussion has perhaps been presented to indicate the thesis of this paper on the assignment "Teaching High-School Students To Write." The thesis is this: The teaching of writing is concerned primarily with considering material which is of importance to the writer and in which he has consequently some faith…. Whatever the material may be, its primary virtue lies in the attempt to tell something to others or to formulate one's own experience. On such a basis there is matter for discussion and for consideration of the relation of the form to the meaning. Since the student has something at stake, he can be expected to work at the problem. (p. 128)

Students learning to write are apt to listen to direct instruction after they have completed a draft of an essay that they have chosen and in which they have invested time and energy to offer their ideas to a real audience. The issue in teaching writing, then, is not *if* we offer direct instruction, but *when* we offer direct instruction.

## Confronting the "When" of Direct Instruction in Teaching Writing in an Era of Rubrics

Teaching writing is influenced negatively by not only the traditional commitment to isolated and direct instruction of grammar, mechanics, and usage, but also the more recent era of rubric-driven writing instruction aimed at high-stakes testing of writing.

As Alfie Kohn has discussed, rubrics can accomplish some narrow assessment goals, but they tend, like grammar drills, to impact negatively our goal of fostering independent and effective writers:

> Just as standardizing assessment for teachers may compromise the quality of teaching, so standardizing assessment for learners may compromise the learning. Mindy Nathan, a Michigan teacher and former school board member told me that she began "resisting the rubric temptation" the day "one particularly uninterested student raised his hand and asked if I was going to give the class a rubric for this assignment." She realized that her

students, presumably grown accustomed to rubrics in other classrooms, now seemed "unable to function unless every required item is spelled out for them in a grid and assigned a point value. Worse than that," she added, "they do not have confidence in their thinking or writing skills and seem unwilling to really take risks." (p. 13)[2]

For teachers at the K–12 level, the high-stakes accountability era poses a powerful hurdle to good writing practices; for college professors teaching first-year seminars focusing on writing, a different hurdle exists since students come to college often with narrow template-driven perceptions of writing—linear and sequential writing processes, prompted writing assignments, mechanical frameworks for five-paragraph essays that include introductions with direct thesis sentences, body paragraphs with prescribed sentence-lengths, and redundant conclusions (restate the introduction, goes the guideline).

Here, then, I want to outline briefly how I have approached the first essay with my first-year seminar students focus on genre and adaptations. The weeks leading to the first submitted essay focused on helping students confront their beliefs about writing and essays, including confronting how we define genres and what ways students are often required to write in formal school settings. One way we confronted these assumptions learned in their K–12 experiences is by reading throughout the semester *Style: Lessons in Clarity and Grace* (Joseph Williams and Joseph Bizup); as well, I ask them to read several pieces on authentic expectations at the college level versus how they were asked to write in high school.

As we examined the expectations for writing found in school, we began to compare how the essay is defined in four areas: K–12, college/academia, the "real world," and universal qualities. Before they submitted their first essays, we also learned to read like writers. I read aloud essays and parts of essays from Barbara Kingsolver (*High Tide in Tucson, Small Wonder*), an excerpt from Louise DeSalvo's *Vertigo*, essays by Kurt Vonnegut (*A Man Without a Country*), and others—including students choosing and discussing essays from William Zinsser's *The Writer Who Stayed*.

The goals I focused on before they drafted a first essay included very big and broad concepts of how writers write and why readers read. Primarily, I sought to reset students' assumptions about essays, writing, and school. Once the first essay was submitted—and I required students to choose both the topic and form of the essays they wrote since I was fostering their autonomy as well—I followed this process:

- Students e-mailed their first essay to me, attaching at least one rough draft and a final draft (the final was rewritten and students were aware of this requirement).

- All students brought hard copies of their essays to class the day they were due by e-mail in order to peer-review in small groups of three.
- Before they peer-review, I handed out the first-year writing intensive rubric approved by our faculty (I haven't shared this with them yet), three blank rubric forms (two for peer review and one for self-evaluation), and a prompt analysis guide.*
- I responded to all the essays using track changes and comments features in Word, returned the essays, and required all students to arrange a conference with me before revising and resubmitting the essays. My responses on the first essay were relatively light—in part not to overwhelm them and in part to allow me to ask questions when we conference.
- In the conference I focused on allowing them to ask questions first, and then I asked questions such as: (1) What were you trying to accomplish in this essay? (2) Do you think you accomplished your goal? (3) Who is your audience? (4) What type of essay did you draft, and why?
- The conferences ended with our discussing a few revision strategies ("few" is extremely important), acknowledging that the essay may need several revisions (also students were allowed to abandon these drafts and start over, identifying the abandoned draft as a discovery draft), and requiring the student to set a due date for the revised essay (I do not assign the due date but encourage students to organize their semester so that they can handle the coming additional essays).

Throughout the semester, I also did not assign grades to any assignments, but offered students the opportunity to meet with me and discuss their grades on any assignment or current status in the class. I wanted them focusing on learning and craft—not grades.

The overarching goal of this process was to help students come to see that learning to write is a journey, along with fostering in them an awareness that essay writing is bound by the conventional expectations of the situation: Disciplines view essays differently, and academic writing remains distinct from writing essays for the public. LaBrant argued "Writing Is More than Structure," concluding:

> The end has all along been writing, but somewhere along the way we have thought to substitute mechanical plans and parts for the total. We have ceased to build the house and have contented ourselves with blueprints. Whatever the cost in time (and that is great), and whatever the effort, our students must be taught to write, to rewrite, to have the full experience of

translating ideas into the written word. This is a deep and full experience, one to which each in his own way has a right. (p. 293)[3]

And in the teaching of writing, it is ours to help our students build houses from the blueprints they create—all in a learning environment that places our direct instruction primarily after the students have invested themselves in writing that matters.

## *Prompt Analysis for Genre Awareness

To the students: As you prepare to write, revise, and edit, consider these questions, particularly if you are given a writing task in your academic classroom:

[Note: If you cannot answer these questions from the task you have been given, how do you find out the answers?]

1. GENRE NAME: What is this text called (its genre name)? What do you already think you know about what a text from this genre looks and 'sounds' like? For example, how should the text be organized? What kind of language do you need to use?
2. PURPOSE: What are you supposed to DO as a writer when completing this task? Are you asked to make an argument? To inform? To describe or list?
3. CONTEXT: If you are writing this task in, or for, a classroom, what do you know about the context? What does the discipline require for a text? Under what conditions will you be writing? For example, are you writing a timed, in-class response?
4. WRITER'S ROLE: Who are you supposed to BE in this prompt? A knowledgeable student? Someone else?
5. AUDIENCE: Is your audience specified? If it is your instructor, what are his or her expectations and interests? What goals for students does the instructor have?
6. CONTENT: What are you supposed to write about? Where do you find this content? In your textbook? In lectures? Are you supposed to relate what you have heard or read in some way?
7. SOURCES: What, and how many, sources are you supposed to draw from to write your text? Have the sources been provided in the class? Are you supposed to look elsewhere? Are the sources primary or secondary?
8. OTHER SPECIFICATIONS: What else do you know about the requirements for this text? How long should it be? What referencing style (MLA, APA) should you use? What font type?

9. ASSESSMENT: How will your paper be graded? What does the instructor believe is central to a good response? How do you know? If you don't know, how can you find out?

10. MAKING THE TEXT YOUR OWN: What about the paper you write can be negotiated with the instructor? Can you negotiate the topic? The types of sources used? The text structure? If you can negotiate your assignment, it might be much more interesting to you.

Created and published in Johns, A. M. (2008). Genre awareness for the novice academic student: An on-going quest. *Language Teaching, 41*(2), 237–252.

## ENDNOTES

1. LaBrant (1946).
2. Kohn, A. (2006). The trouble with rubrics. *English Journal, 95*(4), 12–15. See also Wilson, M. (2007). Why I won't be using rubrics to respond to students' writing. *English Journal, 96*(4), 62–66; and Wilson, M. (2006). *Rethinking rubrics in writing assessment.* Portsmouth, NH: Heinemann.
3. LaBrant (1957).

# CHAPTER 40

# ON COMMON TERMINOLOGY AND TEACHING WRITING

## Once Again, the Grammar Debate

In 1971, after years of scrounging and clawing, my parents were able to build their dream home on the largest lot at the new golf course in my home town. This was a redneck working-class vision of what it meant to achieve the American Dream. As a consequence, I lived on and worked at this golf course (called a "country club" without a speck of irony) throughout my adolescence. Some of my formative moments, then, occurred on the golf course while I was working—including discovering that when a teen has been covertly drinking mini-bottles of liquor for hours virtually every adult can see that in about 2 seconds.

The grass on the course itself was over-seeded a couple times a year, and this required the work of all the employees and many of the club members simply volunteering, including my father. One fall, I believe, I was told to drive around the old pickup truck used exclusively on the course. I was likely a year or so away from driving legally. The truck was a 3-speed manual shift on the column and a transmission that worked about as well as you'd imagine for a work truck that never left the fairways of a redneck golf course.

---

*Teaching Writing as Journey, Not Destination:*
*Essays Exploring What "Teaching Writing" Means*, pp. 201–204
Copyright © 2019 by Information Age Publishing

My father hopped in the passenger seat and told me what to do, throwing around terms such as "clutch" as well as all the intricacies of column shifting. I was overwhelmed and terrified. Within moments, he had me start the truck, and lurch forward, coaching me along the way about using the three pedals and finding the sweat spot for engaging and releasing the clutch (I would drive manual transmission cars with glee well into my late twenties when a broken ankle proved to me the practicality of automatic transmissions). Soon I was left alone with this clunky beast of a truck to shuttle whatever was needed all over the golf course. Within hours, I was pretty damn proficient despite the rolling berms of the fairways, the steep hills, and the idiosyncratic transmission in this truck well past its prime.

Once again on an English teacher forum, questions about teaching grammar surfaced, and as I often do, I thought about how we learn to drive cars. Driving a car and composing are quite similar since they are holistic behaviors that require many seemingly simultaneous decisions performed in some type of "rules" environment (driving within laws and writing within conventions, what people commonly call "grammar" to encompass grammar, mechanics, and usage). As well, I am convinced that both are best learned by actually doing the whole thing, preferably with an experienced mentor guiding the learning process. And thus we come to a recurring and powerful question whenever the grammar debate claws its way zombie-like out of the dirt: Do teachers and students need common terminology for the teaching of writing to be effective?

This is a very practical retort to those who caution about isolated direct grammar instruction and a rules-based approach to how language works. It is a very common complaint I hear from teachers of second languages as well. Let me return for a moment to my adventure in a 3-speed pickup truck. My hearing the term "clutch" did me no good at all in terms of engaging and releasing the clutch and actually maneuvering the truck around the golf course. In fact, my dad immediately added "the pedal on the left." So my first response to the question about the importance of common (grammar) terminology in teaching writing is that we must all step back and critically examine if this is really essential.

My sense gained from teaching writing for over 30 years is that students do not need the technical language that teachers must have and that the terms students should acquire are incredibly few. None the less, my professional concern as a teacher and a writer is not *if* students will acquire common terminology (they will and they should), but *how* and *to what extent*. The grammar debate has one aspect in common with the phonics debate: too many see the argument as a yes/no dichotomy (and it isn't).

So a foundational guiding principle for the role of grammar and common terminology in the teaching of writing is to provide students with *the least direct instruction and acquisition of terminology needed* for the students to be fully engaged in the whole behavior. And then during that whole behavior, students continue to build their grammatical awareness and technical terminology storehouse. And that begins to address the how.

I learned to drive the 3-speed truck by driving the truck very badly for an extended amount of time and among a group of experienced drivers who were also incredibly patient and encouraging. There was no pass/fail, and I never took a test on the parts of the truck or how to drive a 3-speed manual transmission. And thus, our students need low-stakes and extended opportunities to write by choice while receiving ample feedback from their teacher, who models the writing process and the technical terminology that helps those students learn and improve.

Ultimately, then, when our goal is to foster students as writers, let's critically interrogate our own assumptions about what students must have to learn to write, and then let's be vigilant about protecting that goal; in other words, prioritize the time students have to practice the full writing process in low-stakes and supportive environments over time spent on isolated and direct instruction that detracts from that foundational commitment.

I will set aside driving a truck for a final example from my teaching writing. In a first-year writing seminar, I use a text that frames effective writing in broad concepts such as cohesion and clarity. I assign the text; students read weekly and submit response journals on key points and questions. In class and during writing conferences, I use these terms—cohesion, clarity—but we have no test and I never explicitly say they need these terms that I typically use along with some concept or analogy building on their existing schema (my father adding "pedal on the left" after "clutch"). Regularly and often throughout the semester, students begin to say "I was trying to work on cohesion like Williams says in our book."

Teaching writing is not well served by either/or debates, especially when warranted practice is about not *if* but *how*. My students when I taught high school (in the same redneck town where I grew up) and then at the college level have almost all acquired common terminology in the context of what they do without a doubt learn—my writing classroom is about composing, and everything we do is in service to that one essential goal.

Just as the recalcitrant grammar debate spurs in me nostalgia for my formative years gaining the All-American rite of passage, driving, it also pulls me once again to my (abrasive) muse, former NCTE president Lou LaBrant, who confronted in 1953: "It ought to be unnecessary to say that writing is learned by writing; unfortunately there is need" (p. 417).[1] Now, we stand on the same worn path, and I conclude here by urging us all who teach writing to keep our bearings: "writing is learned by writing," and anything else we do must not detract from that truism.

# **ENDNOTE**

1. LaBrant (1953).

# SECTION XV

## LaBRANT, LOU

# CHAPTER 41

# *WE TEACH ENGLISH* REVISITED

At times quaint and oddly misguided but unflinchingly confrontational and assertive—the signature tone of her work—Lou LaBrant's *We Teach English* (1951) was a rare book-length text over her 65 years as an educator. While this text for teachers of ELA/English never garnered the status of Louise Rosenblatt's *Literature as Exploration* (LaBrant and Rosenblatt were colleagues at NYU), both works represent a long history of trying to coral the field of ELA/English teaching.

A recent conversation and debate on an NCTE forum about teaching whole-class, assigned novels has reminded me of the enduring tensions of what it means to teach ELA/English—tensions that span K–12 grade levels as well as being grounded in responsibilities to student needs and interests, the field or discipline of English, and literacy broadly. Historically and then magnified during the past thirty years of high-stakes accountability, ELA/English has shared with math demands and expectations that are not as pronounced in other disciplines; despite the limitations and problems with the terms, I characterize those demands as addressing *disciplinary knowledge* (or content) and *literacy skills*.

Our disciplinary knowledge obligations rest with the compulsion to cover established content, such as identifying the parts of speech, analyzing the main characters in *The Scarlet Letter*, or explaining the key ideas expressed by Ralph Waldo Emerson and Henry David Thoreau as American Transcendentalism. Literacy skills comprise reading, writing, speaking,

*Teaching Writing as Journey, Not Destination:*
*Essays Exploring What "Teaching Writing" Means,* pp. 207–211
Copyright © 2019 by Information Age Publishing
All rights of reproduction in any form reserved.

and listening—how we as humans navigate the world through literacy. Some see these skills as a different way to think about content, skills such as comprehension, predicting, narration, and persuasion.

At best, these obligations can and possibly should work in tandem. When we teach a poem, Langston Hughes's "Harlem," for example, we are introducing students to key content about American literature and the Harlem Renaissance while also teaching them about the elements poetry, reading skills (such as analysis), and reading like a writer so they can transfer those rhetorical and literary strategies into their own writing.

Let me pause here to stress that at all levels from K–12, this is a damn high bar for any teacher. It takes a great deal of time and expertise to learn to manage all that effectively. At worst, these obligations become professional and disciplinary battles—ones waged among practitioners often at the expense of students we should be serving. We must teach phonics, but what about the children acquiring the desire and ability to read? We must teach grammar, but what about the children acquiring the desire and ability to write? Everyone must read *The Great Gatsby*, but what if that requirement creates nonreaders?

When we form ideological camps about disciplinary knowledge or literacy, we often fail both our field of ELA/English and students. *We teach English* means something extremely complex and difficult, something that in fact may be too much to expect of any teacher. But this is what we do, this is who we are.

If we return to the debate and discussion about teaching whole-class novels, we are revisiting an enduring debate that captures exactly what teaching English means. To resolve that debate, I believe, we must remain focused on our students, and not on whether or not we address either area of demands in our field. It is not a simple way to resolve the questions, but it is rather simple: When we attend to either disciplinary knowledge (and we should) or literacy skills (and we must), what are the consequences of those lessons in the evidence of learning by our students?

If we require our students to read Charles Dickens, and many do not read because they dislike the work, and many begin or continue the journey to being a nonreader, then we have failed dramatically any obligations as teachers of ELA/English. If a whole-class unit on *Lord of the Flies* or *The Hunger Games* becomes a vibrant adventure in the novel and literacy, and most if not all read the novel, if several become hooked on literature, then we have accomplished everything that can be expected of teaching ELA/English.

In terms of both student reading and writing, there are decades of evidence that show that student choice in what they read and write is most effective in both fostering disciplinary knowledge (because they actually read and write) and literacy skills as well as literacy engagement (because they become eager to read and write). But we as teachers of ELA/English are confronted with the essential problem beneath the call for student choice: students must have acquired some disciplinary and skills knowledge and proficiencies in order to make those choices.

If we can keep a critical eye on the outcomes of the instructional decisions we make—if we can resist dogged commitments to ideologies—then we can make informed choices about what best serves our students in terms of both what disciplinary knowledge they acquire and whether or not they develop as proficient and eager readers and writers. Staying big picture is important—always asking what we are trying to accomplish with students and then paying close attention to what our students show us we are teaching.

In 2004, Donald Graves looked over his career seeking ways to teach students writing; he offered some enduring ideas about "what remains the same":

> The following fundamentals have remained unchanged in the teaching of writing:
>
> 1.  Children need to choose most of their own topics. But we need to show them all the places writing comes from, that it is often triggered by simple everyday events.
> 2.  Children need regular response to their writing from both the teacher and other readers.
> 3.  Children need to write a minimum of three days out of five. Four or five days are ideal.
> 4.  Children need to publish, whether by sharing, collecting, or posting their work.
> 5.  Children need to hear their teacher talk through what she is doing as she writes on the overhead or the chalkboard. In this way, the children witness their teacher's thinking
> 6.  Children need to maintain collections of their work to establish a writing history. Collections show that history when they are used as a medium for evaluation. (p. 91)[2]

Similar to the debate over whole-class novel instruction, if we view Graves's fundamentals as strict rules and teach to these rules—instead of to how we are fostering students as writers—we become lost, and we likely fail.

So, yes, students choosing what they read, especially something as daunting as a novel, is a fundamental, but that doesn't necessarily discredit the possibility of whole-class novels. To answer any instructional questions, then, as a teacher of ELA/English is in our students, not our obligations to disciplinary knowledge or literacy skills—and especially not in covering the mandated standards or preparing students for high-stakes tests. The questions are worthy of discussion and debate among teachers of ELA/ English, but ultimately we must each answer them with each unique group of students we teach.

When faced with the debates and questions about teaching ELA/English, LaBrant could be harsh and demanding—often seeming to teeter on the edge of, if not crossing over into, prescription. However, what LaBrant was demanding about in terms of "we teach English" is not that we follow her rules, or any rules, but that we remain committed to our students and their journeys in both literature and literacy. During war, in 1942, LaBrant became frustrated with national concerns about literacy:

> The induction of American youth into the armed forces, and the attendant examinations and classifications have called attention to a matter long of concern to those who teach reading or who are devoted to the cause of de- mocracy: the fact that in a land which purports to offer universal education we have a considerable number of youth who cannot read intelligently. We are disturbed now because we want these men to be able to read military di- rections, and they cannot. A greater tragedy is that they are and have been unable to read with sufficient understanding to be constructive peace-time citizens.
>
> As is to be expected, immediate explanations have been forthcoming, and immediate pointing-of-fingers has begun. Most of the explanations and pointing have come from those who have had least to do with teaching reading, and who are least conversant with the real problem. (p. 240)[3]

Sound familiar?

LaBrant argued against what became a recurring political and public hand wringing about a reading crisis:

> An easy way to evade the question of improved living and better schools for our underprivileged is to say the whole trouble is lack of drill. Lack of drill! Let's be honest. Lack of good food; lack of well-lighted homes with books and papers; lack of attractive, well equipped schools, where reading is interesting and meaningful; lack of economic security permitting the use of free schools—lack of a good chance, the kind of chance these unlettered boys are now fighting to give to others. Surround children with books, give them healthful surroundings and an opportunity to read freely. They will be able to read military directions—and much more. (p. 241)

Here and for over six decades, LaBrant was a champion of the we who teach English but in the name of those students we teach, especially the most vulnerable students. To that end, when we teach English, *we teach students*.

And there is where our commitments must lie.

## ENDNOTES

1. LaBrant, L. (1951). *We teach English*. New York, NY: Harcourt, Brace and Company.
2. Graves, D. (2004, November). What I've learned from teachers of writing. *Language Arts, 82*(2), 88–94.
3. LaBrant, L. (1942, November). What shall we do about reading today?: A symposium [Lou LaBrant]. *The Elementary English Review, 19*(7), 240–241.

CHAPTER 42

# TEACHING WRITING IN ELA/ENGLISH

## "Not Everything to Do, But Something"

A [hu]man has not everything to do, but something; and because [she/]he cannot do everything, it is not necessary that [she/]he should do something wrong.

"Civil Disobedience," Henry David Thoreau

It is a misguided and unfair reality, but middle and high school ELA/English teachers are in many ways asked to do everything—and they cannot, of course. Traditionally, ELA/English teachers have been charged as the *primary*, if not *exclusive*, teachers of all things literacy as well as their field of English; in other words, charged with teaching students how to read, write, speak, and listen along with covering whatever body of literature a particular grade level is assigned (and about which students may be tested in high-stakes ways).

My dissertation focus and most-times muse, Lou LaBrant was as acerbic as she was brilliant (and she was brilliant). Once when fielding questions, she chastised a teacher that if she did not know how to teach ELA/English, she should quit, learn how, and then return to the field. Not a shining

*Teaching Writing as Journey, Not Destination:*
*Essays Exploring What "Teaching Writing" Means*, pp. 213–217
Copyright © 2019 by Information Age Publishing

moment for LaBrant, and an attitude we must not tolerate. It is not ours to eat our own kind, and it is far past time that no longer allow ELA/English to be under the weight of doing everything.

This has been weighing on my mind because of several conversations around my blog posts challenging the teaching of research papers and the five-paragraph essay. Maybe I was drawn to LaBrant because we share a tendency to seem strident when we are passionate—or maybe studying and writing about LaBrant so deeply infused my passion with a strident streak. Honestly, it is likely the former. So I am guilty too often of allowing my genuine passion to come off as demanding, judgmental, and unyielding. Shame on me.

## "The Kindness of Strangers"

But I am also fortunate to be in the presence of the kindness of strangers—those who ask, prod, challenge, and join the quest. In particular, comments by a beginning teacher and a teacher at a school that seeks to prepare students for college really hit home for me in terms of asking what ELA/English teachers are to teach in terms of writing if they abandon, as I believe they should, the traditional and scripted research paper assignment and the five-paragraph essay.

First, I must stress that for all teachers, and particularly beginning teachers, the transition from traditional practice to warranted or best practice must be through *baby steps*: choosing one or a few changes to practices that are manageable, incorporating them, and then pacing over a long period of time (months, years) further changes as manageable. I cannot stress enough, whether it is about so-called best practice, responding to student writing, or preparing students for college, we must be neither martyrs, nor missionaries. To be a teacher of ELA/English is honorable in itself.

To move from the five-paragraph essay/template approach to writing instruction to a workshop/authentic form approach, then, begins by identifying the components of writing workshop (time, ownership, response) in order to implement some of those components within the current traditional structure. And then gradually adding components until the traditional structure is replaced with writing workshop. If you are not ready to release the five-paragraph essay form, can you drop the prompt and allow student choice in topics? And can you remove some direct instruction for students to draft and collaborate on their essays during class as well as your own conferencing with students as they brainstorm and compose?

Along with baby steps, change is facilitated by purposeful abandonment of traditional practices that are discredited by evidence (both the research base and a teacher's own practice). *No teacher should try to cram in new practice along with old practice.* Incremental change and abandonment allow teachers to take the needed time to prepare themselves for teaching writing more authentically, without templates—finding, reading, and gathering mentor texts of the types of essays they believe their students should be writing, for example, along with honing their craft at guiding students through reading like a writer activities in order to build the writer's toolbox for students. That said, the field of ELA/English as the place where writing is primarily taught is in dire need of recalibration—as I have addressed related to research papers and the five-paragraph essay.

## The Literary Analysis Essay: "Is This Even Necessary Anymore"

Let's go back for a moment to my opening lament about asking ELA/English teachers to do everything—and consider the opening quote from Thoreau. ELA/English teachers must stop carrying the weight of doing everything, but they must do something, with a critical eye toward avoiding doing something wrong. The powerful dilemma, I think, was posed in a question from Elizabeth Hall on the NCTE Connected Community: "How do I teach students to write a literary analysis essay or is this even necessary anymore?"

Teaching literary analysis essays (and the use of MLA in the traditional research project) has its roots, I am sure, in several different reasons: tradition, seeking to address English as a discipline, and preparing students for college directly and indirectly (the Advanced Placement tests). "Because we have always done it" is a shallow reason to keep a teaching practice so I'll set that aside.

Next, do we as English teachers have an obligation to the discipline of English? Just as we feel compelled to teach British lit or American lit, we feel compelled to teach students about literary analysis. And we are quite justified in that—although with two caveats: first, virtually none of our students will become English majors, and second, to teach literary analysis writing should still be couched within authentic writing. Therefore, canned literary analysis is not warranted, just as remaining trapped in New Criticism (and its more recent cousin "close reading") and perpetuating the literary technique hunt are not warranted.

Even when teaching students who needed to do well on AP tests, I started by investigating authentic mentor texts modeling literary analysis—notably Adrienne Rich's "Vesuvius at Home,"[1] which redefined how many viewed Emily Dickinson. Unpacking Rich's masterful interrogation of Dickinson, we found she begins with and depends heavily on personal narrative mode, and her analysis highlights that textual analysis requires substantial quoting of the examined texts that anchors the writer's analysis and synthesis. But Rich has no clunky introduction with the traditional assertive (read: overstated) thesis, and she does not spend time cataloguing Dickinson's use of literary devices. And here is a key point of departure: Rich comes at Dickinson through many analytical lenses, but she does not forefront New Criticism (as most ELA/English teachers do and as AP Literature and Composition exams do).

Further, our high school students, by the way, cannot write with the mastery of Rich, but they can build their toolbox of genre awareness about how professional writers do literary analysis—including being exposed to a much wider set of analytical lenses than teachers have traditionally explored. One answer to Hall's question is "yes," because literary analysis essays can be very valuable for students as critical thinkers (to read and re-read the world, to write and re-write the world), as liberal arts grounding (students knowing the wide array of disciplinary *ways of knowing*), as *one type* of authentic writing, and as a foundation for the few students who will in fact major in English.

Another answer, however, addresses Hall's "is this even necessary anymore." The truth is that first-year writing (back in the day, "freshman comp") and so-called "college writing" have never been well served directly by ELA/English teachers assigning primarily or exclusively literary analysis essays. Again, literary analysis essays are a part of the English discipline and very few high school students will be English majors. So this harder answer is about addressing the "everything" dilemma.

Each ELA/English teacher, then, must not feel compelled to prepare students for college entirely or to address the discipline of English completely. Each ELA/English teacher must be committed to doing something, guarding against doing something wrong (such as making students hate to read and write, demanding student conformity over student agency, or presenting inauthentic templates that inhibit students as readers and writers). That something may include a literary analysis essay, but ELA/English teachers should feel far more obligated to invest time that helps students gain genre awareness and developing themselves as autonomous thinkers and writers through the reading and writing processes—reading and writing workshop grounded in mentor texts and requiring students to produce authentic texts themselves along a wide range of writing types, some of which they will be required to do in college (disciplinary writing).

Middle school teams and high school departments could very easily organize so that teachers who feel more comfortable with some types of writing than others can choose to distribute what writing experiences students have over the course of several years. ELA/English teachers must resist isolated *individual* responsibility for the "everything," something that can be approached (but never accomplished) over six or seven coordinated years as teams and departments. None of this is easy, and I regret to offer, none of this can be scripted for any teacher. But, while I resist suggesting changes are urgent, I do believe they are damned important.

So I return at the end here to LaBrant in a slightly less strident mood:

> Teachers who follow the rule of emphasizing meaning and true communication find children eager to accept conventional form, and to choose words carefully. But the choice is then in terms of the purposes of the writer or speaker, and not in terms of artificial or superficial standards [emphasis added]....Teachers should consider carefully what they are doing with the most intimate subject in the curriculum. (p. 97)[2]

## ENDNOTES

1. Rich, A. (1976). Vesuvius at home. *Parnassus: Poetry in Review, 5*(1). Retrieved from http://parnassusreview.com/archives/416
2. LaBrant, L. (1943). Language teaching in a changing world. *The Elementary English Review, 20*(3), 93–97.

# CHAPTER 43

# TO HIGH SCHOOL ENGLISH TEACHERS (AND ALL TEACHERS)

All teachers are incredibly important, but high school English teachers will always have a special place in my heart. Significant in my teaching journey are being in my area National Writing Project (Spartanburg Writing Project) and then serving as a lead co-instructor in that same project for a couple years. Concurrent with my career as an educator, I have been a serious and published writer for about 30 years. And of course I have been madly in love with books of all kinds since before memory.

I write this specifically to my colleagues who are high school English teachers, but all teachers really, out of my greatest respect for teacher professionalism, importance, and autonomy—as well as my deepest commitment, the sacredness of every single student who enters any teacher's classroom. While at times this may read as scolding, preaching, or prescribing, I am seeking here to invite every teacher to do what I have done my entire career—stepping back from practice as often as possible, checking practice against my most authentic and critical goals, and then changing that practice if those do not match.

I am fortunate that my former students often contact me, e-mail or Facebook are common, and generally they are too kind. Typically, they reach out to thank me for preparing them as writers, and few things could make me prouder to be a teacher. But these moments are tempered at

*Teaching Writing as Journey, Not Destination:*
*Essays Exploring What "Teaching Writing" Means*, pp. 219–222

times because they are speaking from decades ago—during years when I now know my practice was off, sincere but flawed. So I come to teachers with this invitation from many years thinking hard about teaching literacy, focusing on writing, and being a serious writer myself. These thoughts are informed by years teaching English, years teaching young people to be teachers, and years teaching other teachers as well as observing practicing teachers in the field. I have been fortunate to teach many young people who have secured their first teaching jobs as English teachers. Working with them has impacted me profoundly because they are wonderful additions to our field, but also they have encountered a field and practicing teachers who have routinely discouraged them and me about who teaches and how we teach English.

Michelle Kenney's "The Politics of the Paragraph"[1] coming in the wake of two separate debates about the use of "they" as a singular gender-free pronoun along with a literacy graduate course spurred me to the thoughts below—this rising concern about how English teachers impact our students as free people and as literate people. My lessons also are strongly shaded by the history of the field of education broadly and English teaching narrowly as I have come to understand both through the lens of Lou LaBrant. Teaching and teachers have been profoundly and negatively impacted by eternal forces for a century at least, and those corrosive forces have been intensified during the recent 30-plus years of accountability driven by standards and high-stakes testing.

Now, then, I offer this invitation to consider lessons I have learned about teaching English:

- *Begin with and remain true to authentic literacy, and then comply with standards and testing mandates within that greater commitment.* Our planning and practice must start with our students' literacy being sacred—seeking ways to foster eager readers and writers who still must often demonstrate literacy proficiency in the worst possible settings. This is not a call to be negligent, but to be dedicated to the power of literacy first and bureaucracy second.
- *Forefront your expertise and professionalism 24/7.* Teachers have never received the professional respect we deserve, and during the accountability era, our professionalism has been even further eroded by shifting all the authority for how and what we teach to standards and high-stakes test. Our expertise and professionalism are our only weapons for demanding the authority for teaching be with us—not bureaucratic mandates, or commercial programs. Every moment of our lives we are teachers, and every moment we are representing our profession.

- *Teach students—not programs, standards, test-prep, or your discipline.* Especially at the high school level, and particularly during the accountability era, we are apt to lose sight of our central purpose in teaching English—our students.

- *Resist teaching so that students acquire fixed content and instead foster students as ongoing learners.* Once one of my teacher candidates attended a course in which fellow English teachers were adamant they needed students to learn to cite using MLA by memory. My former student resisted this, suggesting that students should understand citation broadly and then be equipped to follow the ever-changing and different citation guides they will encounter as college students and beyond. This exemplifies a central flaw in teaching English that views learning as acquiring fixed content. See Lou LaBrant's "New Bottles for New Wine" (1952), in which she implores: "Do our students know that our language is changing, that it is the product of all the people, each trying to tell what is in his mind? Do they understand their own share in its making and re-creation?" (p. 342).[2]

- *Become and remain a student of language.* What is your background in the history of the English language? How much linguistics have you studied? For me, a key shift in teaching English was embracing a descriptive grammarian stance informed by linguistics and the history of the language. This allows me to view student language use as part of that history, and helps me focus on teaching students to play with language and then to edit and revise their writing, instead of focusing on "correcting." This is central to having a low-stakes classroom that sees language as investigation.

- *Reject deficit views of language and students.* The prescriptive grammarian comes from a history that linked language use with people's character—a false link. While ideas such as the "word gap" is compelling, it is both false (based on one flawed study) and counter to what we know about literacy and power. Language changes, and claims about "correctness" are always more about power than either language development or literacy.

- *Foster genre awareness in students while interrogating authentic texts (and rejecting artificial writing templates).* As Kenney details, writing templates may prepare students for artificial demonstrations of literacy (high-stakes tests), but they ultimately fail authentic writing and literacy goals. Published writing nearly never follows the five-paragraph essay template, and the whole thesis idea is equally rare in published writing. Students as writers need to be eager readers who are encouraged to mine that reading constantly for greater genre awareness about how any writer makes a piece what the writer is seeking to accomplish. What is an Op-Ed? A memoir? Investigative journalism? A feature story on an Olympic athlete? The essay form, even in academia, is a question, not a template.

- *Be a dedicated reader and writer yourself.* While I argue above for being a professional educator 24/7, I caution here about allowing our teacher Selves to erase our literate Selves. My voracious reading life and my co-career as a writer are invaluable and inseparable from my being an effective teacher. Our reading and writing lives keep us grounded in our authentic goals eroded by accountability.
- *Choice, joy, and kindness.* Writing in 1949, LaBrant warned: "On the other hand, we should not, under the guise of developing literary standards, merely pass along adult weariness" (p. 276).[3] How often have we allowed prescription and standards-based, test-prep instruction to instill in our students a distaste for reading and writing? If we demand all students read Shakespeare or *The Scarlet Letter*, and then most of them come to hate reading, if we hammer the five-paragraph essay into students who wish never to write again, what have we accomplished?

And to offer an umbrella under which my invitation to my lessons rest, I believe we must heed John Dewey:

What avail is it to win prescribed amounts of information about geography and history, to win ability to read and write, if in the process the individual loses his own soul: loses his appreciation of things worth while, of the values to which these things are relative; if he loses desire to apply what he has learned and, above all, loses the ability to extract meaning from his future experiences as they occur? (p. 49)[4]

## ENDNOTES

1. Kenney, M. (2016, Summer). The politics of the paragraph. *Rethinking Schools, 30*(4). https://www.rethinkingschools.org/articles/the-politics-of-the-paragraph
2. LaBrant (1952).
3. LaBrant (1949).
4. Dewey, J. (1997). *Experience and education.* New York, NY: Touchstone.

# CHAPTER 44

# SCAPEGOAT

The GEICO "Scapegoat: It's What You Do" commercial transported me to 10th-grade English class with Lynn Harrill, who would become my mentor and friend. Throughout high school, I was living a double life: at school I was a math and science student—the courses in which I made As—but at home, I was collecting and reading thousands of comic books as well as consuming science fiction (SF) novels, including Michael Crichton's *Andromeda Strain* and working through Arthur C. Clark, Larry Niven, and Jerry Pournelle, and other SF writers with the same obsession I brought to collecting and drawing from comic books.

In Mr. Harrill's class, I experienced a paradigm shift about English class because 8th- and 9th-grade English had been spent doing grammar text exercises and days on end of sentence diagramming (assignments that earned me As in junior high). But in Mr. Harrill's class, we wrote essays and spent (what seemed to me) hellish hours doing vocabulary workbook exercises and tests (assignments that pulled my English grade down to Bs). Vocabulary words struck me as a huge waste of time, completely disassociated from my secret home life dedicated to *words*. "Scapegoat" was one of those words that I still associate with feeling *no connection* between the isolated act of studying and being testing on the weekly list of words and being a young man who would in the coming years discover *in spite of formal school* he is a writer and a lover of books.

The word itself, "scapegoat," as the commercial skewers, creates a tension between the word's meaning and the embedded "goat" that triggers most people's prior knowledge. Out of context, studying "scapegoat"

*Teaching Writing as Journey, Not Destination:*
*Essays Exploring What "Teaching Writing" Means,* pp. 223–226
Copyright © 2019 by Information Age Publishing

for a test cheated me—cheats all students—of being engaged with the rich etymology (one blossoming with allusion) of the word. Formal English, I regret to admit, has mostly and continues to treat human communication as separate skills—grammar, phonics, vocabulary—meant for lifeless and mechanical analysis and acquisition. Reading and writing in school are too often reduced to algebra. I hate to confess also that in Mr. Harrill's class I was chastised about reading SF—told I needed to read real literature—and never given any sense that my comic book life was worthy of being considered the foundation of my life as a writer, reader, and teacher.

•

While reading Gary Saul Morson's "Why College Kids Are Avoiding the Study of Literature," I immediately thought also of my high school experience with English and vocabulary—leading again to "scapegoat." "Time and again," Morson explains, "students tell me of three common ways in which most high school and college classes kill their interest in novels." Morson's three ways ("the technical, the judgmental, and the documentary") essentially are reflected in my story above—reducing human communication to algebra, stripping the life out of reading and writing through school-only practices such as five-paragraph, prompted writing and answering multiple-choice answers after reading decontextualized passages. But Morson's criticism sparked for me the scapegoat-de-jour: the Common Core.

While it was fashionable for some to proclaim that the Common Core would save U.S. public education and others to condemn Common Core as the end to all that is good and right in the world, a much more accurate assessment of Common Core is that it reflects more than a hundred years of misguided teaching and about thirty-plus years of horribly misguided education reform.

•

I attended junior and senior high school in the mid- to late-1970s, just a few years before accountability gripped my home state of South Carolina. However, my English classes were dominated by isolated grammar instruction, nearly no original essay writing or drafting, weekly vocabulary lists and tests, prescribed reading lists of novels by white males, and literature textbooks that were mostly god awful. As I mentioned, Lynn Harrill taught me 10th- and 11th-grade English, embodying the teacher I wanted to be, mentoring me as a beginning teacher, and guiding me into a doctoral program as well as eventually a university position as a teacher educator.

Many of our conversations over the years have been about his regrets as a teacher—about how even as a young and seemingly radical teacher himself, he bent to the pressures of traditional teaching that were not supported by research and instilled in the students he loved what Morson laments in his essay above: *English classes often make students hate reading and writing*. How many students, as I did, fell in love with words in spite of school, in spite of their English teachers' practices?

•

That doctoral program to which Lynn Harrill guided me opened another world to me—in much the same way a speech class in college opened the world of poetry high school had hidden and my English professors opened the world of black writers high school had ignored—the world of Lou LaBrant, the eventual subject of my dissertation. "A brief consideration," LaBrant wrote in 1947, "will indicate reasons for the considerable gap between the research currently available and the utilization of that research in school programs and methods" (p. 87).[2] Just as no accountability, standards, or high-stakes testing were mandating the bad practices of my junior and high school English teachers, LaBrant decades ago leveled a charge that resonates today, coincidentally in our Common Core era.

As English teachers, we have a long tradition of abdicating our autonomy to a shifting series of scapegoats: next year's teacher, textbooks, the canon, Standard English, standards, and high-stakes tests (to name a few of the most prominent). Do we love reading and writing, love language? Do we love our students? Each student who trudges through our classes and learns to hate reading, writing, and language suggests our answer is "no."

•

Engulfed in war, the world LaBrant wrote in during 1943 prompted her to note: "Hence teaching is a unique profession, dealing with remote rather than immediate influence over society" (p. 93) adding:

> It is important that we do not set up in our classrooms prejudices or snobberies which will make our students less instead of better able to understand, enjoy, and use this language....
>
> Too frequently we give children books which have enough value that we call them "good," forgetting that there are other, perhaps more important values which we are thereby missing. It is actually possible that reading will narrow rather than broaden understanding....Let us have no more of assignments which emphasize quantity, place form above meaning, or insist on structure which is not the child's....
>
> We are responsible for such writing when we approve the correctly

punctuated, correctly spelled, and neatly written paper which says nothing of importance, as against a less attractive but sincere account or argument. Children can and should learn to write correctly; but first should be sincere, purposeful expression of the child's own ideas....

Similar unsound attitudes can be the result of being taught to "write just anything" (or to write on the teacher's topic); to spend time correcting sentences which someone else has written about nothing of importance; to change one's structure merely to have a variety of sentence forms; and so on through a whole series of assignments based on the principle that form is first and meaning second.... (pp. 94–95)[3]

Today, LaBrant's final warning rings true still: "Teachers should consider carefully what they are doing with the most intimate subject in the curriculum" (p. 97).

•

As Lynn Harrill did with me—his greatest lesson—I now often face myself, the struggling me who stumbled and bumbled his way through teaching English—often badly—as I sought to gain my balance, stand on my own two feet in order to continue my journey toward being that teacher who embodies a love of language and students, to be in some small way the *because* and not the *in spite of*.

## ENDNOTES

1. Morson, G.S. (2015, July 1). Why college kids are avoiding the study of literature. *Commentary.* Retrieved from https://www.commentarymagazine.com/articles/why-college-kids-are-avoiding-the-study-of-literature/
2. LaBrant (1947).
3. LaBrant, L. (1943). Language teaching in a changing world. *The Elementary English Review, 20*(3), 93–97.

CHAPTER 45

# TEACHING ENGLISH AS "THE MOST INTIMATE SUBJECT IN THE CURRICULUM"

On Twitter, John Warner offered a few reviews of his new book of short stories, *Tough Day for the Army*, followed by this Tweet[1]: "I think writers have ideas about the books they write, but they aren't the same ideas the readers have about those books. #agoodthing." Warner's comment is grounded in his being a writer, but I suspect also in his being a reader and a teacher. I want to stress his #agoodthing and use this brief but insightful moment to push further against the mostly dispassionate academy where New Criticism has flourished and laid the foundation for its cousin "close reading."

With a sort of karmic synergy, I read Warner's Tweet above just as I was diving into a new Haruki Murakami short story, "Scheherazade," and the companion interview with Murakami about the story. "Scheherazade" is classic Murakami—odd, awkward, and then ultimately an unmasking of the human condition. As a writer myself (my creative, expressive writing exclusively now poetry), I was laid bare as a reader and writer toward the end of the story:

> It was also possible that he would, at some point, be deprived of his freedom entirely, in which case not only Scheherazade but all women would disappear from his life. Never again would he be able to enter the warm moistness of their bodies. Never again would he feel them quiver in

*Teaching Writing as Journey, Not Destination:*
*Essays Exploring What "Teaching Writing" Means*, pp. 227–230
Copyright © 2019 by Information Age Publishing
All rights of reproduction in any form reserved.

response. Perhaps an even more distressing prospect for Habara than the cessation of sexual activity, however, was the loss of the moments of shared intimacy. What his time spent with women offered was the opportunity to be embraced by reality, on the one hand, while negating it entirely on the other. That was something Scheherazade had provided in abundance—indeed, her gift was inexhaustible. The prospect of losing that made him saddest of all.[2]

A recurring motif of my creative self is confronting exactly what Murakami states directly: "Perhaps an even more distressing prospect for Habara than the cessation of sexual activity, however, was the loss of the moments of shared intimacy." And it is this type of lucidity in stories, novels, poems, and films when I often cry because I am *filled too full of feeling deeply* what the author has both expressed and felt (I assume), what I know as well.

If we turn to the interview by Deborah Treisman,[3] however, we can see Warner's point above clearly since Murakami repeatedly deflects Treisman's efforts to mine meaning from the story; for example, Murakami replies to two separate questions with:

> Sorry, but I don't know the exact circumstances that brought about the situation, either....Because what's important isn't what caused Habara's situation but, rather, how we ourselves would act in similar circumstances....
> I don't know, but things certainly don't look very good for Habara....

What matters to Treisman as a reader (and interviewer) appears insignificant to Murakami.

These exchanges highlight that text has both author intent and reader inference (think Rosenblatt's reader, writer, text triangle)—but the exchanges also allow us to consider (or reconsider) that text meaning often depends on a power dynamic that involves *who decides what matters* and *how*. Murakami's "Scheherazade" focuses on an unnamed character (called "Scheherazade" by Habara, the other character in the story) who is a source of both sex and storytelling for Habara, who is mysteriously restricted to his house:

> Habara didn't know whether her stories were true, invented, or partly true and partly invented. He had no way of telling. Reality and supposition, observation and pure fancy seemed jumbled together in her narratives. Habara therefore enjoyed them as a child might, without questioning too much. What possible difference could it make to him, after all, if they were lies or truth, or a complicated patchwork of the two?
> Whatever the case, Scheherazade had a gift for telling stories that touched the heart. No matter what sort of story it was, she made it special. Her voice, her timing, her pacing were all flawless. She captured her listener's attention, tantalized him, drove him to ponder and speculate, and

then, in the end, gave him precisely what he'd been seeking. Enthralled, Habara was able to forget the reality that surrounded him, if only for a moment. Like a blackboard wiped with a damp cloth, he was erased of worries, of unpleasant memories. Who could ask for more? At this point in his life, that kind of forgetting was what Habara desired more than anything else.

As readers, we share with Habara a brief journey through Scheherazade's episodic tales of her own adventures, leading to the end where Murakami appears to suggest that her storytelling is more intimate for Habara, and thus more important, than the sex she shares.

Just as Murakami's interview reveals the range of *what matters* in text, that Habara "enjoyed [Scheherazade's stories] as a child might, without questioning too much" (and we might add, as Treisman does in the interview) speaks against the dispassionate ways in which formal schooling frames text and dehumanizes the reading experience for and with children and young adults (hence, New Criticism, close reading, and the enduring "evidence hunt" of reducing text to what can—or should—be mined from that text). And thus, in her "Language Teaching in a Changing World," Lou LaBrant (1943) warned:

> Too frequently we give children books which have enough value that we call them "good," forgetting that there are other, perhaps more important values which we are thereby missing. It is actually possible that reading will narrow rather than broaden understanding. Some children's books, moreover, are directed toward encouraging a naive, simple acceptance of externals which we seem at times to hold as desirable for children.... Let us have no more of assignments which emphasize quantity, place form above meaning, or insist on structure which is not the child's. (p. 95)[4]

LaBrant, then, builds to her key point: "Teachers should consider carefully what they are doing with the most intimate subject in the curriculum" (p. 97).

Teaching English as "the most intimate subject in the curriculum" is connected to, as LaBrant explains in "The Place of English in General Education" (1940), the essential element of being human: *Language is a most important factor in general education because it is a vital, intimate way of behaving. It is not a textbook, a set of rules, or a list of books*" (p. 364).[5] Decades since LaBrant made these arguments, we must ask—especially in the context of Warner's Tweet and Murakami's story and interview—why do we persist in reducing text to the dispassionate responses demanded in the academy, whether that sits within the mechanistic processes of New Criticism or the decontextualized demands of close reading? Where in formal schooling is there room to "[enjoy] [text] as a child might, without questioning too much?"

In the answer-driven classrooms that have traditionally and currently mis-served both the text being analyzed and the students evaluated by how they analyze those texts, Murakami sends a much different message:

> Habara is a man who has experienced an irrevocable turning point in his life. Was the turning point moral, or legal, or was it a metaphorical, symbolic, psychological kind of thing? Did he turn the corner voluntarily, or did someone force him? Is he satisfied with the results or not? I don't know the answers to any of these questions. The instant he turned that corner, though, he became a "desert island." Things can't go back to the way they were, no matter what he does. I think that is the most important aspect of this story.

As author of this story, Murakami is interested in the questions raised, what is left unknown to him: "I don't know. Scheherazade is a riddle to me, as well—what she is thinking, what she is looking for."

Fiction and poetry seek the mysteries of the human condition, the unknown, the unanswerable. As LaBrant and Murakami tell us, language and teaching are about the *intimacy of being human*—not about the dispassionate calculation of meaning, the objective pose that is both misleading and efficient as well as manageable. Unlike Habara, we are not in fact trapped in the house of such dispassion; we have chosen to remain there. Instead we should step outside, to enjoy text "as a child might, without questioning too much."

## ENDNOTES

1. https://twitter.com/biblioracle/status/519229314533838848
2. Murakami, H. (2014, October 13). Scheherazade. *The New Yorker.* Retrieved from https://www.newyorker.com/magazine/2014/10/13/scheherazade-3
3. Treisman, D. (2014, October 6). This week in fiction: Haruki Murakami. *The New Yorker.* Retrieved from https://www.newyorker.com/books/page-turner/fiction-this-week-haruki-murakami-2014-10-13
4. LaBrant (1943).
5. LaBrant, L. (1940, May). The place of English in general education. *The English Journal, 29*(5), 356–365.

# CHAPTER 46

# TEACHING LITERACY IN PURSUIT OF "A WHOLESOME USE OF LANGUAGE"

> Because, in the final analysis,
> the language we speak constitutes who we are as a people.
>
> "Yesterday," *Men without Women*, Haruki Murakami

"Let us look at this English tongue with which, as English teachers, we profess to deal," proposes Lou LaBrant in her "The Place of English in General Education," published in *English Journal* in 1940 (p. 356).[1] As LaBrant's biographer, I immediately pause at "profess" and recognize that a scolding is about to commence—one that is blunt, smart, and unlikely to achieve her goals because of her scathing tone and style as well as the recalcitrance of far too many who teach literacy at all levels of formal education. During my interviews with people who had known LaBrant, one spoke directly to her essence: "She never suffered fools gladly," he said.

And about language and their uses, we have always been and remain surrounded by foolishness about language—in William Butler Yeats's trap: "The best lack all conviction, while the worst/Are full of passionate intensity." Among her many points addressing how educators teach literature/reading and writing, LaBrant makes a foundational demand:

---

*Teaching Writing as Journey, Not Destination:*
*Essays Exploring What "Teaching Writing" Means*, pp. 231–235
Copyright © 2019 by Information Age Publishing
231

Mental hygiene calls for a wholesome use of language. Schools do much to set up the opposite attitude. By the very nature of the school, its experiences become a standard of sort. Language used in school is characterized as "good" in contrast to language which cannot be used in school. By our taboo on sex words, on literature which deals frankly with life-experiences, and on discussion of love and romance, we set up inhibitions and false values. Only by discussing frankly and unemotionally vital matters can we develop individuals who use language adequately and without embarrassment....Our people use [language] timidly, haltingly. They fear to speak directly, call frankness vulgarity, fear to discuss love, beauty, the poetry of life. They ban honest words and prefer circumlocutions. The language teacher, the teacher of English, carries a goodly share of responsibility for the mental hygiene of young people. (p. 362)

Formal schooling, LaBrant confronts, creates an unhealthy attitude about language in young people—and thus, corrupting what young people believe, how they think, and ultimately how they navigate the world. These failures of formal schooling have roots, she notes, in misguided practice: "As training for independent thinking and clear self-expression, how appropriate is it to ask children to punctuate bad sentences some textbook-maker has written, or to write endless papers on topics chosen by a teacher or committee?" (pp. 363–364). And thus, LaBrant concludes: "*Language is a most important factor in general education because it is a vital, intimate way of behaving* [emphasis original]. It is not a textbook, a set of rules, or a list of books" (p. 364).

## Teaching Literacy in Pursuit of "a Wholesome Use of Language"

Since about 2008, my university has been offering faculty seminars focusing on teaching writing/composition to first-year students. The university switched from a traditional English 101/102 model (though we never used those labels) to a pair of first-year seminars with one being writing-intensive. That shift included a commitment to inviting and allowing faculty across the disciplines to teach writing/composition—despite virtually none of them (included some in the English Department) having formal training in teaching composition or being writers. Next, we created a year-long seminar, Faculty Writing Fellows (FWF), and appointed a Director of Writing who leads these seminars and all aspects of the writing program, which now includes the writing-intensive first-year seminar (the second one has been dropped) and an upper-level writing/research requirement.

When the opening session of one cohort of FWF began their journey, and during one presentation, I sat listening to a colleague explore with the participants how to decide if and how to engage with students whose writing includes so-called problems with grammar, mechanics, and usage (a set of distinctions that most professors lump as "grammar"). This colleague teaches history of the English language and upper-level grammar courses; she was very patiently and kindly—unlike LaBrant—making a case for descriptive grammar and stepping back from focusing in an unhealthy way on correctness in order to begin with student expression, while also carefully unpacking what students do and don't know about conventional uses of language (instead of rules).

I could listen to this colleague all day; she is a measured and gifted scholar of language who embodies how linguists talk about and *think* about language (it is more about *marveling at* and *wondering about* than preserving some arcane and misguided rule). Then the inevitable happened. A participant asked about a rule, concerned that we professors have an obligation to maintain the rules of the language but also worried that she may be addressing a rule that no longer applies.

My colleague was steadfast. Instead of making a declaration on the said rule, she walked the point back to our overarching obligation to address the ideas of students as expressed in their writing. Despite her kindness, patience, and *authoritative* reply, I fear that she had no more success than LaBrant did with her abrupt mannerisms. Far too many teachers charged with teaching literacy as their main obligation and teachers who necessarily engage with literacy anchored to what they would call teaching about disciplinary knowledge/content remain trapped in thinking that *correctness* trumps all else in teaching writing/composition and speaking in formal settings.

In the session about responding to student writing, then, we were derailed into chatter about splitting infinitives, ending sentences with prepositions, and the use of "they" as a gender-neutral singular pronoun. My colleague's message, I regret, was lost in the feeding frenzy, the language itself left bleeding and battered in the wake of the grammar police circling and attacking like sharks. And here is what was lost.

First, our obligations with teaching literacy must begin with two primary goals: fostering an accurate and healthy attitude about language (descriptive grammar grounded in the history of language development) concurrent with initially addressing the ideas expressed by students (accuracy, originality, complexity) through coherent, clear, and concise language use (diction, style, organization). Next, nested in that first dual obligation, we must raise *student awareness* that conventional uses of language, although always shifting, carry *status marking* in many circumstances. Language use, then, impacts directly and indirectly a person's credibility as well as the effectiveness of the ideas being expressed.

Here, let me emphasize that this obligation allows any of us to teach directly to students that people continue to function under the rule mentality, but along with that, we should make them aware of several important caveats:

- Prescriptive grammar often fails in the context of historical patterns of language, and many so-called rules are illogical in that historical context: not splitting infinitives and not ending sentences with prepositions both grew from imposing Latin grammar onto English in order to raise its status as a language; rejecting double negatives the result of garbling mathematical and linguistic concepts; and constructions such as "Aren't I?" highlighting the often foolish pursuit of rules over naturally occurring usage (the latter being how "they" has become a singular pronoun).

- Teaching students *about* a rules approach to language must include pulling back the curtain, sharing with students that many so-called rules are in fact the topic of heated debate among experts on language (again, the "they" debate).

- Language use cannot be divorced from *discussions of power*; the standard dialect versus non-standard dialect dichotomy is about who has power and how those in power manipulate language correctness to marginalize and silence some groups (LaBrant addresses this in her 1940 essay quoted above). Despite many who call for no politics in teaching, to teach standard English in a rules-based way is a blunt political act itself. Instead of taking a false objective stance about rules, invite students to read, for example, James Baldwin on Black English, or Silas House's "In My Country."

Finally, and I am making a sequential case here, *once a student has presented an artifact of a quality that deserves it* (after purposeful drafting and conferencing), we must wade into editing, where we do have an obligation to address conventional grammar, mechanics, and usage. But even as we confront conventional language use, we must know the status of the language ourselves, and we must also continue to focus on issues that are status marking for the student's attention in editing.

Dangling and misplaced modifiers are likely to garble meaning while split infinitives, not so much. Subject/verb agreement (common when students are ambitious, writing longer sentences with subordinations that separate the subject and verb) can scar credibility while pronoun/antecedent agreement or a comma failure, not so much.

Ultimately, no teacher can do everything in any one course. We are all forced, then, to make priorities. In terms of literacy and language, we must first do no harm—foster and honor "a *wholesome* use of language" that cannot be separated from the autonomy and agency of our students as purposeful, ethical, and informed people.

## ENDNOTE

1. LaBrant (1940).

# SECTION XVI

**LITERACY AND THE LITERARY TECHNIQUE HUNT**

# CHAPTER 47

# FORMAL SCHOOLING AND THE DEATH OF LITERACY

My privilege is easily identified in my being White and male, but it is the story of my life that better reveals my enormous privilege established by my mother when I was a child. I entered formal schooling with such a relatively high level of literacy and numeracy that from those first days I was labeled "smart"—a misnomer for that privilege. From *Green Eggs and Ham* to *Hop on Pop*, from canasta to spades, from Chinese checkers to Scrabble—games with my mother and often my father were my schooling until I entered first grade. And none of that ever seemed to be a chore, and none of that involved worksheets, reading levels, or tests.

Formal schooling was always easy for me because of those roots, but formal schooling was also often tedious and *so much that had to be tolerated* to do the things I truly enjoyed—such as collecting, reading, and drawing from thousands of comic books throughout my middle and late teens. I was also voraciously reading science fiction and never once highlighting the literary techniques or identifying the themes or tone.

During my spring semester as a college professor of education, I spend a great deal of time observing preservice English/ELA teachers, and once I had an exchange on Twitter about the dangers of grade retention, notably connected to third-grade high-stakes testing. And from those, I began musing more than usual about how formal school—how English/ELA teachers specifically—destroy literacy, even when we have the best of intentions. From the first years of K–3 until the last years of high school, students have their experiences of literacy murdered by a blind faith in and complete abdication to labeling text by grade levels and narrow approaches to literary analysis grounded in New Criticism and what I call the "literary technique hunt."

## Misreading the Importance of Third-Grade Reading

As I have addressed often, reading legislation across the U.S. is trapped in a simplistic crisis mode connected to research identifying the strong correlation between so-called third-grade reading proficiency and later academic success. Let's unpack that by addressing the embedded claims that rarely see the light of day. The first claim is that labeling a text as a grade level is as valid as assigning a number appears. While it is quite easy to identify a text by grade level (most simply calculate syllables per word and words per sentence), those calculations entirely gloss over the relationship between counting word/sentence elements and how a human draws meaning from text—key issues such as prior knowledge and literal versus figurative language.

An important question, then, is asking in whose interest is this cult of measuring reading levels—and the answer is definitely *not* the student. This technocratic approach to literacy can facilitate a certain level of efficiency and veneer of objectivity for the work of a teacher; it is certainly less messy. But the real reason the cult of measuring reading levels exists is the interests of textbook companies who both create and perpetuate the need for measuring students' reading levels and matching that to the products they sell. Reading levels are a market metric that are harmful to both students and teaching/learning. And they aren't even very *good* metrics in terms of how well the levels match any semblance of reading or learning to read.

The fact is that all humans are at some level of literacy and can benefit from structured purposeful instruction to develop that level of literacy. In that respect, everyone is remedial and no one is proficient. Those facts, however, do not match well the teaching and learning industry that is the textbook scam that drains our formal schools of funding better used elsewhere—almost *anywhere* else. Remaining shackled to measuring and labeling text and students murders literacy among our students; it is inexcusable, and is a root cause of the punitive reading policies grounded in high-stakes testing and grade retention.

## The Literary Technique Hunt

By middle and high school—although we continue to focus on whether or not students are reading at grade level—we gradually shift our approach to text away from labeling students/ texts and toward training students in the subtle allure of literary analysis: mining text for technique. Like reading levels, New Criticism's focus on text in isolation and authoritative meaning culled from calculating how techniques produce a fixed meaning benefits from the veneer of objectivity, lending itself to selected-response testing. And thus, the great technique hunt, again, benefits not students, but teachers and the inseparable textbook and testing industries.

The literary technique hunt, however, slices the throat of everything that matters about text—best represented by Flannery O'Connor:

> I prefer to talk about the meaning in a story rather than the theme of a story. People talk about the theme of a story as if the theme were like the string that a sack of chicken feed is tied with. They think that if you can pick out the theme, the way you pick the right thread in the chicken-feed sack, you can rip the story open and feed the chickens. But this is not the way meaning works in fiction.
>
> When you can state the theme of a story, when you can separate it from the story itself, then you can be sure the story is not a very good one. The meaning of a story has to be embodied in it, has to be made concrete in it. A story is a way to say something that can't be said any other way, and it takes every word in the story to say what the meaning is. You tell a story because a statement would be inadequate. When anybody asks what a story is about, the only proper thing is to tell him to read the story. The meaning of fiction is not abstract meaning but experienced meaning, and the purpose of making statements about the meaning of a story is only to help you experience that meaning more fully.[1]

In other words, "A poem should not mean/But be," as Archibald MacLeish explains.

Texts of all genres and forms are about human expression, about the aesthetic possibilities of creativity. No writer, like no visual artist, writes in order to have the words or artwork replaced by the reductive act of a technocratic calculating of meaning through the algebra of New Criticism. To continue the hokum that is "reading level" and to continue mining text for techniques—these are murderous practices that leave literacy moribund and students uninspired and verbally bankrupt.

The very best and most effective literacy instruction requires *no textbooks*, *no programs*, and *no punitive reading policies*. Literacy is an ever-evolving human facility; it grows from reading, being read to, and writing—all by choice, with passion, and in the presence of others more dexterous than you are. Access to authentic text, a community or readers and writers, and a literacy mentor—these are where our time and funds should be spent instead of the cult of efficiency being sold by textbook and testing companies.

## ENDNOTE

1. O'Connor, F. (n.d.). Flannery O'Connor on meaning [Web log]. *On the Way to Writing*. Retrieved from https://lpei4.wordpress.com/on-writing-esp-fiction-and-creative-process/flannery-oconnor-on-meaning/

# SECTION XVII

## PLAGIARISM

CHAPTER 48

# "STUDENTS TODAY...."

## On Writing, Plagiarism, and Teaching

College instructor Rick Diguette offers a grim picture of first-year college writing:

> Once upon a time I taught college English at a local community college, but not any more. Don't get me wrong, I'm still on faculty and scheduled to cover three sections of freshman composition this fall. But it has become obvious to me that I am no longer teaching "college" English.
>
> Every semester many students in my freshman English classes submit work that is inadequate in almost every respect. Their sentences are thickets of misplaced modifiers, vague pronoun references, conflicting tenses, and subjects and verbs that don't agree when they remember, that is, that sentences need subjects. If that were not bad enough, the only mark of punctuation they seem capable of using with any consistency is the period.[1]

I read this just after I had been mulling Jessica Lahey's "What a 12 Year Old Has in Common With a Plagiarizing U.S. Senator,"[2] and I recognize in both pieces several overlapping concerns that deserve greater consideration as well as some warranted push back.

*Teaching Writing as Journey, Not Destination:*
*Essays Exploring What "Teaching Writing" Means*, pp. 245–251
Copyright © 2019 by Information Age Publishing
All rights of reproduction in any form reserved.

## "Students Today..."

In both Diguette's and Lahey's pieces, we must confront a problematic although enduring sense that *students today* are somehow fundamentally different from students in the past, and that difference is always that students today are worse. Students today can't even write a complete sentence (Diguette), and students today are cheating like there is no tomorrow (Lahey). This sort of "students today" crisis discourse fails us, I believe, because it is fundamentally skewed by our tendency to be nostalgic about the past as well as by shifting far too much focus on lamenting conditions instead of addressing them.

I offer, then, a broad response to both Diguette's and Lahey's central points: *Let's not address student writing and plagiarism/cheating as if these are unique or fundamentally worse concerns for teachers and education now than at any other point in modern U.S. education.*

And for context, especially regarding students as writers, I offer the work of Lou LaBrant on teaching writing and my own examination of teaching writing built on LaBrant's work; in short:

> In "Writing Is More than Structure," LaBrant (1957) says that "an inherent quality in writing is responsibility for what is said. There is therefore a moral quality in the composition of any piece" (p. 256). For LaBrant, the integrity of the content of a student's writing outweighs considerably any surface features. In that same article, she offers a metaphor that captures precisely her view of the debate surrounding the teaching of writing—a debate that has persisted in the English field throughout this century: "Knowing about writing and its parts does not bring it about, just as owning a blueprint does not give you a house" (p. 256)....
>
> LaBrant sought ultimately through writing instruction the self-actualized literate adult, the sophisticated thinker. She never wavered in her demand that writing instruction was primarily concerned with making sincere and valuable meaning—not as a means to inculcate a set of arbitrary and misleading rules, rules that were static yet being imposed on a language in flux.
>
> Lou LaBrant remained paradoxically rigid in her stance: The writing curriculum had to be open-ended and child-centered; the content of writing came first, followed by conforming to the conventions; and English teachers had to be master writers, master descriptive grammarians, and historians of the language. It all seemed quite obvious to her, since she personified those qualities that she demanded. LaBrant was one of many who embodied the debates that surround the field of teaching English, and she left writing teachers with one lingering question: Do we want our students drawing blueprints or building houses? The answer is obvious. (pp. 85, 89)[3]

Instead of framing student writing and plagiarism, then, within crisis discourse, we must view the teaching of writing and the need to instill scholarly ethics in our students as *fundamental and enduring aspects of teaching at every level of formal schooling.* In other words, the problems in student work we encounter as teachers—such as garbled claims; shoddy grammar, mechanics, and usage; improperly cited sources; plagiarism—are simply the *foundations upon which we teach.* Along with the essential flaw of viewing *students today* as inferior to students of the past, the urge to lament that students come to any of us poorly prepared by those who taught them before is also misleading and more distraction.

We certainly could and should do a better job moving students along through formal education, but the simple fact is that each teacher must take every student where they are is and then move that student forward as well as possible. Formal standards and implied expectations about where all students should be mean little in the real world where our job as teachers is bound to each student's background, proclivities, and all the contexts that support or impede that student's ability to grow and learn.

Now, before moving on, let me introduce another point about our perceptions of how and when students learn literacy. Consider the common view of children learning to read by third grade, for example. Although reported commonly throughout mainstream media, the widespread assumption that students *must* acquire reading by third (or any) grade is flawed because children and adults *continue to evolve* as readers (and writers) in ways that defy neat linear categories. Thus educator professor and scholar Peter Smagorinsky notes in his response to Diguette, "Education is very complex, and it's rare that one problem has a single cause."[4]

## On Writing, Plagiarism, and Teaching

None of what I have offered so far relieves teachers of this truth: All students need (deserve) writing instruction and that must include serious considerations of proper citations as well as focusing on the ethical implications of being a scholar and a writer (and citizen, of course). And while I disagree with claims that *students today* are fundamentally worse writers or more prone to plagiarism than students in the past, I do recognize that we can expose why students perform as they do as writers and why students plagiarize and settle for shoddy citation.

Whether we are concerned about the claims or organization in a student writing sample, the surface features (grammar, mechanics, and usage), faulty attribution of citations, or outright plagiarism, a central root cause of those issues can be traced to the current 30-years cycle of public school accountability built on standards and high-stakes testing. As Smagorinsky does, I want to urge anyone concerned about student writing to consider the conclusions drawn by Applebee and Langer[5] regarding the teaching of writing in middle and high school.

Applebee and Langer present a truly disheartening examination of the consequences related to the accountability era as they impact student writing: Although teachers are more aware than ever of best practices in the teaching of writing (due in no small part to the rise of the National Writing Project in the 1970s and 1980s), throughout middle and high school, students *are not writing* in ways that foster their abilities to generate original ideas; establish, support, and elaborate on credible claims; and polish writing that conforms to traditional conventions for language.

The primary reasons behind this failure are not "bad" teachers or lazy/stupid students, but the demands linked to high-stakes accountability. Just as one example, please consider the unintended and corrosive consequences of writing being added to the SAT in 2005. The writing section of the SAT negatively impacted the teaching of writing in the following ways, all of which can be found in contexts related to preparing students for other high-stakes testing situations related to state-based accountability:

- Writing (composition) has been reduced to what can be tested in multiple-choice format. In other words, students were being taught and assessed for writing in *ways that are not composing*. Here we have the central failure of allowing testing formats to correlate with holistic performances, and thus, students are not invited or allowed to spend the needed time for developing those holistic performances (composing). See LaBrant's "Writing Is Learned by Writing."[6]

- Students write primarily or exclusively from detailed prompts and rubrics assigned by teachers or formulated by test designers. Ultimately, by college, few students have extended experiences with confronting the wide range of decisions that writers make in order to form credible and coherent ideas into a final written form. If many college students cannot write as well as professors would like, the reason is likely that many of those students have never had the opportunity to write in ways that we expect for college students. Students have been drilled in writing for the Advanced Placement tests, the SAT, and state accountability tests, but those are not the types of thinking and writing needed by young scholars.

- Students have not experienced extended opportunities to draft original essays over a long period of time while receiving feedback from their teachers and peers; in other words, students have rarely experienced workshop opportunities because teachers do not have the time for such practices in a high-stakes environment that is complicated by budget cut-backs resulting in enormous class sizes that are not conducive to effective writing instruction.

The more productive and credible approach to considering why students write poorly or drift into plagiarism, then, is to confront the commitments we have made to education broadly. The accountability era put a halt to best practice in writing for our teachers and students so we should not be shocked about what college professors see when first-year students enter their classes. But another source of shoddy student writing must not be ignored.

Within that larger context of accountability, student writing that is prompted tends to have much weaker characteristics (content as well as surface features including proper citation) than writing for which students have genuine engagement. In other words, while students are not composing nearly enough in their K–12 experiences (and not receiving adequate direct instruction of writing at any formal level), when students do write, the assignments tend to foster the worst sorts of weaknesses highlighted by Diguette and Lahey.

Shoddy ideas and careless editing as well as plagiarism are often the consequences of *assigned writing* about which students do not care and often do not understand. (Higher quality writing and reducing plagiarism[7] can be accomplished by student choice and drafting original essays over extended time with close monitoring by the teacher, by the way.) And this leads back to my main argument about how to respond to both Diguette and Lahey: As teachers in K–12 and higher education, we have a moral obligation to teach students to be writers and to be ethical. Period.

To be blunt, it doesn't matter why students struggle with writing or plagiarism at any level of formal education because we must address those issues when students enter our rooms, and we must set aside the expectation that students come to us "fixed." In other words, like most of education, *learning to write and polishing ones sense of proper citation as well as the ethical demands of expression are life-long journeys, not goals anyone ever finishes*. However, in the current high-stakes accountability era of K–12 education—and the likelihood this is spreading to higher education—I must concur with Smagorinsky:

> If you want kids to learn how to write, then put your money to work to provide teachers the kinds of conditions that enable the time to plan effective instruction, guide students through the process, and assess their work thoughtfully and considerately.
>
> Otherwise, you may as well add yourself to the list of reasons that kids these days can't write.

And I will add that if college professors want students who write well and ethically, they (we) must commit to continuing to teach writing throughout any students formal education—instead of lamenting when those students don't come to us already "fixed."

Writing and ethical expression have never been addressed in formal schooling in the ways they deserve; both have been mostly about technical details and domains of punishment. The current accountability era has reinforced those traditional failures (see Chapter 56). I find Diguette's and Lahey's pieces both very important and seriously dangerous because they are likely to result in more misguided "blaming the victims" in that too many of the conclusions drawn about why students write poorly and often plagiarize remain focused on labeling teachers and students as flawed. That students write poorly and often plagiarize is evidence of systemic failures, first and foremost. In order for the outcomes—effective and ethical student writers—to occur, then, we all must change the conditions and expectations of formal education, including understanding that all teachers are obligated to identify our students' strengths and needs in order to start there and see how far we can go.

## Final Thoughts: Adult Hypocrisy

Many of you may want to stop now. The above is my sanitized response, but it isn't what I really want to say so here goes. If you wonder why students write poorly and too often plagiarize, I suggest you stroll into whatever room has the biggest mirror and look for a moment. As someone who is a writer and editor, I work daily with scholars and other writers who submit work far more shoddy than my students submit. And as an increasingly old man, I witness the adult world that is nothing like the idealized and ridiculous expectations we level moment by moment on children.

Plagiarism? You too can become vice president of the U.S.! (See Joe Biden).

Lazy student? You can become president of the U.S.! (See George W. Bush).

Now, I absolutely believe we must have high expectations for our students, including a nuanced and powerful expectation for ethical behavior, but many of the reasons that children fail at their pursuit of ethical lives must be placed at our feet. The adults in the U.S. (especially if you are white, if you are wealthy, if you are a man) play a much different ethical game than what we tell children. Children see through such bunkum and that teaches a much different lesson that doesn't do any of us any good.

## ENDNOTES

1. Diguette, R. (2014, August 3). Welcome to college, or grade 12½. *The Atlanta Journal-Constitution.* Retrieved from https://www.myajc.com/news/opinion/welcome-college-grade/ZPqjM4CHxVisd0awpbhlVL/

2. Lahey, J. (2014, July 24). What a 12 year old has in common with a plagiarizing U.S. senator. *The Atlantic.* Retrieved from https://www.theatlantic.com/education/archive/2014/07/plagiarism/374999/

3. Thomas, P.L. (2000, January). Blueprints or houses? Lou LaBrant and the writing debate. *English Journal, 89*(3), 85–89.

4. Smagorinsky, P. (2014, July 28). Bad student writers: You get what you pay for [Web log]. *The Atlanta Journal-Constitution.* Retrieved from http://www.petersmagorinsky.net/About/PDF/Op-Ed/BadWriters.html

5. Applebee & Langer (2013).

6. LaBrant (1953).

7. Thomas, P.L. (2007, May). Of flattery and thievery: Reconsidering plagiarism in a time of virtual information. *English Journal, 96*(5), 81–84.

## CHAPTER 49

# PLAGIARISM

## Caught Between Academia and the Real World

An international student enrolled in a U.S. university presents her first speech for an introductory public speaking course. English is not her first language so writing and delivering the speech present for her problems not faced by students native to the United States. All students in the course also submit their speeches to the professor electronically so that the texts can be run through plagiarism detection software. This international student's speech is flagged for two passages being over 40% unoriginal, word-for-word identical in many areas to a high-profile political speech easily found online.

In academia, students accused of plagiarism and then proven to have plagiarized face dire consequences—failing the assignment, failing the entire course, and/or expulsion. Having taught high school English and then first-year writing, and having served on a university academic discipline committee, I have witnessed a wide range of problems with how academia defines plagiarism (including different bars for plagiarism from professor to professor in the same university), how professors detect and address plagiarism, and how students are taught *and not taught* the ethical and technical aspects of proper citation and use of sources in original writing.

*Teaching Writing as Journey, Not Destination:*
*Essays Exploring What "Teaching Writing" Means,* pp. 253–256
Copyright © 2019 by Information Age Publishing
253

The scenario above, however, was very publicly presented through the speech offered by Melania Trump at the 2016 Republican National Convention. While Melania Trump's speech became fodder for parody and humor as well as partisan bickering over whether or not it was plagiarism and whether or not it mattered, several key aspects of this act of plagiarism in the real world was ignored, especially as it informs how we treat plagiarism in academia at all levels.

Here is the ugly truth we in the academy fail to teach students: In formal schooling (and most scholarship), plagiarism is punished harshly, especially when the plagiarist is a student; but in the real world, plagiarism occurs quite a bit, especially in politics,[1] and with very few negative consequences—mostly because the plagiarists are powerful people (consider Rand Paul as just one example). The significant gap between the consequences for plagiarism by a student in school and for powerful people in the real world offers some important lessons for both academia and the public.

In K–12 and higher education, students are subjected to a high level of focus on and scrutiny about plagiarism. However, much of that is about *detection* and *punishment*—while too little time is spent *directly teaching* students about the ethics and technical aspects of choosing, using, and citing sources for original work. When Rand Paul faced multiple cases of his work, including speeches and publications, being flagged for plagiarism, his response is important to consider (and in many ways parallels defenses of Melania Trump's plagiarism):

> Paul has argued that his speeches aren't meant to be meticulously footnoted academic papers. He has also noted that he cited the movies he talked about and, in the case of his book, that the Heritage Foundation study and Cato were cited in the endnotes. Heritage and Cato have both released statements saying they don't take issue with Paul's use of their work.[2]

For students, this real-world situation seems to suggest that only in academia is plagiarism a big deal, and thus, the academia is over-reacting.

Ultimately, plagiarism in any setting is about attribution of words and ideas to others. From Rand Paul to countless students, the ease with which words and ideas can be lifted from Wikipedia combined with seeing education as mere credentialing or seeing a speech as just a functional thing is a dangerous formula—if ethical considerations matter at all in either academia or the real world. Melania Trump's plagiarism deserved scrutiny, and plagiarism must remain a line not to be crossed in academic and scholarly work. While the real world will likely continue to allow some people to skirt consequences for plagiarism, I believe the academy needs to think carefully about how we address plagiarism and the adequate citation of people's ideas and words.

Here, then, are some guiding thoughts about what must be confronted about plagiarism in the academy:

- Proper citation and plagiarism are ethical considerations; therefore, formal schooling needs to increase requirements for courses in philosophy (to know the body of thought about ethical considerations) as well as embedding greater time spent on ethics within all disciplines.

- Students deserve honest discussions of how plagiarism and its consequences are about *power* as that intersects ethics. Inviting students to investigate real-world cases of plagiarism is an important gateway to their understanding what it entails as well as why they should be making ethical choices in their own education and beyond.

- Formal schooling needs to reconsider the intensity placed on detecting and punishing plagiarism (including rejecting technology as a central device for the detection[3]) and to place more time and value on teaching students how to gather, use, and cite sources for their work. *Too often students are simply told their work is incorrect or plagiarized; too rarely are students then guided through a revision process that requires and allows them to complete their work ethically and properly.*

The phrase "merely academic" is a damning one because it captures the gulf between what we do and profess in formal schooling as that is refuted by the real world. When students see the real world functions under significantly different norms than formal schooling, they are apt to tolerate (at best) schooling until they can be released into the real world—too often unmotivated to be critical of or to seek ways to change that real world. If education is more than credentialing (and currently it may not be), and if education seeks to be transformative for both the students and the society the schools and universities serve, that gulf must be bridged.

Our society and our politics are neither equitable nor ethical. Our schools and universities have a duty to address both—but we must do it through rich and robust teaching and learning, not mere detection and punishment.

## ENDNOTES

1. Tran, M. (2016, July 19). A short history of political plagiarism. *The Guardian.* Retrieved from https://www.theguardian.com/us-news/2016/jul/19/short-history-political-plagiarism-melania-trump

2. Blake, A. (2013, November 4). Rand Paul's plagiarism allegations, and why they matter. *The Washington Post*. Retrieved from https://www.washingtonpost.com/news/the-fix/wp/2013/11/04/rand-pauls-plagiarism-allegations-and-why-they-matter/

3. Schorn, S. (2016, November 7). Cheating students: How plagiarism detection software defrauds learners and teachers. Retrieved from https://prezi.com/vtvlgsaftpf9/cheating-students-how-plagiarism-detection-software-defrauds-learners-and-teachers/

# SECTION XVIII

## POETRY

# CHAPTER 50

# WHAT MAKES POETRY, POETRY?

On Valentine's Day 2016, I spent the morning with poetry. So when I came across Peter Anderson's blog post,[1] I was suitably primed to do something I believe I had failed to do formally—write about teaching poetry as a poet. A couple years before I would discover that I am a teacher (the fall of my junior year of college), I was sitting in my first-year dorm room in the spring when I wrote my first real poem, and thus, had that quasi-religious experience of becoming a poet. Being a poet is not something I chose to do, not something I can control. There are weeks, maybe months, when no poems come, and then there are manic days and days and days when they come like tidal waves, avalanches—unbidden but gathered frantically out of the writer's fear that at any moment this may end, abrupt as a fatal aneurism.

Now comes the really embarrassing part, where poet/writer intersects with teacher. The first moment my foot touched the floor of *my* classroom, I envisioned myself as a teacher of writing, but also a teacher who would instill in my students my love for reading (devouring) literature, especially poetry. I worked hard, intensely—as I am prone to do—to teach my students to write, willing all the while the love of literature and poetry into their adolescent hearts and minds. Yet—this is embarrassing—I was casually murdering everything I loved, and scrubbing the life and blood from my students' *possibilities* as writers, poets, and the sorts of joyous readers I had envisioned.

*Teaching Writing as Journey, Not Destination:*
*Essays Exploring What "Teaching Writing" Means*, pp. 259–260
Copyright © 2019 by Information Age Publishing

My godawful teaching of poetry and efforts at having my students write poetry—despite my precious poetry unit built around the music of R.E.M.—were all mind and no heart. The most important aspect of ending these horrible practices as a teacher who had divorced himself uncritically from his Poet Self was dropping my transactional methods (opening the poetry unit by *giving* students "the four characteristics of poetry" [all nonsense, by the way] and then asking them to apply those to their analysis of a poem they chose [I thought the choice part was awesome]) and embracing an overarching discovery approach driven by a broad essential question: What makes poetry, poetry?

Early and often as we meandered through dozens of poems and R.E.M. song lyrics, my students and I kept returning to a Thoreau moment: "Simplify, simplify, simplify." No matter how hard we tried, we could discover nothing a poet did that writers of other types of writing didn't also do—except for the purposeful formation of lines and stanzas (including that prose poets create poetry by the *negative* of avoiding the conventions of lines and stanzas in poetry). Prose, we recognized, is driven by the formation of sentences and paragraphs, as a contrast, but poetry is almost exclusively as well composed of complete sentences (despite the argument by most students that poetry is a bunch of "fragments," leading to examinations of enjambment). Reading and writing poetry became investigations, opportunities to play with words and witness the joy they can bring.

All writing, including the work of the poet, including the work of any artist, is a creative act endured in the context of some structures that the writer/artist either embraces or actively reaches beyond. What makes poetry, poetry? The purposeful construction of words into lines and stanzas. "A poem should not mean/But be," poses Archibald MacLeish. But as a young teacher, I sullied that simple dictum. Instead, I committed the *act of teaching*, about which Marianne Moore declares: "I, too, dislike it: there are things that are important beyond/all this fiddle."

School and *teaching* can and often are the death of poetry, of writing, of the magnificent joy of human expression. As poet/writer and teacher, mine is to resist "all this fiddle," and to allow for students the moment when poetry comes, unexpectedly while your dog sleeps on your feet.

## ENDNOTE

1. Anderson, P. (2015, July 13). Line and stanza breaks in free verse poetry —NVWP Summer Institute—Day 5 pt. 1 [Web log]. *Mr. Anderson Reads and Writes.* Retrieved from https://mrandersonwrites.wordpress.com/2015/07/13/line-and-stanza-breaks-in-free-verse-poetry-nvwp-summer-institute-day-5-pt-1/

# CHAPTER 51

# TEACHING ESSAY WRITING THROUGH POETRY

As a writer and teacher, I am pained to admit, but in the big picture I do agree with Kurt Vonnegut who opens "Teaching the Unteachable" with "You can't teach people to write well. Writing well is something God lets you do or declines to let you do. Most bright people know that...."[1] My caveat, however, is about what we mean by "writing well." Vonnegut above and my agreement are confronting what I would call those who are by their nature and inclinations *writers first*—those who labor over poetry, fiction, essays, and the like for months and even years (and decades) without any real hope anyone will ever publish that work. These are writers who write because they *have* to, but not necessarily because they want or need to.

Throughout my career, I have taught primarily high school and undergraduate students to write—but that effort is rarely about the sort of writer mentioned above; instead I am teaching writing that is essentially functional and disciplinary. And it is there that I diverge from Vonnegut because I know for a fact that we can teach people to write well in the disciplines, often extremely well even when they do not particularly like to write, even when they insist they are not very good writers.

One of the most effective approaches to teaching disciplinary-based essay writing is to focus on large concepts about effective writing and then to ground that in examining poetry in order to teach those concepts. Using poetry to reinforce essay writing helps highlight the universal qualities of powerful writing and continues to push students in their awareness of genre, form, and medium as they impact expression.

## Kingsolver's "What the Janitor Heard in the Elevator" and the Essay

Barbara Kingsolver from her collection *Another America/Otra America* begins "What the Janitor Heard in the Elevator" with "The woman in the gold bracelets tells her friend:"[2] and then continues:

> I had to fire another one.
> Can you believe it?
> She broke the vase
> Jack gave me for Christmas.
> It was one of those, you know? That worked
> with everything. All my colors.
> I asked him if he'd mind
> if I bought one again just like it.
> It was the only one that just always worked.
>
> Her friend says:
> Find another one that speaks English.
> That's a plus.
>
> The woman in the gold agrees
> that is a plus.

In class, we begin to read and examine this poem, but I use this discussion to highlight the *craft of writing* (especially as that relates to disciplinary essay writing), not to do the traditional poetry analysis most students expect. Here are some of the elements of effective writing I highlight:

- After we begin discussing the poem, I steer the students back to the title, which in this case is extremely important. Thus, I emphasize the *importance of the title* as well as discuss the art and craft of subheads in disciplinary essays. Many students have not focused on titles, and often submit essays without titles so this is typically a key lesson for first-year students.
- Next, we highlight the use of "gold" in the opening line and the final stanza. The points I stress are about *word choice, connotation,* and *framing*. I believe essay writing must begin at the word level for young writers; they need a greater sense of *purpose* in the words they choose, notably *specificity, concreteness, appropriateness* (key here

is that words have specialized meanings in the disciplines), and *clarity*. And that connects with connotations of words; in the poem, "gold" carries a great deal of important information about the scene, issues related to wealth and privilege. My students are quick to admit that Kingsolver has chosen "gold" with *intent*, purpose. Further, "gold" serves as a framing motif since she incorporates the word in the opening line and the end. I stress to students that essays are often framed (and to avoid the mechanistic introduction and conclusion format they have learned in high school). *Framing* and *motifs* add powerful and concrete elements to writing that young writers often lack.

- We also confront Kingsolver's use of "one" and "it," especially the latter since I have stressed the problems with the pronoun to my students. In this poem, "one" and "it" create meaning in their repetition but also in their mixed implications about both the domestic worker and the vase. The point of emphasis is that Kingsolver, again, chooses and repeats words with purpose to create meaning, and this contrasts how students are apt to repeat and use empty or vague language from carelessness.

- Finally, we discuss the effectiveness of writing with characters and plot as well as the impact of showing versus telling. *People doing things* are powerful, much more powerful than abstractions. Kingsolver in her poem trusts the reader to know the abstractions she is showing; however, young writers tend to make many grand announcements (often overstated) and fail to show or support those claims.

Often I follow the discussion of Kingsolver's poem with Martin Luther King Jr.'s "Letter from Birmingham City Jail," and the result is impressive. We are able to identify these craft lessons immediately in King's essay; students are also significantly more willing to embrace the concepts once we worked through the poem and then into King's writing.

While there is a cynical irony to Vonnegut's claims about teaching the unteachable—written by a writer who often taught at writing conferences and legendary writing workshops—ones that do elicit laugher, I am convinced that we teachers of writing who serve primarily students who will have to write while in formal education and then may go on to write in the disciplines can be very successful, but only if we take the teaching of writing seriously, and seek ways in which students can grow as writers. Focusing on the universals of effective writing and then allowing students to examine and practice those universals are essential. And to do that, I find that poetry is an excellent resource for teaching the writing of essays.

# ENDNOTES

1. Vonnegut (1967).
2. Kingsolver, B. (1998). *Another America/Otra America.* (R. Cartes, Trans.). Berkley, CA: Seal Press.

# SECTION XIX

## PUBLIC INTELLECTUAL (WRITING FOR THE PUBLIC)

# CHAPTER 52

# WRITING FOR THE PUBLIC

## A Framework

In several undergraduate courses (a May course on education documentaries, first-year seminars, and an upper-level writing/research course) and a graduate course (current trends in literacy) I teach, students write public pieces that challenge them to examine a common misconception and then help a general audience better understand the issue. The piece is created as an online document as well—requiring that students explore citing and supporting their claims with hyperlinks to credible and effective sources.

Having written public pieces in mainstream and alternative publications regularly for over a decade and then writing online (in different types and for different venues) blogs for about five years, I have learned a great deal about writing from a specialized perspective for the public. As a university-based academic, I have also come to advocate that public work is at least as important for scholars as traditional publishing (peer-reviewed journals, books)—if not more important since the social/practical impact and scope of reach are often much greater for public work. As a genre (commentary), a distinct medium (virtual/online), and advocacy, writing for the public is incredibly difficult and too often discouraging.

Primarily for K–12 teachers, academics, and scholars/researchers, this discussion of a framework for public writing also argues that we need more informed public voices—especially from educators, academics, and

*Teaching Writing as Journey, Not Destination:*
*Essays Exploring What "Teaching Writing" Means*, pp. 267–270
Copyright © 2019 by Information Age Publishing
267

researchers. Public writing is an especially important genre of writing for stepping away from traditional views of essays and argumentation (as taught in formal schooling)—rejecting introduction (thesis), body, and conclusion templates; reconsidering paragraphing (short is better).

Openings (and even the title) of public works should seek to accomplish three goals (sometimes simultaneously): (1) engaging the reader by being interesting, (2) focusing on or preparing the reader for the central topic and major claim of the piece, and (3) establishing for the reader your expertise or unique perspective related to the topic (consider that readers likely are reading you for the first time and have no context for your credibility). For educators, academics, and scholars/researchers, public writing must purposefully and carefully recognize that popular perceptions about issues tend to be simplistic or even misinformed. That reality means the audience will be antagonistic and nearly impossible to sway.

Powerful examples of this for me have been writing about grade retention, corporal punishment, and the word gap—all topics routinely misrepresented by the media and misunderstood by the public (and political leaders). In all three situations, the evidence is overwhelming (or significantly complex, as with the research on literacy and social class) but also counter to those misrepresentations and misunderstandings. For writers with expertise and experience in a field, public writing must remain constantly aware of that public while also navigating the high standards of traditional scholarship.

That means opening a public piece by being interesting can be accomplished by following a key guideline from Joseph Williams (*Style*): write with characters and plot. Readers are often interested in people doing things—narrative; and people are really interested in real people doing real things. For teachers and professors, we can often share actual classroom stories, but public writing can also mine the rich world of journalism for real-world stories that accurately reflect the broader generalizations found in high-quality research. Yes, qualitative data (narratives) can be outliers or misleading, but our job as experts is to choose and shape narratives that are *representative*, while also engaging the general public.

Within a few opening paragraphs, then, we want to engage and focus our readers while establishing our credibility; this is a much different and much harder task for a writer than the formulaic introduction/thesis. Here, we need to acknowledge that public commentaries generally fall in a word-count range of about 750–1,250 words (typically at the lower end). This is really brief for complex topics (ones that academics may cover in 6,000–7,000 words), and many feel writing public commentaries has more in common with writing poetry (concision, concision, concision) than other forms of prose. I agree—since I am also a poet. The bulk of your piece, however, must be the main claims, evidence (hyperlinked) and elaborations that constitute the body. In the body, typically you are challenged to make complicated and sometimes technical information accessible to the general public.

Word choice, sentence formation, use of evidence—these are the really hard parts of doing public writing (and there is no template). And while your evidence is essential, hyperlinks must be used as if readers will not follow them, and the credibility of the evidence (just as you do initially with yourself) must be established in a way that is *compelling to the average* (non-expert) reader. And here is the truly frustrating part of public writing: although, for example, I noted that major medical organizations and the American Psychological Association all have research-based stances against corporal punishment of any kind, many of the responses I have received completely ignore or even discount that evidence (evidence that in the academic world would carry a great deal of weight).

Since public pieces are brief, as well, your agenda is best served by having a clear major claim/argument and then a few supporting claims; keep the argument as simple as possible without being simplistic. Just as a narrative is engaging as an opening, the bulk of your discussion must be carried by concrete and vivid details; always give the reader as many sensory triggers as possible.

Now, as we think about an ending, I want to make a counterintuitive claim: The traditional view of the essay (as we have been taught in formal schooling) includes that the body is the meat of an essay; thus, the part that matters most. However, in public writing, the opening captures the reader's attentions, and then the ending leaves the reader with the impression that likely works or doesn't in terms of making your case. Instead of thinking about a conclusion as a restatement of the introduction (horrible advice, by the way, that serves no purpose in any type of writing), the ending often is most effective when you work on *framing* your argument. Framing also depends heavily on the use of the concrete. Once you establish a story— or even a refrain—in your opening, you can return to that image, those people, that event, or the refrain in the final paragraph or two. That motif, then, gives your piece coherence in the reader's mind, establishing an internal logic to the piece that may have a stronger influence on the reader intuitively than the rational arguments of the body.

As a final point—something I stress to my students since their writing often will be evaluated, graded: work diligently to have a final few sentences, a final few words that are vivid and leave the reader with the new idea or new impression that is at the center of your argument. "What I have most wanted to do throughout the past ten years is to make political writing into an art. My starting point is always a feeling of partisanship, a sense of injustice," explained George Orwell in "Why I Write," adding, "I write it because there is some lie that I want to expose, some fact to which I want to draw attention, and my initial concern is to get a hearing."[1]

"The job is to reconcile my ingrained likes and dislikes with the essentially public, non-individual activities that this age forces on all of us," Orwell continued; however, "It is not easy. It raises problems of construction and of language, and it raises in a new way the problem of truthfulness." As educators, academics, and scholars/researchers, we are well prepared to tackle "the problem of truthfulness," and if we the informed do not, we are leaving that important task to others less credible.

## ENDNOTE

1. Orwell, G. (1946). Why I write. Retrieved from http://orwell.ru/library/essays/wiw/english/e_wiw

# SECTION XX

## PUBLISHING

CHAPTER 53

# ADVICE FOR SUBMITTING WORK FOR PUBLICATION

While I often blog about submitting work as a student and author, I want to focus here on submitting work for publication in academic, scholarly, or professional venues, especially work submitted by K–12 teachers and university scholars. For those new to submitting work for publication, an important first step is understanding academic and professional publishing. Academic/professional journals and books are edited and managed often by teachers and professors who are rarely paid for that work, and thus, must edit and manage along with maintaining their full-time academic work. Therefore, this is important: Submit your work in such a way that you honor the time and professionalism of the editor(s). What does that entail?

*Do your homework.* Before submitting, and even before writing your submission, *read and carefully consider the publication (journal) or publisher (books) for which you are seeking publication.* You should read and familiarize yourself with the work of the editor(s) as well. Especially if you are submitting to a journal, read and analyze several *recent* works in the journal or column you are targeting. Journals and columns can change significantly under different editors, so "recent" is key.

*Draft with the publication in mind.* Writing your submission must include maintaining a focus on the journal, column, or book call for manuscripts. Original pieces drafted after seeing the call or revising/reshaping existing work (such as a thesis or dissertation completed for degree work) must be

*Teaching Writing as Journey, Not Destination:*
*Essays Exploring What "Teaching Writing" Means,* pp. 273–276
Copyright © 2019 by Information Age Publishing
All rights of reproduction in any form reserved.

crafted to fulfill the call focus and guidelines, including conforming to the word count. Never submit a thesis/dissertation excerpt or manuscript for publication without revising/reshaping the work to meet the call you are targeting.

*Format manuscript to citation/publication specifications.* Two important points here: (1) manuscripts must be formatted and texts cited properly (impeccably), and (2) formatting should honor "less is always better." Formatting your Word document should conform to some standard guidelines:

- Use Times New Roman (or similar standard font—although never submit a work with different fonts in body, headers, etc.) and 12 pt. font; double space throughout with the standard 1/2" indent for paragraphing and 1" (or per style sheet) margins.

- Use appropriate header/footer requirements of style sheet identified by the publication, but avoid decorative formatting of headers/footers (lines, images, etc.). Editors want and need clean files. All submitted work will be reformatted if published so your decorations are time wasting. (Don't use italics, bold, or quote marks unless necessary—as in proper formatting required by the style sheet identified. Quote marks should *never* be used for emphasis.)

- Note proper formatting for your title, subheads (academic/professional writing tends to have subheads), and references. Take great care not to mix citation conventions for levels of headings and designation of citations as well as the listing of sources (such as the use of footnotes/endnotes, in-text citations, and heading for references). Note that citation generating software or apps should be avoided since they are often flawed and also embed formatting that can be problematic; if used, export as a text-only file and then carefully edit.

- Be sure to use your word processor appropriately. Know how to format paragraph indentations, hanging indents (citations), and block quotes with the ruler or menu options (and not manually with Return>Tab).

- Include your name (as it should be once published) and contact information on the manuscript as noted in the publication guidelines. Also, be sure to have a reliable e-mail address that you check often.

In academic/professional publishing, there simply is not room for muddled citation and documentation formatting. Yes, the many and varied style sheets are mind-numbing (APA, MLA, Chicago, Harvard), and the odd changes publications will make to those standards are a maze ("use

MLA but also for this publication…"), but citation conventions constitute a significant part of the professionalism of your work. Check, double-check, and have a peer check your citations—the consistency, accuracy, and formatting.

*Submit a clean document.* Submitted manuscripts send a powerful message to editor(s). Sloppy manuscripts (poorly copyedited, mangled formatting, improper citation, active track changes/comments) suggest the writer isn't serious and the piece isn't ready for consideration (note the "honor the time and professionalism of the editor(s)" above). Rolling over a manuscript from one submission to another can be a problem if you are not careful to fully revise and reformat a piece. Never submit with the caveat you'll properly revise to fit the guidelines if accepted. Here, again, asking a colleague to read for edits is essential.

*Make your contact with the editor(s) count.* The actual submission of the work is a last and important step. Use e-mail or postal as required, but make sure that the file or hard copy conforms exactly to the publication requirement (many publications have limits on Word file types; some hard copy submissions must have multiple copies included; and always note the guidelines for cover page and author identification on the manuscript). Since most submissions are now electronic (either by e-mail or through a submission system), be sure to name the electronic manuscript file as required (or if no requirements, be simple and practical, such as naming the file your name), put required or practical information in the "subject" line (if no requirement, your last name and call date/topic are helpful), and include a brief but effective cover letter.

The cover letter should, again, consider the time and professionalism of the editor(s)—so brief is excellent. However, be sure to include the title of your piece, the call topic/date you are addressing, and then a few details that may help your piece:

- Note your professional context and why this piece is something only you could have written or is credible because of your background/expertise.
- Identify your understanding of the publication by referencing a previous article, another work by the publisher, and/or some relevant work by the editor. These must be sincere gestures of your having researched the publications, however, and are not intended as merely cozying up to the editor.
- Include any required information from the call, and verify you are available by a reliable e-mail address.
- If your submission is in any way *unlike* what the publication tends to accept or *varies* from the call in some significant way, you should

note those differences with a brief explanation of why you think they are justified.

Blanch Dubois relied on the kindness of strangers. In academic/professional publishing, *mutual* kindness is a must. Those submitting work should do so with the labor and time of the editor(s) in mind, and then the editor(s) must handle those submissions with the sort of care they would appreciate.

# SECTION XXI

## READING LIKE A WRITER

# CHAPTER 54

# GUIDED ACTIVITY

## More Reading Like a Writer

After walking through a reading like a writer (scholar) class session using an essay by Barbara Kingsolver (see Chapter 23), I want to offer briefly a guided activity for students to complete in groups in order to practice reading like a writer as one step in their own growth as writers. For example, I ask students to read "Water Is Life" by Barbara Kingsolver, and then, to discuss and answer the following questions:

- What appears to be Kingsolver's target/primary audience? What is the evidence from the essay to support that?
- How does Kingsolver create an effective opening? What techniques (literary, rhetorical), strategies does she employ? Give specific examples.
- What are Kingsolver's major claims? How does she elaborate on those claims? What evidence does she use to support her claims? Give specific examples.
- Identify one or two of the best sentences in this essay. What makes them effective?
- Does Kingsolver break the "rules" of grammar[1] or that you were taught in school? Examples? What is her purpose in these situations?

*Teaching Writing as Journey, Not Destination:*
*Essays Exploring What "Teaching Writing" Means*, pp. 279–280
Copyright © 2019 by Information Age Publishing

- What is the guiding tone of this essay? How does Kingsolver create that tone? Give specific examples. Does she ever break that tone? Example(s)?
- What does Kingsolver want her audience to know or do? Give specific examples.
- How does Kingsolver frame this essay in her closing paragraph(s)? Give specific examples.

These questions are common in the writing conferences I hold with students about their own original essays so this activity helps further reinforce the need for writers to be aware of and purposeful about these elements of essay writing.

## ENDNOTE

1. Landrum, J. (2007). Students: Do experts follow the rules you're taught? *Journal of Teaching Writing, 23*(1). Retrieved from https://journals.iupui.edu/index.php/teachingwriting/article/view/1355/1304

# SECTION XXII

## RUBRICS

CHAPTER 55

# KEN LINDBLOM'S "IS INTERESTING TO READ" AND THE RUBRIC DILEMMA REDUX

At the 2003 National Council of Teachers of English annual conference in San Francisco, I met Ken Lindblom, then a column editor for *English Journal* and later an outstanding editor for the same. Ken is among an important nucleus of NCTE colleagues and friends who have enriched my professional life in ways I can never repay; I have served as a column editor for EJ under two different tenures of editors and as the Council Historian just after the centennial along with being awarded the 2013 George Orwell Award—just to name some of the personal accomplishments that I cherish as examples of the collegiality and kindness found in the NCTE community of teachers and scholars.

So Ken's "The Rubric Criterion That Changed Everything" has put me in a predicament since I value Ken as one of my go-to thinkers on teaching writing but I also have a long and firm stance against grades, tests, and rubrics. The central point addressed by Ken captures exactly why his post inspires me and gives me pause:

> Once I was reading a stack of papers, and I remember thinking, "Man, I wish these papers were more interesting!" Then it hit me: Students will work on what's listed on a rubric. In my next paper assignment, I added this to the rubric: "Is Interesting to Read."[1]

*Teaching Writing as Journey, Not Destination:*
*Essays Exploring What "Teaching Writing" Means*, pp. 283–285
Copyright © 2019 by Information Age Publishing
All rights of reproduction in any form reserved.

Rubrics—as Maja Wilson and Alfie Kohn deconstruct—often become the *chore to fulfill* when students write, and while they can provide structure and clarity in grading for both students and teachers, rubrics can often be nightmares for those same teachers when student writing flounders but fulfills the rubric or soars in ways that the rubric never addresses.

Instead of rubrics, then, I offer students guiding questions, and do agree that students need structure (see Chapter 39). Regardless of using rubrics or guiding questions, I want to stress that raising student awareness of being interesting is both powerful and essential. That awareness, however, must be fostered by examining with students the many ways in which writers accomplish being interesting.

First, we must highlight that embedded in "Is Interesting to Read" is a focus on audience. In my first-year writing seminars, I stress that I want students to stop writing for me, and to develop essays with clear and real audiences in mind. This is part of my on-going goal of encouraging students to stop thinking as students and to start thinking as writers. Some of the concrete strategies that we focus on that contribute to being interesting as a writer include the following:

- Creating openings, instead of writing mechanistic introductions, that are compelling first and then focus the reader on the central purpose of the essay. We do several reading like a writer activities (see Chapters 23, 54) throughout the semester, but focus on openings in the first few weeks.

- Expanding tone beyond the faux academic pose of objectivity, and acknowledging the power of humor. Notably in our reading of Barbara Kingsolver, for example, students notice that essays are often humorous (especially in the opening), and thus, more interesting.

- Emphasizing the power of narrative (and description) as a mode that creates interest. Drawing on *Style*, we think about nonfiction essays in terms of fiction—character, plot, and setting. Inherent in narrative, as well, is the importance of details (see Chapter 47).

- Allowing drafting to be an act of discovery (see Chapter 60), brainstorming. Another key aspect of resisting the traditional introduction/thesis approach is helping students recognize that drafting often leads writers to their purpose; in other words, drafting as discovery opens the door to *finding the interesting* instead of trying to fulfill the obligation of a predetermined thesis.

- Reimagining the essay form not as an introduction/thesis, body, and conclusion but as a cohesive form better served by *framing*— developing a few opening and closing paragraphs that share a story, detail, or compelling element that both engages and compels the reader (thus, interesting).

I remain less optimistic than Ken that rubrics can serve our goal to foster students as writers who are aware of their audience and committed to being interesting. I do believe, however, seeking ways to encourage specific strategies for being interesting as a writer is achievable, but it is also essential, as Ken argues, not simply something extra.

## ENDNOTE

1. Lindblom, K. (2018, January 2). The rubric criterion that changed everything [Web log]. *Edukention.* Retrieved from https://edukention.wordpress.com/2018/01/02/the-rubric-criterion-that-changed-everything/

# CHAPTER 56

# MORE ON FAILING WRITING, AND STUDENTS

Throughout the 1980s and 1990s, I taught English in the rural South Carolina (SC) high school I attended as a student. Many of those years, I taught Advanced Placement courses as part of my load (I taught all levels of English and usually sophomores and seniors) and was department chair. Over the years, I worked hard to create an English department that served our students well. We made bold moves to provide all students in each grade the same literature textbooks (not different texts for different levels, as was the tradition, thus labeling students publicly) and to stop issuing to students grammar texts and vocabulary books (teachers retained classroom sets to use as they chose).

And a significant part of our English classes was the teaching of writing—having students write often and to produce multiple-draft essays. I stressed the need to end isolated grammar instruction (worksheets and textbook exercises) and urged that grammar, mechanics, and usage be addressed directly in the writing process. Even though the principal was supportive and a former English teacher, at one faculty meeting while the administrators were discussing recent standardized test scores for the school (yes, this test-mania was in full force during the 80s and 90s in SC), the principal prefaced his comments about the English test scores with, "Keep in mind that the English scores may not reflect what we are doing here since we don't teach grammar."*

*Teaching Writing as Journey, Not Destination:*
*Essays Exploring What "Teaching Writing" Means*, pp. 287–293
Copyright © 2019 by Information Age Publishing
All rights of reproduction in any form reserved.

In a nut shell, that sort of mischaracterization and misunderstanding about best practice is at the foundation of Joan Brunetta's writing about how standards- and test-based schooling had failed her.[1] In that context, I want to address below not only how we still fail the teaching of writing but also how that failure is a subset of the larger failure of students by traditional approaches to teaching that are teacher-centered and committed to core knowledge.

## Revisiting "The Good Student Trap" in the Accountability Era

Adele Scheele has coined the term "the good student trap," which perfectly captures how schools create a template for what counts as being a *good student* and then how that template for success fails students once they attend college and step into the real world beyond school. My one caveat to Scheele's ideas is that especially during the accountability era—a ramping up of traditional practices and norms for education—this *trap* affects *all* students, not just the good ones. And the trap goes something like this, according to Scheele:

> Most of us learned as early as junior high that we would pass, even excel if we did the work assigned to us by our teachers. We learned to ask whether the test covered all of chapter five or only a part of it, whether the assigned paper should be ten pages long or thirty, whether "extra credit" was two book reports on two books by the same author or two books written in the same period. Remember?
> We were learning the Formula.
>
> - Find out what's expected.
> - Do it.
> - Wait for a response.
>
> And it worked. We always made the grade. Here's what that process means: You took tests and wrote papers, got passing grades, and then were automatically promoted from one year to the next. That is not only in elementary, junior, and senior high school, but even in undergraduate and graduate school. You never had to compete for promotions, write résumés, or rehearse yourself or even know anyone for this promotion. It happened automatically. And we got used to it....
> What we were really learning is System Dependency! If you did your work, you'd be taken care of. We experienced it over and over; it's now written in our mind's eye. But nothing like this happens outside of school. Still, we remain the same passive good students that we were at ten or fourteen or twenty or even at forty-four. The truth is, once learned, system dependency stays with most of us throughout our careers, hurting us badly. We

keep reinforcing the same teacher-student dichotomy until it is ingrained. Then we transfer it to the employers and organizations for whom we'll work.[2]

This model of traditional schooling includes a teacher who makes almost all the decisions and students who are rewarded for being compliant—and that compliance is identified as "achievement."

In English classes, a subset of this process is reflected in how we teach, and fail, writing. Hillocks and others have noted that traditional commitments to the five-paragraph essay (and cousin template-models of essays) and a return to isolated grammar exercises have resulted from the rise of high-stakes testing of writing. As well, the accountability era has included the central place of rubrics driving what students write, how teachers respond to student writing, and how students revise their essays. So what is wrong with five-paragraph essays, grammar exercises, and rubrics?

Let's focus on rubrics to examine why all of these are ways in which we fail writing and students. Alfie Kohn explains:

> Mindy Nathan, a Michigan teacher and former school board member told me that she began "resisting the rubric temptation" the day "one particularly uninterested student raised his hand and asked if I was going to give the class a rubric for this assignment." She realized that her students, presumably grown accustomed to rubrics in other classrooms, now seemed "unable to function [emphasis added] unless every required item is spelled out for them in a grid and assigned a point value. Worse than that," she added, "they do not have confidence in their thinking or writing skills and seem unwilling to really take risks."[3]

Rubric-based writing and assessment, then, reflect the exact problem noted by Applebee and Langer: teachers know more today than ever about how to teach writing, but commitments to accountability and testing prevent that awareness from being applied in class; as Kohn explains:

> What all this means is that improving the design of rubrics, or inventing our own, won't solve the problem because the problem is inherent to the very idea of rubrics and the goals they serve. This is a theme sounded by Maja Wilson in her extraordinary new book, *Rethinking Rubrics in Writing Assessment*. In boiling "a messy process down to 4–6 rows of nice, neat, organized little boxes," she argues, assessment is "stripped of the complexity that breathes life into good writing." High scores on a list of criteria for excellence in essay writing do not mean that the essay is any good because quality is more than the sum of its rubricized parts. To think about quality, Wilson argues, "we need to look to the piece of writing itself to suggest its own evaluative criteria"—a truly radical and provocative suggestion.

Wilson also makes the devastating observation that a relatively recent "shift in writing pedagogy has not translated into a shift in writing assessment." Teachers are given much more sophisticated and progressive guidance nowadays about how to teach writing but are still told to pigeonhole the results, to quantify what can't really be quantified. Thus, the dilemma: Either our instruction and our assessment remain "out of synch" or the instruction gets worse in order that students' writing can be easily judged with the help of rubrics.

Once fulfilling the expectations of the rubric becomes the primary if not exclusive goal for the student, we have the SAT writing section and the unintended consequences, as Newkirk explains about students writing to prompts and rubrics for high-stakes testing:

> George Hillocks Jr. has shown that another persistent problem with these types of prompts concerns evidence—the writer must instantly develop instances or examples to be used for support. In a sample of the released papers from the Texas state assessment, some of this evidence looks, well, manufactured.... When I first read this essay, I imagined some free spirit, some rebel, flaunting the ethics of composition and inventing evidence to the point of parody. But when I shared this letter with a teacher from Texas, she assured me that students were coached to invent evidence if they were stuck [emphasis added]. In my most cynical moment, I hadn't expected that cause. And what is to stop these coached students from doing the same on the SAT writing prompt? Who would know?[4]

As but one example above, "the good student trap," is replicated day after day in the ways in which students are prompted to write and then how teachers respond to and grade that writing. The failure lies in who makes almost all of the decisions, the teacher, and who is rewarded for being mostly compliant, students.

While core knowledge advocates and proponents of rubric-driven assessment tend to misrepresent critical and progressive educators who seek authentic learning experiences for students with charges of "not teaching X" or "So what shall we teach?" (with the implication that core knowledge educators want demanding content but critical and progressive educators don't), the real question we must confront is not *what* content we teach and students learn, but *who decides* and *why*. If we return to rubrics, well designed rubrics do everything *for* students, everything writers need to do in both college and the real world beyond school.

Rubric-driven writing is asking *less* of students than authentic writing in a writing workshop. Traditional core knowledge classrooms are also deciding for students what knowledge matters, and again, asking less of students than challenging students to identify what knowledge matters in order to critique that knowledge as valuable (or not) for each student as well as the larger society. *The tension of this debate is about mere knowledge acquisition versus confronting the norms of knowledge in the pursuit of individual autonomy and social justice—making students aware of the power implications of knowledge so that they live their lives with purpose and dignity instead of having life happen to them.*

My call is not for ignoring the teaching of grammar, but for confronting the norms of conventional language so that students gain power over language instead of language having power over them. Why do we feel compelled not to end a sentence with a preposition? Where did that claim come from and who benefits from such a convention? Why does academic writing tend to erase the writer from the writing ("No 'I'!") and who benefits from that convention?

You see, critical approaches to teaching go *beyond* the mere acquisition of knowledge that some authority has deemed worthy (what Freire labels the "banking concept" of teaching). Yes, knowledge matters, but not in the fixed ways core knowledge advocates claim and pursue. Critical approaches to knowledge honor the dignity of human autonomy in children, something that many adults seem at least leery if not fearful of allowing in their classrooms. Core knowledge, rubrics, templates, prescriptions, and prompts are all tools of control, ways to trap students in the pursuit of compliance. They aren't challenging (or "rigorous" as advocates like to say), and they aren't learning. As Scheele explains:

> System dependency is not the only damaging thing we learned in the context of school: We learned our place....
>
> Yet most of us were falsely lulled into a false self labeled "good" by fulfilling the expected curriculum. The alternative was being "bad" by feeling alienated and losing interest or dropping out....
>
> So what's the problem? The problem is the danger. The danger lies in thinking about life as a test that we'll pass or fail, one or the other, tested and branded by an Authority. So, we slide into feeling afraid we'll fail even before we do-if we do. Mostly we don't even fail; we're just mortally afraid that we're going to. We get used to labeling ourselves failures even when we're not failing. If we don't do as well as we wish, we don't get a second chance to improve ourselves, or raise our grades. If we do perform well, we think that we got away with something this time. But wait until next time, we think; then they'll find out what frauds we are. We let this fear ruin our lives. And it does. When we're afraid, we lose our curiosity and originality, our spirit and our talent-our life.

## Beyond Rigor, Templates, and Compliance

In my position at a small and selective liberal arts university, I teach mostly good students in my writing-intensive first-year seminars. Students are asked to read and discuss *Style*, a descriptive look at grammar, mechanics, and usage that raises students' awareness and skepticism about conventional uses of language, but rejects seeing conventions as fixed rules. (We ask why teachers in high school tend to teach students that fragments are incorrect when many published works contain fragments, leading to a discussion of purposeful language use.)

Throughout the course, students are invited to plan and then write four original essays that must be drafted several times with peer and my feedback. The focus, topic, and type of essay must be chosen by the student. To help them in those choices, we discuss what they have been required to do in high school for essays, we explore what different fields expect in college writing, and we read and analyze real-world essays in order to establish the context for the choices, and consequences of those choices, that writers make—specifically when those writers are students.

I offer this here in case you think somehow I am advocating "fluffy thinking" or a "do-your-own-thing philosophy" of teaching, as some have charged. And I invite you to ask my students which they prefer, which is *easier*—the template, prompt-based writing of high school that created their good student trap or my class. [HINT: Students recognize that five-paragraph essays and rubrics are easier, and they often directly ask me to just tell them what to write and how. As Mindy Nathan noted above, good students are "*unable to function* [emphasis added] unless every required item is spelled out for them in a grid and assigned a point value."]

My students reinforce for me every class session that we have failed the teaching of writing and those students by *doing everything for them in school*. They are nearly intellectually paralyzed with fear about the consequences of their own decisions. When challenged and supported to be agents of their own learning, their own coming to understand the world, and their own decisions about what knowledge matters and why, however, they are more than capable of the tasks. And with them in mind, I must ask, who benefits from compliant, fearful students as intellectual zombies, always doing as they are told?

———

* Although he phrased his comment poorly, my principal was, in fact, making a valid point that a multiple-choice English (grammar) test was unlikely to fairly represent what our students had learned about composing original essays. He intended to make a swipe at the quality of the test, although he did so gracelessly.

## ENDNOTES

1. Brunetta, J. (2013, November 27). A Massachusetts student writes: How MCAS changed my education [Web log]. *Living in Dialogue. Education*

*Week/Teacher*. Retrieved from http://blogs.edweek.org/teachers/living-in-dialogue/2013/11/a_student_writes_how_mcas_dera.html
2. Scheele (2004).
3. Kohn, A. (2006). The trouble with rubrics. *English Journal, 95*(4). Retrieved from https://www.alfiekohn.org/article/trouble-rubrics/
4. Newkirk (2005).

# CHAPTER 57

# MODELS, MENTOR TEXTS, AND (MORE) RESISTING RUBRICS

In the discussion spurred by Ken Lindblom's adding "interesting to read" to his writing rubrics (see Chapter 55), Tim Ogburn posed on a discussion thread: "So, along with rubrics (or not), I wonder how folks use models (or not)?" Ogburn's question coincided with my first offering of an upper-level writing/research course at my university: Scholarly Reading and Writing in Education. After the first class meeting, I have been revising and adding to the course guidelines and materials. Part of that work has been looking carefully at how I can use and expand my materials from my first-year writing seminar, which I have taught in various forms for about a decade now.

To answer Ogburn directly, I want to admit that my teaching writing practices are significantly grounded in using models and mentor texts. But here's the caveat: My experience and the research base both show that using models is *only a weak strategy* when teaching writing. For one example of research, *Writing Next* ranks using models as the 10th out of 11 effective strategies:

**Study of Models (Effect Size = 0.25)**

The study of models provides adolescents with good models for each type of writing that is the focus of instruction. Students are encouraged

---

*Teaching Writing as Journey, Not Destination:*
*Essays Exploring What "Teaching Writing" Means,* pp. 295–298
Copyright © 2019 by Information Age Publishing

to analyze these examples and to emulate the critical elements, patterns, and forms embodied in the models in their own writing. The effects for all six studies reviewed were positive, though small. It was not possible to draw separate conclusions for low-achieving writers, as none of the studies specifically addressed this population.[1]

None the less, I incorporate models and mentor texts while always seeking ways to increase their effectiveness.

Here, then, is how I use models for my four essay assignments in my first year writing seminar:

**Essay Requirements**

**Essay 1: See our shared prompt HERE (link to document provided).**

    Examples of personal narratives:

    "Everybody's Somebody's Baby," Barbara Kingsolver

    "Letter to My Son," Ta-Nehisi Coates

    "The Secret Lives of Inner-City Black Males," Ta-Nehisi Coates

    "They Can't Turn Back," James Baldwin

**Essay 2:** Compose and draft an essay of about 1,250–1,500 words in blog/ online format (see examples below) that offers an **expository** or **argumentative mode** for a general public audience from the perspective of expertise. Incorporate images, video, or other media.

**SAMPLE submission format (link to document provided).**

Examples (online pieces by me):

    "Should We Marvel at a Black Captain America?"

    [See scholarly version: "Can Superhero Comics Defeat Racism?"]

    "There is no debate about hitting children—it's just wrong"

    "Corporations Are Behind The Common Core State Standards—And That's Why They'll Never Work"

    "Gaiman's Mythical Folding of Childhood into Adulthood"

**Essay 3:** Compose and draft a substantially cited essay of about 4-6 double-spaced pages that presents a **discipline-based examination of a topic or poses a discipline-based argument.** Citations must conform to APA style guidelines. [See "Writing for Specific Fields" (link provided).]

Examples:

> Properly formatted APA sample essay (link to document provided)
>
> "Universal Public Education—Our (Contradictory) Missions"
>
> "Of Rocks and Hard Places—The Challenge of Maxine Greene 's Mystification in Teacher Education"

**Essay 4:** TBD in a conference

And then, how I have adapted that approach in an upper-level writing/research course (as embedded in submission guidelines):

**Annotated bibliographies:** Submit annotated bibliographies in both the initial and final submissions (all drafts should be complete and in proper format, even when submitting "rough" or initial drafts) as Word files and attach to e-mail with "annotated bibliographies" in the subject line. See some guidelines and a sample annotated bibliography **here** (note APA version). Submit each annotated bibliography as a separate Word file, and format in Times New Roman font, 12 pt., double space, with 1" margins. Each file should be named "lastname AB#.docx" (each file numbered from 1 through 8 or 10).

**Research project essay:** Submit research project cited essay in both the initial and final submissions (all drafts should be complete and in proper format, even when submitting "rough" or initial drafts) as Word files and attach to e-mail with "research project essay" in the subject line. See APA guidelines **here** and a sample APA essay **here.** Submit essay as a Word file, and format in Times New Roman font, 12 pt., double space, with 1" margins. Each file should be named "lastname essay.docx" (as you revise and resubmit, add RW, RW2, RW3, and so forth, to the file name to designate multiple drafts).

**Public commentary:** Submit your public commentary in both the initial and final submissions (all drafts should be complete and in proper format, even when submitting "rough" or initial drafts) as Word files and attach to email with "public commentary" in the subject line. See a sample public commentary **here.** Submit essay as a Word file, and format in Times New Roman font, 12 pt., single space, with 1" margins. Each file should be named "lastname OpEd.docx" (as you revise and resubmit, add RW, RW2, RW3, etc., to the file name to designate multiple drafts).

Finally, what, then, is the case for models and mentor texts—especially as ways to resist rubrics?

- Authentic (published) models and mentor texts are powerful alternatives to templates and artificial writing forms such as five-paragraph essays and anchor texts for standardized testing.
- Models and mentor texts are rich and engaging materials for *reading like a writer* and other critical reading activities, and thus, offer far more than simply teaching writing.
- If resisting and not outright rejecting rubrics, teachers and students can mine models and mentor texts in order to develop rubrics and/or guiding questions for composing together.
- Models and mentor texts are essential for developing genre awareness in students as well as fostering in students a greater understanding of writer purpose, audience, writing forms, conventional expectations (grammar, mechanics, and usage), and so forth.

As I continue to witness, teaching writing is a journey, and with that concession, using models and mentor texts to teach writing is an excellent example of how we must be neither a slave to nor ignorant of the research base and our own practiced experiences with methods. Grounding the teaching of writing in models and mentor texts proves to be *both* essential and in some ways inadequate, leaving us with "miles to go before [we] sleep."

## ENDNOTE

1. Graham & Perin (2007).

# SECTION XXIII

## TEACHING ENGLISH

# CHAPTER 58

# READERS, WRITERS, TEACHERS, AND STUDENTS

## "The Pointlessness of So Much of It"

> I wonder who I would have been, without those shelves, without those
> people and those places, without books.
>
> I would have been lonely, I think, and empty, needing something for
> which I did not have words.
>
> "Four Bookshops," The View from the Cheap Seats: Selected Nonfiction,
> Neil Gaiman

I was sitting in my university's second workshop designed to help university professors teach writing when I had an epiphany about teaching writing that I believe has helped me understand better why the teaching of writing remains so contentious. Both the formal teaching of reading and writing—notably at the secondary and undergraduate levels—is conducted by one of two essential groundings: teaching literacy as a reader and/or writer versus teaching literacy as a hyperstudent/teacher.* While my teaching and advocacy for teaching rests solidly in the former, I am not here suggesting one is better than the other, but that these two perspectives are at the core

*Teaching Writing as Journey, Not Destination:*
*Essays Exploring What "Teaching Writing" Means,* pp. 301–304
Copyright © 2019 by Information Age Publishing

why discussing and confronting so-called "best practices" often comes off as a heated debate instead of a productive conversation.

Many English majors, including those certifying to teach secondary English and those who attain doctorates to teach at the university level, are primarily prepared to teach a very narrow version of literary criticism—mostly addressing fiction and poetry, and mostly through analysis of literary technique and writer's craft. During the accountability era when *what we teach* and *what students learn* have been reduced to how students are tested, reading and writing have been reduced to artificial (as in how we address them in school and how we test them) forms: reading snippets of texts to answer multiple choice questions (no real-world readers do this), writing from a prompt in order to be assessed by a rubric and/or against an anchor paper (at best a bastardization of real-world writing, but honestly, again, no real-world writers do this).

I will not explore this fully here, but we cannot ignore as well how the commodification of education has eroded the authenticity of reading and writing. Textbooks and teaching materials feed the accountability dynamic narrowly but also speak to viewing reading and writing as students and teachers, not as readers and writers.

## A Case for Readers and Writers in Formal Schooling

Neil Gaiman's *The View from the Cheap Seats: Selected Nonfiction* is an adventure in a writer's-writer offering essay after essay about his love affair with books, writers, libraries, and genre, and is both a pure joy for me as reader and writer as well as yet another journey into trying to understand better the teaching of reading and writing. Gaiman is an incredibly successful writer who cannot resist constantly reminding his readers how his life as a writer grew from his love affair with books and writers, how bookstores and libraries were his sanctuaries. His is also a testament to the power of a wide variety of genres and media in the life of avid readers and writers.

"The Pornography of Genre, or the Genre of Pornography" and "What the [Very Bad Swearword] Is a Children's Book, Anyway? The Zena Sutherland Lecture" are powerful essays about the importance of teaching literacy as readers and writers (and thus at least tempering teaching literacy as hyperstudents/teachers) but also about how literacy is a journey, not something to be acquired or mastered. To focus on the second essay noted above, Gaiman shares a story of his telling a joke to a fellow eight-year-old, a joke including the word "fuck"; the controversy that followed, including the friend's parents removing that child from the private school, taught Gaiman "two very important lessons":

The first was that you must be extremely selective when it comes to your audience.

And the second is that words have power. (p. 79)[1]

This essay on children's literature is also about children, as Gaiman explains: "Children are a relatively powerless minority, and, like all oppressed people, they know more about their oppressors than their oppressors know about them" (p. 80).

And then, Gaiman confronts formal schooling—reinforcing something I have found to be a pattern among some of the most well regarded writers:

> For the record, I don't think I have ever disliked anything as long or as well as I disliked school: the arbitrary violence, the lack of power, the pointlessness of so much of it....
>
>   My defense against the adult world was to read everything I could. I read whatever was in front of me, whether I understood it or not.
>
>   I was escaping. Of course I was—C.S. Lewis wisely pointed out that the only people who inveigh against escape tend to be the jailers. ( pp. 80–81)**

And here is where I believe the tension I noted earlier comes into play.

   Again, I am not arguing here that teaching literacy as a reader/writer is necessarily *better* than teaching literacy as a hyperstudent/teacher, but I am extremely concerned that the latter dominates formal schooling to an extreme that is harmful to both literacy and basic human dignity and agency. Gaiman's essays, however, shout to those of us who teach literacy that formal schooling and teaching literacy as hyperstudents/teachers stood between Gaiman and works such as his wonderful *The Ocean at the End of the Lane*, that Gaiman has become a gifted and treasured writer in spite of his formal education (like Louise DeSalvo in her memoir *Vertigo*, Gaiman honors the coincidental lessons of libraries and bookstores).

   I am fairly certain now that lumping all sorts of literacy instruction into a course called "English" is a really bad idea—teaching literary analysis is often at odds with fostering a love of reading, but being a teacher of reading and/or literature is simply not the same thing as teaching writing. So much of my antagonism about how we teach literacy isn't at us teachers so much as at the system itself—how formal schooling too often is rightly analogized as prison, how many of us have excelled in many ways in spite of our education.

   As a lover of books, libraries, and bookstores; as a writer who views nearly every moment of this life through writer's eyes; as someone who, like Gaiman, remains moment by moment aware of the "powerlessness" and "helplessness" of being a child or teen, of being a student—I make the case often that the teaching of literacy (reading and writing) needs less school- and test-only versions of reading and writing, but much more authentic reading and writing.

At the end of his contemplation on what makes a book for children (or adults), Gaiman returns to a point he makes early in the talk: "But then, you do not come to authors for answers. You come to us for questions. We're really good at questions" (p. 90). It is here that I think we have a better way for formal schooling—the pursuit of questions with the joy and wonder of a child. So I'll thus end with a question: What value is there in rules, tests, templates, and requirements if in the end our classrooms have resulted in children seeking ways to escape "the pointlessness of so much of it?"

——

\* Many if not most teachers and professors are *hyperstudents*, having excelled at and achieved within formal schooling where literacy is reduced to tests, templates, and narrow views of what counts as "good" and "bad" language and texts. Once anyone has excelled in that culture, it is difficult to view it critically or to reject it for what avid readers and writers would call "authentic" literacy.

\*\* See from "On Science Fiction," C.S. Lewis:

> They are as refreshing as that passage in E. M. Forster where the man, looking at the monkeys, realizes that most of the inhabitants of India do not care how India is governed. Hence the uneasiness which they arouse in those who, for whatever reason, wish to keep us wholly imprisoned in the immediate conflict. That perhaps is why people are so ready with the charge of 'escape'. I never fully understood it till my friend Professor Tolkien asked me the very simple question, 'What class of men would you expect to be most preoccupied with, and most hostile to, the idea of escape?' and gave the obvious answer: jailers. The charge of Fascism is, to be sure, mere mud-flinging. Fascists, as well as Communists, are jailers; both would assure us that the proper study of prisoners is prison. But there is perhaps this truth behind it: that those who brood much on the remote past or future, or stare long at the night sky, are less likely than others to be ardent or orthodox partisans. (p. 67)[2]

## ENDNOTES

1. Gaiman, N. (2016). *The view from the cheap seats: Selected nonfiction.* New York, NY: HarperCollins.
2. Lewis, C.S. (2002). *Of other worlds: Essays and stories.* Eugene, OR: Harvest Books.

CHAPTER 59

# ANALOGIES LIKE LAND MINES

## Treading Carefully When We Discuss
## Teaching Writing

Metaphor is a powerful element in the craft of language. Writers and speakers seek metaphors, similes, and analogies to produce rich expression, but the analogy is a part of everyday discourse and all types of public expression and debate. One of the staples of my years teaching high school English was Flannery O'Connor's "A Good Man Is Hard to Find," a dark satire and enduring example of the brilliance found in Southern literature. My students and I always paused early in that story, the second paragraph, that begins:

> Bailey didn't look up from his reading so she wheeled around then and faced the children's mother, a young woman in slacks, whose face was as broad and innocent as a cabbage and was tied around with a green head-kerchief that had two points on the top like a rabbit's ears. (p. 117)[1]

*As a cabbage?* we would always ponder. The early descriptions establish O'Connor's use of contrast to cause tension between some of the cartoonish elements with the grim reality of the story's plot.

But I also feel in the cabbage simile that O'Connor was poking a bit at metaphorical language itself—something like a meta-metaphor. Less as craft and more as a strategy for argument, however, Donald Trump, apparently, has posed that he avoids exercise because, he claims, humans are like batteries, having a finite amount of energy. He believes we waste that energy store when exercising. Both of these example highlight, I think, that we must always investigate the use of analogy for the essential validity of the relationship being presented.

At different times in the past, the mind, for example, has been characterized as a blank slate and a muscle—and then, evidence and careful consideration of these analogies have been discredited. Where analogy fails, it seems, is when we take a position and then reach for a comparison that confirms the position. Trump, in his baseless battery analogy, simply clamored for something to justify his position—one that falls apart if we interrogate the comparison. Yet, the analogy is a powerful tool, and often compelling because analogy brings the concrete and the understood into complex and often abstract settings: the mind as a blank slate or muscle is far more manageable for the average person than how the mind actually functions, a domain for specialists.

As a writer and a teacher, I find my world is often deeply entrenched not only in language, but also in investigating how language works (and doesn't) to create warranted meaning. Both as a writer and reader, I have come to live by a guideline that helps remind me of the need to resist the uncritical allure of the analogy: *Just because someone can make a comparison doesn't mean that the comparison is valid.*

### Writing Is Like?

Notably, I have had several experiences with people making analogies in order to understand writing (composing) and teaching writing: writing like learning to ride a bicycle (starting with training wheels to justify teaching the five-paragraph essay), writing like playing a piano (moving from scales to playing a full piece). Both of those are recurring analogies, and thus, they must be compelling. However, here I am asking us all to think more carefully about these analogies. Writing (composing) is nothing like riding a bicycle, and is also nothing like playing the piano, because writing (composing) is creating something from nothing, an act of synthesis.

"Writing" as a term can cause some of the problem, in fact, so let's first consider writing (as handwriting) versus writing (as composing). Even in behaviors that depend on something like rote actions (such as handwriting, riding a bicycle, and playing a piano), the repetition of behaviors must be "correct" (or you are learning to do something "wrong") while also incrementally moving from something like novice to proficient to expert.

Let me risk next an analogy between coaching a scholastic sport and teaching. As a soccer coach, I worked hard to maintain some level of quality in *drills during practice* (isolated and rote), for the fact above, to prepare players for *playing an actual soccer match* (holistic and autonomous, although conforming to a body of rules); but my work as a coach would have been much different if I were helping the team create a whole new game instead of teaching them how to conform to an existing system.

Now we have come against the inherent flaw in the analogies about writing like riding a bicycle or playing a piano because writing (composing) is not of the same *kind* of behavior. Instead, writing is more validly analogous to visual art such as painting or drawing. While writing (composing) and visual art do in fact have discrete skill sets that can and should be honed in isolated and somewhat artificial ways, practice, composing a written piece and visual art come from trying the whole thing inexpertly at first and then continuing to do the whole thing in incrementally more proficient ways until some level of expertise is achieved.

Writing (composing) and visual art begin by facing blank paper, acts of synthesizing and creating from nothing to something. And thus, in pursuit of a more valid analogy, just as we do not teach painting by first asking students to paint-by-number, we should avoid at least an overuse of templates (five-paragraph essay, etc.) when teaching composition. Further, the field of composition has ample evidence (as do those of us who teach writing/composition) that once students have been prompted to conform to a template, they are dogged in never letting go; the template, sigh, is not a set of training wheels easily removed.

Metaphor, simile, and analogy are powerful tools, but the pursuit of analogy is like navigating a field littered with land mines; we should tread more carefully when making our comparisons, avoiding the Trump error above (selecting the analogy to confirm a belief without investigating if the comparison is accurate, without starting with a credible claim itself). Just as we scramble to understand better how the brain/mind works, often resorting to analogy, we who write and teach writing (composing) are confronted with something equally complex, and are rightfully looking for how to better navigate that understanding.

In that pursuit, I believe the bicycle and piano analogies to writing mislead us and our students. Let us seek instead analogies grounded in capturing the holistic and chaotic nature of rendering meaning from nothing and presenting comparisons that are of the same kind.

## ENDNOTE

1. O'Connor, F. (1971). *The complete stories.* New York, NY: Farrar, Straus, and Giroux.

# SECTION XXIV

## WRITING PROCESS

CHAPTER 60

# WRITING AS DISCOVERY

## When Process Defaults to Script

For most people, I imagine, vacations spur thoughts of welcomed relief from day-to-day routines and obligations. But as a writer—one who writes almost daily—I find vacation's necessary break from routine is almost unbearable. My ideal existence would include waking early, 5:30 A.M. or 6, and then shuffling through my morning ritual online—some things practical and some, quasi-recreational/quasi-professional—while drinking coffee.

And then I would write for several hours.

For example, one summer I was on a 6-day cycling trip to Asheville, NC, and did not have any of those usual routine options for the first few days. While cycling and touring the breweries of Asheville were wonderful, I grew increasingly anxious about not writing. Friday, then, we took a break from cycling and ventured that morning to a donut and coffee shop where I did begin a blog post about the trip after taking care of bills and some of the typical online patterns of my normal life. While I was still meandering into that post, we decided to shift to a local bookstore in town so I stopped mid-blog. As we heading to the bookstore, I talked about what I was blogging and realized it was about political bravery—realizing and saying aloud I should have titled the blog "Brave."

Once settled in to writing again at the bookstore, I revised the title, and waded back into the blog post with a renewed sense of what I was

*Teaching Writing as Journey, Not Destination:*
*Essays Exploring What "Teaching Writing" Means,* pp. 311–314
Copyright © 2019 by Information Age Publishing

trying to examine. The piece is typical of my public blogging—a weaving of personal, political, and literary remnants that I quilt together, hoping to produce a cohesive whole. A better title and a clearer understanding of what my purpose as writer seemed to be, however, still did not fulfill me; I was nearly paralyzed with a sense that I had nowhere to go, no way to bring the post to an end.

I paused my drafting and scrolled through my Twitter feed, discovering an interview with Arundhati Roy. As I read, I recognized that Roy was herself discussing political bravery, what I was investigating in my blog post about visiting Asheville and watching the train wreck of debate about healthcare in the U.S. Returning to my draft, I weaved in a bit about reduced circumstances from Margaret Atwood's *The Handmaid's Tale* and then included some key points from Roy's interview. I had throughout that morning *discovered* what I was writing and had also *discovered* the elements I needed to create something more cohesive than I had when I sat down to write.

I must emphasize that I had none of that before I drafted, what most people would call "writing." Stopping and restarting, talking through the post with someone else, and reading had all charged and shifted what that post became. Of course, I had some initial urge to write, some focus in terms of content, but most of that post is similar to the vast majority of my work as a writer—the thing itself does not come into focus until after the drafting. So when I came across Ann Curzan's "Why I Don't Ask Students to Write the Thesis Statement First," I was immediately drawn to her central points:

> In the well-intentioned effort to help college writers find strong theses, we as instructors can put the cart before the horse....
> I want students to have that experience of using writing to explore and figure things out, even when they are doing it for a course assignment (i.e., a requirement). The best essays, I believe, start with questions: questions about something we are curious about, a puzzle we can't seem to figure out yet, a position or a text or an event or a kind of human behavior that we are struggling to understand. I fear that when we ask students to start with a thesis—an argument or a defined position—rather than a question, before they even begin the process of writing, we are setting them up to write less interesting essays. And we don't set up essays from the very beginning as a chance to explore. When I came to this realization, it changed my pedagogy.[1]

As a writer and teacher of writing, I have had the same discomfort with the writing process as I experience with the five-paragraph essay template—authentic writing guidelines are reduced to harmful practices when a script supersedes the authenticity in the practice. In *English Journal*, Nicole

Boudreau Smith argues for principled practice in writing instruction, what I call warranted practice (see Chapter 28). Two of her principles are Component #1: Writers Need Process, Not Product and Component #2: Writers Need Strategies, Not Formulas.[2]

Curzan's piece on the predraft thesis and then writing to that thesis helps us investigate how our students of writing need process, but how we also need to be wary of reducing the process to a script. In other words, for many writers, *drafting is brainstorming*—yet teachers often portray brainstorming as a step *before* drafting, just as teachers often require a clear thesis statement before students write. I come back, then, to being a writer who teaches writing as well as the never-ending pursuit of authentic practice. I reject completely the template approach to the essay, the five-paragraph form, but I also push against teaching students *the* writing process instead of helping student experiment with and discover in order to refine *their* writing process.

Brainstorming, drafting, conferencing, revising and editing—these are common elements of the writing process, but they are not sequential or linear, and they are not exhaustive; abandoning drafts, reading, taking breaks—these are also aspects of the process that students must be aware of and then allowed to investigate. More broadly than requiring a thesis and demanding a sequential writing process (which must be documented by the student for the teacher), we as writing teachers need to foster in students *writer's purpose*, the urge to write that then intersects with process and form as well as the myriad aspects of creating a coherent text for an audience. Asking students to identify their text outcome before they draft may be one of the most prohibitive practices in our classrooms. *Writing as discovery* has the potential to unlock the writer in our students that we often lament not seeing.

When teachers, especially teachers of writing, reach for templates and scripts, I believe that urge comes from a good place, the recognition that students who are novice or developing need structure. However, I also recognize that templates and scripts tend to do more harm than good; we have ample evidence that students rarely release rigid templates if they have worked for them (in other words, students who made A's using the five-paragraph essay have been conditioned that the template is effective). The writing process is incredibly important for students learning to write, and asking them to work from blank paper can be far too daunting.

Instead of reducing the writing process to a script and demanding a definitive thesis from students before they draft, we should offer structure through a broader array of ways to begin a text—questions, problems, provocative passages from other writers, personal stories, an exciting turn of phrase, a title. To return to Smith's principled practice (my warranted practice), I suspect that we all must step back from time to time and investigate if our practice matches our goals. When, how, and if students write with or to a thesis is a set of practices that may be better replaced by seeking ways to help students see writing as discovery.

## ENDNOTES

1. Curzan, A. (2017, July 25). Why I don't ask students to write the thesis statement first. *The Chronicle of Higher Education.* Retrieved from https://www.chronicle.com/blogs/linguafranca/2017/07/25/why-i-dont-ask-students-to-write-the-thesis-statement-first
2. Smith, N.B. (2017). A principled revolution in the teaching of writing. *English Journal, 106*(5), 70–75.

# CONCLUSION

## The Struggle Itself

In "What's Wrong with Writing Centers," Rose Jacobs reports on Lori Salem's "quantitative analysis of Temple University's writing center, which she has directed since 1999. The assistant vice provost wanted to understand its role by investigating who doesn't visit as well as who does." Salem discovered:

> [T]hat practices that are near-orthodoxy in writing centers—such as nondirective instruction, in which tutors prompt students to come up with the right answers themselves; and a resistance to focusing on grammatical errors—cater to individuals who already have a strong grounding in grammar and composition, the sort of students who never turn up. That leaves the most frequent visitors underserved: female students, minority students, and those who grew up speaking a language other than English at home.[1]

Salem admits her study is just a beginning since it focuses on one center at one university, but as someone who has been teaching writing for almost four decades, both as a high school English teacher and a college professor of first-year and upper-level writing courses, I can confirm that many of the dilemmas uncovered by Salem ring disturbingly true.

Those two distinctly different teaching experiences have shaped me within a broader unifying way: I have mostly taught myself how to teach

*Teaching Writing as Journey, Not Destination:*
*Essays Exploring What "Teaching Writing" Means,* pp. 315–320
Copyright © 2019 by Information Age Publishing
All rights of reproduction in any form reserved.

315

writing, having only one real formal experience with learning how to teach writing through the National Writing Project's summer institute. I don't have any degree in composition, and didn't formally study composition in any undergraduate or graduate courses. As a high school teacher for almost twenty years, I learned mostly by trial-and-error, and then was saved by my regional NWP affiliate, the Spartanburg Writing Project, where I also was a co-lead instructor for a few summers before heading to higher education full time.

But the last decade has been an incredibly fertile and difficult journey with how writing is taught in higher education. I have been teaching first-year writing, along with an upper-level writing course, and I briefly held a small administrative role in guiding our first-year seminars. Over that time, my university has (finally) formalized a writing program by naming a Director of Writing Programs and seeking ways to make the writing and media lab and program more cohesive (adding the upper-level writing/ research requirement to the curriculum, for example). The teaching of writing is also being more directly addressed by creating Faculty Writing Fellows, faculty who participate in a year-long seminar addressing writing instruction.

As I have participated in and witnessed these recent growing pains at my university, I can offer some anecdotal, but I think credible, observations that match well with Salem's research:

- Writing instruction at the course/class/individual faculty level suffers from a lack of purpose and cohesion without a school/college unifying mission and set of shared goals. In other words, how does any class/course contribute to some set of outcomes related to writing *all* students should have experiences in as integral to graduating?
- Class-level writing instruction and writing centers/labs must guard against two corrosive but alluring perspectives: (1) viewing writing instruction as remediation, and (2) seeing any course or session on "how to write" as some sort of one-shot inoculation against "errors" (a deficit view).
- Both learning to write and teaching writing are journeys, and must remain grounded in clearly defined contexts. Disciplinary writing in high school and college is much different than becoming a writer of fiction or poetry. For example, composition faculty and K–12 English teachers define "writing workshop" differently than creative writing faculty (think MFA).
- Teaching writing always involves tension among concerns about craft, content, and correctness. A writing program, and writing center practices, must address how these elements will be taught

as well as how each is weighted (not if, but when, how, and why). Many who come to teaching writing from disciplines outside English or composition are overconcerned with correctness (teaching writing is correcting grammar, mechanics, and usage) and significantly focused on disciplinary content and the logic of student claims, evidence, and elaboration in writing.

- Teaching writing is enhanced by those teachers *being writers themselves*, but this expectation must be navigated carefully since few faculty are writers and some may write mostly out of necessity, not out of a drive to be writers.

- The inequity unmasked by Salem's study often presents itself in the teaching of writing through *which students* receive *what instruction*. So-called reluctant or remedial students (disproportionately black, brown, and/or poor) receive instruction on correctness (grammar, mechanics, usage) often in isolation (worksheets on skills) and are allowed or required to compose very little or not at all. The so-called advanced or gifted students (disproportionately white and affluent) compose more often and are allowed to venture into "creative" writing, experimentation, and choice. These instructional choices perpetuate inequity.

Writing centers and programs, then, are necessarily integral parts of equity and academic goals in any school, college, or university. Students must be better served at the class/course level as well as over the entire school/college experience through a cohesive writing program that rejects seeing the teaching of writing as remediation or an inoculation, but embraces authentic purposeful instruction. Just as Salem's data show that students view writing centers as ineffectual, thus unimportant, faculty often marginalize the status of teaching writing—something to be done by someone else or not relevant to their discipline.

Writing, however, is an essential tool of not only students and academics, but also being fully human. Learning to write and teaching writing are both being misserved in formal education, with the shortcomings of writing centers as one example, and as a consequence, so are our students and those charged to teach them.

## "good enough for one of your blogs but ..."

Once, I had the kind of experience with a scholarly submission that I wish I could someday identify as rare, but the truth is, this is essentially typical—even among the progressive and critical colleagues, scholars, and publications where I place a good deal of my academic and scholarly work.

I submitted a chapter and was prompted to revise and rewrite it multiple times (I, in fact, appreciate and thrive on substantial editor feedback in my work, especially since much of my public work—see below—is produced in isolation). Often, when editors ask for revisions of my academic work, the initial comments revolve around the work being too conversational—too much personal narrative. As a sort of inverse of that dynamic, when I submit public work, the editorial complaint is my work is too scholarly.

In both the academic/scholarly press and the public media, I have a very purposeful commitment to submitting work that simultaneously offers a message I am seeking to share while using the mode, discourse, genre, and medium to confront the norms of both contexts; I want to challenge the academic/scholarly norms of discourse, and I want to challenge the public norms of discourse. My work with journalists has been some of the best on-the-job training I have ever experienced as a writer. While I remain often frustrated about certain entrenched conventions for public work (journalism is too cavalier about citations, for example), I have learned a great deal from careful editing, questions, and suggestions when working with journalists.

As I turn back to the opening experience with a recent piece (which eventually found a home at *AlterNet*, by the way), I must say that I am troubled by the entrenched expectations for discourse among academics and scholars—notably critical scholars who want radical and critical messages wrapped in reductive, stilted, traditional discourse conventions. And what is more troubling, I think, is the not-so-subtle condescension found among academics, including the "this piece is good enough for one of your blogs but…" refrain.

Traditional academic and scholarly discourse has much to learn from the world of blogging and online discourse. My blogs, for example, allow me to pursue the quilting I have begun to examine here, first inspired in me by the hybrid scholarship of Maxine Greene, whose writing in educational philosophy opened up to me a world in which literary, historical, and personal references were weaved with the so-called weightier business of philosophical *rigor* (an ugly word that should never be used in the positive contexts people do use it).

I have been using Joseph Williams' *Style* (a work that comes in enough versions and editions to set some Guinness World Record I suspect) with students since the mid-1990s when a member of my doctoral committee, Craig Kridel, held up the book at our first doctoral meeting and told us everyone should read it and know it. A key point made by Williams that has remained with me as a writer is the concept that we humans are interested in *people doing things*, even better is *real people doing real things*. Vivid writing of all genres, modes, and forms is concrete, and the most engaging case any writing can make involves personal narrative (see Robert Nash's

*Liberating Scholarly Writing*). But as Greene models, I also think that claims, evidence, and elaboration become effective and compelling with a richness that quilting can offer, pulling from literature, history, quantitative statistics, personal narrative, journalism, philosophy, and non-print media such as films, music lyrics, and graphic texts.

In one blog post, I came to see that teaching is an invisible profession, and that idea was made more engaging for me when I began to consider Ralph Ellison's *Invisible Man*. So I grabbed a copy (after looking through the previews at amazon and google books), eventually rereading the Prologue and Epilogue. In that reconnection with literature, I also came to see that teachers have been hibernating, like Ellison's unnamed narrator. The finished piece is more rich for my literary research, but also for my shaping the finished piece around those passages.

When journalism ignores the power of citation and when academics/scholars belittle blogging and the thriving online media, both seriously fail to seek discourse that public intellectuals can engage with the wider public in ways that bring about change. While it stings to have my own work negatively criticized and eventually dropped from a project I very much supported, I am much more concerned about the entrenched insular nature of academia and scholarship.

In academic publishing and processes such as tenure and promotion at the university levels, peer-reviewed journals and traditional forms of discourse remain not just honored but exclusively tolerated and rewarded—despite the tremendous imbalance of few (if any) people reading the peer-reviewed works while thousands are exposed to public work (I had an online piece in *The Atlantic* that reached 1,000+ Facebook "likes" in a few days; my blog allows me to see daily visits of 350 or more).

The work of scholars as writers needs to be about what we say, of course, and there must be great care in making informed claims within and from ones field of expertise. But academics must not ignore how we communicate and especially to whom. To put a twist on a cliched riddle, If an academic publishes an essay in a peer-reviewed journal and no one reads it ...

•

And this, so far, has been my journey as a writer and as a teacher of writing, a journey in which those two aspects of my being inform each other in ways that make separating them in any way difficult for me. I end this collection of essays on teaching writing and being a writer with an investigation of writing centers and a brief meditation on being trapped between different expectations for my writer self because I know only one thing clearly: The journey itself is enough to fill a writer's heart, a teacher's heart.

## ENDNOTE

1. Jacobsm R. (2018, February 5). What's wrong with writing centers. *The Chronicle of Higher Education*. Retrieved from https://www.chronicle.com/article/What-s-Wrong-With-Writing/242414

# ABOUT THE AUTHOR

**P. L. Thomas,** Professor of Education (Furman University, Greenville SC), taught high school English in rural South Carolina for 18 years before moving to teacher education. He is a former column editor/co-editor for *English Journal* (National Council of Teachers of English) and series editor for *Critical Literacy Teaching Series: Challenging Authors and Genres* (Brill Publishers). He has served on major committees with NCTE and was a recipient of the NCTE's George Orwell Award. Previous books with IAP include *Ignoring Poverty in the U.S.: The Corporate Takeover of Public Education* (2012) and *Parental Choice?: A Critical Reconsideration of Choice and the Debate about Choice* (2010). He has also published or edited volumes on Barbara Kingsolver, Kurt Vonnegut, Margaret Atwood, Ralph Ellison, James Baldwin, and Haruki Murakmai. His scholarly work includes dozens of works in major journals—*English Journal, English Education, Souls, Notes on American Literature, Journal of Educational Controversy, Journal of Teaching Writing*, and others. His commentaries have been included in Room for Debate (*The New York Times*), The Answer Sheet (*Washington Post*), *The Guardian* (UK), *Truthout, Education Week, The Daily Censored, OpEdNews, The State* (Columbia, SC), *The Post and Courier* (Charleston, SC) and The Greenville News (Greenville, SC). His work can be followed at Radical Eyes for Equity (https://radicalscholarship.wordpress.com/) and @plthomasEdD on Twitter.

Made in the USA
Las Vegas, NV
06 February 2021